THE BARBARIAN REBORN

Weaponry & Survivalism

VIKING AGE BARBARIAN

The Barbarian Reborn: Weaponry and Survivalism
Viking Age Barbarian

Thema Classification:
JBG (Controversial Knowledge), VSZ (Self-Sufficiency), QDX (Popular Philosophy), SR (Combat Sports & Self-Defense), SRM (Martial Arts), JWM (Weapons & Equipment).

978-0-6487660-1-8

MANTICORE PRESS
WWW.MANTICORE.PRESS

For my Enemies, Past, Present and Future

To crush your enemies, to see them fall at your feet – to take their horses and goods and hear the lamentation of their women. That is best.

- Attributed to Genghis Khan (1162-1227)[1]

[1] Cited from Harold Lamb, *Genghis Khan: The Emperor of all Men* (Thornton Butterworths, London, 1928), p. 112.

TABLE OF CONTENTS

PREFACE

In the previously published Manticore book, *Zombie Apocalypse Now! Why the Collapse of Civilization is Nigh*, by Thorfinn Skullsplitter,[2] it was argued that the present-day cultural preoccupation with zombies and the zombie apocalypse has more substance to it that just crude reductionist commercial exploitation. There is a deep structured, collective unconsciousness-based social angst about the stability and sustainability of modern Western, or now more generally, techno-industrial civilization.[3] In short: we are, or will be the walking dead, of sorts.

This existential angst is completely justified in the light of a vast array of scientific evidence relating to the environmental crisis, considering problems from biodiversity decline, the depletion of soil, water quality decline and water quantity depletion, peak oil, resource depletion, and climate change, to name but a few of a set of converging and compounding crises. That was his vision of the Kali Yuga, Ragnarök, call it what you will. We can also cite as an expert evidence witness, the example of Pentti Linkola,[4] as one seeing doom soon on the business as usual scenario, as the present techno-industrial system destroys itself, and us.[5]

---

[2]   Thorfinn Skullsplitter, *Zombie Apocalypse Now! Why the Collapse of Civilization is Nigh*, (Manticore Press, 2019).

[3]   P. Goodchild, *Tumbling Tide: Population, Petroleum, and Systematic Collapse*, (Insomniac Press, Ontario, 2013); T. J. Kaczynski, *Anti-Tech Revolution: How and Why*, (Fitch & Madison, Scottsdale, 2016).

[4]   Pentti Linkola, *Can Life Prevail? A Revolutionary Approach to the Environmental Crisis*, (Arktos, London, 2011).

[5]   Craig Dilworth, *Too Smart for Our Own Good: The Ecological Predicament of*

The best-selling *Zombie Apocalypse Now!* reviewed this evidence and concluded that on a business-as-usual scenario—and remember, unending economic growth/resource consumption is not negotiable generally—civilization is likely to collapse by around 2030.[6] Indeed, examining many ethno-social variables, social decay is already occurring and decline will continue until our world falls apart like a badly glued box. This vision of doom was examined by Skullsplitter using the zombie and the inevitable zombie apocalypse as convenient metaphors for our decline and fall. There is likely to be a great die off of the vast majority of humanity, with survivors living in a New Dark Age, darker than the one that followed the collapse of ancient Rome. The insane leveling effects of economic globalism, where everyone (except the top 1%) will be equal on the bottom of the wheelie bin, will mean that this time the entire planet will fall. We will face degradation of the environment (even from social breakdown alone[7]), such as the meltdown of nuclear reactors and radioactive pollution, and ecological catastrophes that the ancients could not imagine, even in their most drug-induced nightmares. It will be worse than *The Walking Dead*.

Skullsplitter then advocated hardcore survivalism, going beyond prepping popular today, but he did not go into what I believe is the more important short-term question, of personal defense, as the world burns, and the gangs roam and purge, destroying at will, in wastelands such as Baltimore and London. I am, however, in agreement with Skullsplitter on most of his points, with some skepticism about his claim that climate change will be worse than the mainstream predicts. As an agnostic about these complex science matters, not being a physical scientist myself, but rather a fighter, I say: we shall see ultimately who is right. Nevertheless, I agree that for a multitude of reasons techno-industrial civilization of the West is, to use a technical term, *fucked*, but I believe that the real crisis

---

Humankind, (Cambridge University Press, Cambridge, 2010).

[6]   Colin Mason, *The 2030 Spike: Countdown to Global Catastrophe*, (Earthscan, Abington, 2003).

[7]   D. Orlov, *The Five Stages of Collapse: Survivors Toolkit*, (New Society Publishers, Gabriola Island, 2013).

will be felt, and is already being experienced, at a street level, with the coming of what I call hyper-violence, and a new age of blood and steel, as the values of so-called civilized order expire. After a brief outline of the contents of this book, I go into more detail of my vision of collapse, which supplements the pessimism of Skullsplitter.

It will be argued that the post-apocalyptic survivor needs to embrace a physical culture of strength with a quasi-religious fervor, making toughness part of one's very being. Along with this comes a belief in the fellowship of weaponry, both guns, while they last, and melee weapons, as humanity goes medieval, and then plunges into a new (scrap) Iron Age, then crashes back to the Stone Age (or oblivion). The philosophy of weaponry, and our possible salvation through it, is discussed.

A return of nature will also mean that the remnants of humanity may become prey for wild animals, including huge numbers of feral dogs that will prey upon humans. There is some evidence that wolves and bears could be serious threats in some regions, but such threats are minor compared to the dangers posed by "man's best friend."

The philosophical treads are tied together, and we see the new barbarian. This warrior will go beyond the ideas of Friedrich Nietzsche (1844-1900), who believed that philosophy teaches us the imperative to "become who you are," famously said in his *Thus Spake Zarathustra* (1883-1891), and instead will hold that the point of human existence is to become, who we are *not* – to transcend our fate in acts of cosmic defiance. The neo-barbarian will reject all of the crumbling ideologies of modernity and postmodernity, and failed belief systems such as Christianity, which will be evident when hell comes to Earth and no one is saved, and Godot never comes. The neo-barbarian as a "super-man" (*Übermensch*) will endure the world with all its horrors, and struggle to overcome. He will "just survive somehow," to use a memorable phrase from episode 2, season 6 of *The Walking Dead*. He will be a worshiper of the old gods of his people, be they Norse, Germanic, African, or native American or Aboriginal, based on his tribal origins. None of these belief systems will be judged to be true or false, because rational argument-based philosophy will have mercifully ended, and we will be too busy struggling to survive to have leisure time for logic-chopping, which most writing today is. Things will just be, and that is all. Here, the present author follows his tribal ways, that of the Vikings, and others are free to go their own tribal way.

Three fellow travelers in the wild world of barbarianism are Bronze Age Pervert, Jack Donovan, and James LaFond, and for honor, I need to acknowledge my intellectual and literary betters. Then, readers who may be frustrated with this book, and are still in an apocalyptic virginal state, will be able to reach a literary climax and penetrate The Great Collapse.

Best known of the three gentlemen, perhaps, is Bronze Age Pervert, whose book, or "exhortation," *Bronze Age Mindset*,[8] has recently received a number of reviews, followed by a number of responses to a youthful energetic book serving up atavistic nihilism, shaken but not stirred, with an effervescent neo-Nietzschean revolt against the modern world. It's that good.

Bronze Age Mindset is like a rampage style, hit and run video game, where every cherished dogma of the establishment "this world of refuse," gets smashed by a nude bodybuilder. The Pervert proclaims: "Because unfortunately in the long run the development of civilization and comfort leads to the proliferation of damaged life, the innovation of mankind leads to unspeakable abortions of life, and men on the periphery who want to preserve the natural order begin to plot the end of everything."

Where BAP sees the modern barbarian as ever-ready to push the crumbling system over the edge, much as the *Germani* barbarian did in say, Peter Heather's account of the fall of the Roman Empire,[9] James LaFond sees the system as already well advanced in decay, maggots eating the corpse of the West, his home town of Baltimore ("harm city") serving as an exemplar of what is to come, soon.[10]

---

[8]   Bronze Age Pervert, *Bronze Age Mindset*, (Kindle/Independently published, 2018).

[9]   Peter Heather, *The Fall of the Roman Empire: A New History of Rome and the Barbarians*, (Oxford University Press, Oxford, 2007).

[10]   James LaFond and Jesse James Bowie, *Letters from the Fall; Civilization Decomposes*, (Independently Published, 2019).

In a myriad of superb, but vastly under-appreciated books, both fiction and non-fiction, LaFond has explored the same theme as BAP, namely how civilization has emasculating, castrating effects upon traditional manhood, turning men once-warriors, of the Bronze and Iron and Steel Ages, into something we often know-not-what, in this age of silicon and consumer softness.[11] LaFond, in *At the End of Masculine Time*, sees civilization as a "Faustian matrix whereby the collective and individual souls of men are incinerated on The Altar." The self-destructive nature of civilization was a view held to with varying degrees of strength by earlier masculine writers such as Edgar Rice Burroughs (1875-1950), Jack London (1876-1916), Robinson Jeffers (1887-1962), H. P. Lovecraft (1890-1937), and the creator of Conan the Barbarian, Robert E. Howard (1906-1936), so James is in very good company.[12]

LaFond, in his book *Taboo You*,[13] gives a clear expression of the mindset of the modern barbarian:

> I reject philosophy as the whining of old men and the fantasies of soft women hiding behind ideas. I am a barbarian. ... I reject all faiths; all religions; all political ideologies; all economic models; all martial arts systems; all beliefs. I am a barbarian.[14]

I endorse this attitude, even against Evola, and Nietzsche. And the practical actions of the barbarian:

---

[11]   James LaFond, *Of Lions and Men: Masculinity and Tribalism in the Western Tradition*, (A Dark Eyed Girl Book, (2015)), *At the End of Masculine Time: A Case for Cultural Resistance*, (Punch Buggy Books, 2015), *Under the God of Things: The Masculine Condition within the Belly of the Soul-Eating Beast Known as Civilization*, (CreateSpace, 2016), *Masculine Axis: A Meditation on Manhood and Heroism*, (CreateSpace, 2017), *Man Gearing: Building an Unapologetic Masculine Mindset in an Effeminate World*, (A Jerk House Book, 2018).

[12]   James LaFond, *A Thousand Years in His Soul: The Poets – Part One. Five Aryan Mystics at the Dawn of the Atomic Age*, (Punch Buggy Books, 2015). LaFond pursues the theme of demographic collapse, and a coming Reconquista, in his science fiction novel, *Reverent Chandler* (2016), the prequel, *Malediction Song* (2017), and the sequel, *Nightsong of the Nords* (2018), taking the work of Jack London and Robert E. Howard, much further.

[13]   James LaFond, *Taboo You: Way of the Terminal Man*, (Harm City Book, 2014).

[14]   As above, p. 126.

> Most people, if shipwrecked with the Mona Lisa, would cling to it as they eked out a living, in the hopes of being credited with or rewarded for preserving the world's greatest masterpiece once rescued. I would use it for kindling to light my campfire.[15]

However, the barbarian is not necessarily a "savage," living from hand to mouth, lacking a moral code and guiding principles of life, like the intelligentsia.[16] The ancient Greeks saw barbarians as folk living outside of their culture, which was a civilization of the day.[17] In particular, the barbarian is a tribal being in general, having a commitment to his group of people, usually all known to him, over all others. This is where we can introduce the great work of Jack Donovan. As Jack notes in his magnificent book *Becoming a Barbarian*,[18] tribes are honor groups, the pillar of barbarism being honor. The various warrior virtues, or qualities, that also, in turn, define manliness, "what is best and what is usual in him,"[19] include strength, courage, mastery as well as honor.[20] The barbarian, whether the tall, muscular, hyper-violent Yamnaya, who swept through Europe between 5,000 and 4,000 years ago,[21] the pagan Vikings of over a thousand years ago, or those of us men today, seeking with Donovan to become "more complete beast(s),"[22] will be committed to

---

[15]   As above, p. 120.

[16]   Roy Coleman, "The Neo-Barbarian University," August 8, 2016, at https://emotionalstates.wordpress.com/2016/08/08/the-neo-barbarian-university/.

[17]   James LaFond, *Barbarism Versus Civilization: Seeking a Postdomesticated Life*, (A Crackpot Book, 2018).

[18]   Jack Donovan, *Becoming a Barbarian*, (Dissonant Hum,2016).

[19]   H. C. Mansfield, *Manliness*, (Yale University Press, New Haven, 2006), p. 194.

[20]   Jack Donovan, *The Way of Men*, (Dissonant Hum, 2012). Arguably there are other warrior virtues besides these four; the warrior code of bushido, for example lists seven: *yuki* (courage); *jin* (benevolence); *rei* (etiquette); *makoto* (honesty); *chugi* (loyalty); *gi* (Rectitude) and *meiyo* (honor).

[21]   David Anthony, *The Horse, the Wheel, and Language: How Bronze-Aged Riders from the Eurasian Steppes Shaped the Modern World*, (Princeton University Press, Princeton, 2010).

[22]   Jack Donovan, *A More Complete Beast*, (Dissonant Hum, 2018); Friedrich Nietzsche, *Beyond Good and Evil*, (Penguin Books, 1975); Liam Gooding, *How to Become a Modern Viking: A Man's Guide to Unleashing the Warrior Within*, (Kindle, 2016), http://liamgooding.com.

the warrior virtues over the so called values of civilization, especially our present consumer slug values of the "Empire of Nothing."

As I see it, taking the juicy bits and pieces from all of the above writers, the neo-barbarian rejects the universalistic values of modernity and post-modernity, and the technologies and ideologies associated with modern civilization (at best seeing such technologies and sciences as only of instrumental value, rather than having some fundamental truth about reality as scientific realism supposes[23]). Instead, the barbarian looks back to the warrior virtues of our past, to an age of blood and iron, if not bronze, or stone, and the conception of manhood of those wild and woolly times. The reason for this given in this book, is that we are headed back to the past anyway from a collapse of civilization, so we, therefore, need to dress for the occasion.

However, as Donovan argues, in *A More Complete Beast*, traditional masculinity is no longer needed in the cosmopolitan society, so it is a philosophical problem justifying and outlining how and why one would become a noble beast, or even any kind of beast at all.

In this book, we will see that the collapse of civilization, coming up fast, will destroy these forces weakening people, weak people too, and lead to a return of "social Darwinism" and the struggle for life.[24] The weak, the vast majority will fall in a great die-off, as Skullsplitter argued in his magnificent book. The barbarian returns, and with the collapse of modernity and post-modernity, and all associated with it, the old war gods return as well, if they were ever really gone. It will be in our power to "restart the world," as Jack Donovan describes it:

> The Noble man has a great reverence and respect for strength. The Noble man chooses his own values because he believes in himself and his own worth and judgment … [a] more Noble approach to a desire for change is to take on the mindset of the conqueror. The conqueror creates change according to his liking … not because of any theoretically objective sense that it is morally

[23]   K. Brad Wray, *Resisting Scientific Realism*, (Cambridge University Press, Cambridge, 2018).

[24]   James Hill, *The Resurrection of Social Darwinism*, (Kindle).

good or evil. The revolutionary wants to 'fix' the world by turning the moral wheel one way or the other, while the conqueror creates the world he wants.[25]

Nietzsche also wrote:

At the base of all these noble races one cannot fail to recognize the beast of prey, the splendid *blond beast* who roams about lusting after booty and victory; from time to time this hidden base needs to discharge itself, the animal must get out, must go back into the wilderness: Roman, Arab, Germanic, Japanese nobility, Homeric heroes, Scandinavian Vikings – in this need they are all alike. It is the noble races who have left the concept "barbarian" in all their tracks wherever they have gone; indeed within their highest culture a consciousness of this betrays itself and every pride in it ... This "boldness" of noble races – mad, absurd, sudden in its expression; the unpredictable, in their enterprises even the improbable ... their indifference and contempt toward all security, body, life, comfort; their appalling light-heartedness and depth of desire in all destruction, in all the delights of victory and cruelty – all was summed up for those who suffered from it in the image of the "barbarian." [26]

Thus, let us now relearn how to be barbarians and conquerors!

---

[25] Jack Donovan, *A More Complete Beast*.

[26] Nietzsche, *On the Genealogy of Morality*, pp. 22-23.

PART I

The Apocalypse Begins

1.

Apocalypse Cometh

Man was, and is, too shallow and cowardly to endure the fact of the *mortality* of everything living. He wraps it up in rose-coloured optimism, he heaps upon it the flowers of literature, he crawls behind the shelter of ideas so as to not see anything. But impermanence, the birth and the passing, is the *form of all that is actual* – from the stars, whose destiny is for us incalculable, right down to the ephemeral concourses on our planet. The life of the individual—whether this be animal or plant or man—is as perishable as that of peoples or culture. Every creation is foredoomed to decay, every thought, every discovery, every deed, to oblivion. - *Oswald Spengler*[27]

It is always a good idea to keep an eye on what the global financial elite are up to. The mega-money class have acute, near-prehistoric survival instincts, combined with super-cunning and phenomenally good fortune (usually) and know when the blood will flow in the streets, even if it is their own.[28] Hence, we should pay keen attention to news items that report that the capitalist super-class are so concerned about the coming prospects of social breakdown, that they are buying up "bolt holes," or survival retreats, in places like New Zealand and Chile, but presumably not Australia, which

---

[27]   Oswald Spengler, *Man and Technics: A Contribution to a Philosophy of Life*, (George Allen and Unwin, London, 1932), pp. 13-14.

[28]   J. D. Davidson and W. Rees-Mogg, *Blood in the Streets*, (Grand Central Publishing, 1988).

no doubt the elite regard as already destroyed, facing a near-term economic Armageddon, with record foreign debt, record household debt, and a housing bubble that could burst at any time, destroying the livelihoods of millions of Australians.[29] Australia is not "the future" but seems to be accepted to be an expendable society, much like Sweden, a failed social experiment.[30]

Super-entrepreneur Peter Thiel, who co-founded PayPal, considers New Zealand to be "the future." In 2016, it was revealed that Thiel and Sam Altman, a Silicon Valley entrepreneur, intended to board a private jet and fly to Thiel's property in the land of *The Lord of the Rings*, in the case of some apocalyptic events, such as nuclear war, a synthetic virus breakout ("zombie apocalypse"), or if other sets of the compounding and converging catastrophes mentioned in this volume, happened.[31] Once they got there, it was not clear what they would then do, perhaps sitting out the collapse of civilization until a reboot occurred, if ever.

While the doomsday billionaire preppers are shipping bunkers to New Zealand,[32] the government has passed a new law to ban many foreigners from buying properties.[33] However, survival preps continue across the world, as the richest and best-informed people get ready for … what?

---

[29]   On Australia's economic doom, see: http://stocksnews.com.au/2018/06/18/six-scenarios-of-the-coming-economic-armageddon.

[30]   Kajsa Norman, *Sweden's Dark Soul: The Unravelling of a Utopia*, (Hurst & Company, London, 2019); S. P. Leonard, *Travels in Cultural Nihilism: Some Essays*, (Arktos, London, 2017).

[31]   T. Friend, "Sam Altman's Manifest Destiny," October 10, 2016, at https://www.newyorker.com/magazine/2016/10/10/sam-altmans-manifest-destiny; M. O'Connell, "Why Silicon Valley Billionaires are Prepping for the Apocalypse in New Zealand," https://www.theguardian.com/news/2018/feb/15/why-silicon-valley-billionaires-are-prepping-for-the-apocalypse-in-new-zealand.

[32]   G. Birchall, "Apocalypse-Fearing Billionaires are Shipping Bunkers to New Zealand," September 6, 2018, at https://nypost.com/2018/09/06/apocalypse-fearing-billionaires-are-shipping-bunkers-to-new-zealand/; D. Rushkoff, "Survival of the Richest," July 5, 2018, at https://medium.com/s/futurehuman/survival-of-the-richest-9ef6cdddocc1.

[33]   J. Smyth, "Billionaire Bolt-Holes' Under Threat in New Zealand," March 2, 2018, at https://www.ft.com/content/0dcabab4-1c44-11e8-aaca-4574d7dabfb6.

Cutting to the chase, there are numerous destructive forces, both man-made and natural (also human influenced), which will tear apart the fabric of social reality as we know it. These forces could include the violent clash of ideologies (seen most dramatically in the cultural war battles in America between nationalists and cosmopolitan progressives), resource depletion crisis, ethnic conflict, and ecological degradation (largely a product of human population expansion). These forces will destroy techno-industrial society, probably before 2030, and perhaps sooner, as many have already predicted. The world as we know it is going to come crashing down, much like the airship in the Hindenburg disaster (May 6, 1937).

There is little political will to confront this civilizational threat front-on, which would require a homogeneous, unified society to co-ordinate in an all-out "war effort." Instead, what we have as a result of the destructive modernist philosophy is inevitable tribalism,[34] combined with the fanatical religion of economic growth unending on a finite planet,[35] leading inexorably to national dissolution,[36] most probably through civil war.[37]

America, and much of Europe, are regarded by some writers as failed, or ungovernable states.[38] A survey conducted by Rasmussen Reports of 1,000 Americans found that 31 percent of the sample believed that Civil War 2.0 was likely in the next five years, with 44

[34] A. Chua and J. Rubenfeld, "The Threat of Tribalism," October, 2018, at https://www.theatlantic.com/magazine/archive/2018/10/the-threat-of-tribalism/568342.

[35] D. Worster, *Shrinking the Earth: The Rise and Decline of American Abundance*, (Oxford University Press, Oxford, 2016); C. Dilworth, *Too Smart for Our Own Good*, (Cambridge University Press, Cambridge, 2009).

[36] M. Hart, *The Rise and Fall of the United States*, (VDARE Books, Litchfield, 2018).

[37] C. DeGroot, 'America Needs a Civil War," February 23, 2018, at http://takimag.com/article/america_needs_a_civil_war_christopher_degroot/#axzz5WJ4jf2sV.

[38] M. Snyder, "Is the United States on a Road to Becoming Ungovernable?" http://theeconomiccollapseblog.com/archives/is-the-united-states-on-a-road-to-becoming-ungovernable; C. Hedges, "America The Failed State," July 1, 2018, at https://www.truthdig.com/articles/america-the-failed-state/; C. Hedges, *America: The Farewell Tour*, (Simon and Schuster, New York, 2018).

percent of Blacks seeing such a conflict coming.[39] So, forget about civic nationalism, for the decay is way beyond that now.[40] Victor Orbán, prime minister of Hungary, states that:

> Those who want to mould the European Union into a European empire are all, without exception, supporters of immigration. They have made the admission of migrants the litmus test of being European, and expect every country and nation to become multicultural without delay. Now we can see that they deliberately failed to use their enormous police and military capability, and they deliberately failed to defend Europe from the migrant masses. If they were able to do it, they could have done so too. What was lacking was not the ability, but the will. Even today, the Brussels vanguard and the other leaders who are opposed to nation states see migration as a chance, an opportunity. They see it as a chance to replace the European Union of nation states with a multicultural empire of mixed populations, smoothed into a unity: a Europe without nation states; an elite separated from its national roots; an alliance with multinational power groups; a coalition with financial speculators.[41]

If this scenario was true, the results are likely to be a repeat of the fall of the Roman Empire, with "barbarians" playing the usual role.[42]

Civil War 2.0 could also spread like wild fire across the West. It will be a conflict much like that described below, of house-by-house horror, as Gerard VanderLeun accurately describes:

> How do I mow my lawn, given that my neighbor may shoot me dead? How does he smoke his dope in his backyard, given that he has the same fear from his gun collecting, kook-fringe, fascist, racist, neighbor that is just aching to force his dusty religion upon him?

---

[39] http://www.rasmussenreports.com/public_content/politics/general_politics/ june_2018/31_think_u_s_civil_war_likely_soon.

[40] T. Chittum, *Civil War Two: The Coming Breakup of America*, (American Eagle Publications, 1997); D. Blight, "'The Civil War Lies on Us Like a Sleeping Dragon': America's Deadly Divide – and Why it has Returned," August 20, 2017, at https://www. theguardian.com/us-news/2017/aug/20/civil-war-american-history-trump; J. Walker, "Are We Headed for a Second Civil War?" August 20, 2017, at http://www.latimes.com/opinion/ op-ed/la-oe-walker-second-civil-war-20170820-story.html.

[41] From: http://www.kormany.hu/en/the-prime-minister/the-prime-minister-s-speeches/ prime-minister-viktor-orban-s-speech-on-the-62nd-anniversary-of-the-1956-revolution-and-freedom-fight.

[42] P. Heather, *The Fall of the Roman Empire: A New History of Rome and the Barbarians*, (Oxford University Press, Oxford, 2007).

How do I fly airplanes, given that I can't leave the house? How does he take the ferry to Seattle to practice law? How does the Sheriff deputy leave his house, given that his two daughters would be in danger from his Democrat-Socialist neighbor? Who drives the food trucks? Who operates the local power plant? Who delivers the gasoline?

Nobody. Society grinds to a halt, and there are too many guns and too much hatred (cultural) to impose any kind of order through martial law. The US is too big. Once the shooting gets underway, it is here for good. It will be neighbor on neighbor until ghettos are cleared out and warlords rise. … The money supply will become glacial. Nobody will have money since the banking system will undoubtedly collapse, since nobody is working. That will put gasoline on a raging fire of hatred. The grand experiment in civic nationalism will be, yet again, a failure. Tribal loyalties will come to the fore, for no other reason than survival.[43]

Matters will be much worse though in a grid-down, end of the rule of law, collapse scenario. The threat from neighbors, people in one's locality, could be even more sinister than that of the "golden hordes" of "mutant zombie bikers (MZB),"[44] who are at least recognizable. Research has indicated that at least four percent of people are clinically psychopaths/sociopaths, being on the surface seemingly normal, but beneath that, exposed to triggering environmental stimuli, expose their true selves, as amoral, manipulative, lacking remorse, guilt, and empathy, exhibiting "ice-cold" emotional blankness and are ruthlessly callous.[45]

There is no sharp line between sociopathology and psychopathology, with those who make some sort of a distinction saying that the sociopath has a very weak conscience (which is ineffective and can be practically discarded, and the psychopath having no conscience at all; so that the psychopath is the most

[43] G. VanderLeun, "Civil War? If it Starts it will be Uglier than Anyone Can Imagine," October 15, 2018, http://americandigest.org/wp/civil-war-if-it-starts-it-will-be-uglier-than-anyone-can-imagine/.

[44] http://mutantzombiebikers.blogspot.com/.

[45] R. D. Hare, *Without Conscience: The Disturbing World of the Psychopaths Among Us*, (Guilford Press, New York, 1993); K. Fisher, *Sociopath and Psychopath: The Worst of Both Worlds*, (CreateSpace, 2016); M. Stout, *The Sociopath Next Door*, (Harmony, New York,2006).

extreme version of the sociopath. The more technical term, "anti-social personality disorder," is usually used by professional psychologist/psychiatrists.[46] But, for our purposes, any such fine distinction is irrelevant. The psychos may not be mass murderers yet, but come the collapse they will remorselessly kill,[47] if need be, maybe just for the "fun" of it, when the rule of law bites the dust. The neighbors/friends/family members-relatives who are openly hostile have shown their cards, and can be "lovingly caressed" when the time comes, but those who have acted friendly may get under one's guard. Even if they are not clearly obvious killers, in the "right" circumstances, all human primates potentially are threats when you stand in the way of their survival.[48] Most, in the US at least, will be armed, as we enter what could be Fifth (not Fourth) Generational Warfare, the Hobbesian war of all against all.[49]

Already, humanity has been dumbed down so much that it will not take too long to descend to the drinking-blood-from-skulls mode. Most people exist at the moron level, concerned only with creature comforts such as booze and drugs, and whatever degeneracy that is presently going down, an issue that will be returned to throughout this book. According to the Dunning-Kruger effect,[50] people of low cognitive ability, namely significant proportions of modern populations, have delusional beliefs about the superiority of their cognitive abilities, but lack the metacognitive capacity to be able to discern this; in short, such people are too stupid to be aware of their stupidity, lacking the cognitive skills and ability to know

---

[46] https://www.nhs.uk/conditions/antisocial-personality-disorder/.

[47] https://www.psychologytoday.com/au/blog/wicked-deeds/201702/psychopathic-killers-hide-in-plain-sight.

[48] R. Ardrey, *The Territorial Imperative: A Personal Inquiry into the Animal Origins of Property and Nations*, (Collins, London, 1967); K. Lorenz, *On Aggression*, (Methuen, London, 1966).

[49] W. S. Lind (et al.), "The Changing Face of War: Into the Fourth Generation," *Marine Corps Gazette*, October 1989, pp. 22-26.

[50] J. Kruger and D. Dunning, "Unskilled and Unaware of It: How Difficulties in Recognizing One's Own Incompetence Lead to Inflated Self-Assessments," *Journal of Personality and Social Psychology*, vol. 77, 1999, pp. 1121-1134.

that they are incompetent morons.[51] From a survivalist perspective, this could go either way, simply being eliminated by Darwinian natural selection when faced with survival events (as in the Darwin Awards[52]), or they could luck out in surviving for a time and become further depraved and predatory. Dumbed down imbecility, mixed with the IQ-lowering, and the aggression-producing recreational drugs of today, has readily produced tribes of ferals who will lack morality, conscience and any shape of decency. The moron may not be as dangerous as the psychopath, but I hazard a guess that these degenerates will constitute a much larger proportion of the population. Once their money, drugs, and booze ends, they will come to raid, rape and kill, blaming those with resources for their plight. And, these savages will be of all shapes and colors, so this revolt is a universal socio-cultural decay.[53] Therefore, things will be messy, miserable and violent when the collapse comes, precisely as depicted in the description of Ragnarok in *Völuspá* Stanza 45:

> Brothers will fight
> and kill each other,
> sisters' children
> will defile kinship.
> It is harsh in the world,
> whoredom rife
> - An axe age, a sword age
> - shields are riven -
> a wind age, a wolf age -
> before the world goes headlong.
> No man will have
> mercy on another.[54]

Of course, not everyone will be a wolf, because for every predator, there will be countless poor little lambs for the wolves to slaughter.

[51]   E. Dutton and M. Woodley of Menie, *At Our Wit's End: Why We are Becoming Less Intelligent and What That Means for the Future*, (Imprint Academic, Exeter, 2018).

[52]   https://darwinawards.com/.

[53]   T. L. Stoddard, *The Revolt Against Civilization: The Menace of the Underman*, (Charles Scribner's Sons, New York, 1922; Forgotten Books, London, 2015).

[54]   U. Dronke, *The Poetic Edda: Volume II: Mythological Poems*, (Clarendon Press, Oxford, 1997).

For example, two young female backpackers, one from Denmark the other from Norway, were beheaded by ISIS terrorists in the village of Imlil in Morocco's High Atlas Mountains.[55] A video recorded by the killers shows the likely raped victim, lying on her stomach as two men speak Arabic. One then begins to saw the back of her neck with a long kitchen knife. There was much written about this covering various angles, but beyond all the politics, it is clear that this was a situation where two unthinking white lambs went into an ultra-dangerous area, unprepared. There was no "situational awareness" or "threat assessment." If these women had to venture into this territory as a matter of necessity, which was not the case, they should have prepared. Even in this highly weapons-restricted region, it would not have been too difficult to have obtained superior weapons to these cheap knives, assuming that this was all they had. With training, two women with, say, quarterstaffs cut from local trees, determined to use them, could have defended themselves. It may have been possible to drive them off, as most predators in the animal kingdom fear injuries. But, these were children of modernity, were sadly not pre-modern "shield-maidens," so they were slaughtered like animals in an abattoir. This, alas, will become common as the great culling begins, as such news demonstrates.[56] And, another young female backpacker, seeking self-realization in the village of San Juan la Laguna, Guatemala, whose naked and beaten body was found on a lonely trail, on March 11, 2019, can be added to this tale of woe.[57]

Let us not forget the males either. According to the reports, four tree surgeons were working in Rochdale, England.[58] They had

---

[55] https://www.news.com.au/travel/travel-updates/incidents/family-urges-public-not-to-watch-scandinavian-tourist-decapitation-video/news-story/cb8d0318432609d83a5da743c025ab27.

[56] https://www.dailymail.co.uk/news/article-6738131/SAS-troops-severed-heads-50-Yazidi-sex-slaves-close-barbaric-ISIS.html.

[57] https://www.dailymail.co.uk/news/article-6795959/Guatemalan-search-party-jacket-belonging-missing-British-backpacker-two-miles-hostel.html.

[58] "UK: 20-Strong Gang Target 'White Bastards,' Cut off Teenager's Hand with Axe," October 20, 2019, at https://www.breitbart.com/europe/2019/10/20/uk-20-strong-gang-target-white-bastards-cut-off-mans-arm-axe/.

stopped an individual from abusing an elderly woman. The said individual was "incensed" that he had been "disrespected" on his "territory." So, he assembled his gang, armed with a collection of weapons, such a claw hammer, knives, machetes, a knuckle duster, and an axe, and tracked the workers to the property where they were presumably cutting down trees using cutting tools such as chain saws. An 18-year old tried to be a "peacemaker," and had an axe smashed into his chest, collapsing a lung. The next axe blow from the incensed individual, aimed at his head, was blocked by the youth raising his arm which was then severed at the wrist. Then another worker's nose was shattered by the gang member's knuckle duster. Only at this point did one of them decide to start up a chain saw, which led to the gang fleeing.

The Coming of the New Dark Age

No plan of operations extends with any certainty beyond the first contact with the main hostile force. - *Helmuth von Moltke the Elder*

Everybody has a plan until they get punched in the mouth. - *Mike Tyson*

Many thinkers who have proposed that Western civilization, and in turn, the modern techno-industrial paradigm, is at an end, and facing imminent collapse.[59] Perhaps though, a more appropriate metaphor, other than the classic structural/architectural one, where collapse is a singular destructive event like a bridge collapse, is *decay*, a breakdown and decomposition, occurring more slowly much as

---

[59] D. Orlov, *The Five Stages of Collapse: Survivor's Toolkit*, (New Society Publishers, Gabriola Island, 2013); J. M. Greer, *Dark Age America: Climate Change, Cultural Collapse, and the Hard Future Ahead*, (New Society Publishers, Gabriola Island, 2016); P. R. Ehrlich and A. N. Ehrlich, "Can a Collapse of Global Civilization be Avoided?" *Proceedings of the Royal Society B*, vol. 280, 2013, 20122845: http://dx.doi.org/10.1098/rspb.2012.2845; P. R. Ehrlich, "Overpopulation and the Collapse of Civilization," November 5, 2013 at http://mahb.stanford.edu/blog/overpopulation-and-the-collapse-of-civilization/.

disease and ultimately death creeps up and kills an individual.[60] In either case though, the eventual consequence is that our civilization and people, expires.[61]

Factors listed include the "cancerisation of the European social fabric," the degrading of Western culture and the rise of postmodern nihilism,[62] mass immigration, the complete polarization of most Western societies between "localists/nationalists" and "cosmopolitans/globalists,"[63] the economic and military threat of China,[64] technological displacement of labor and the end of work,[65] and the coming economic collapse from factors ranging from the illusions and contradictions of fiat money.[66] Interacting as a threat multiplier with all of these crises is the possibility of an ecological catastrophe. Economic collapse is most likely to be the first stage of collapse.[67] Apart from the long-discussed problems of fiat money, most countries, including China, face numerous existential economic problems, all sufficient to produce a new Great

---

[60] H. Nyborg, "The Decay of Western Civilization: Double Relaxed Darwinian Selection," *Personality and Individual Differences*, vol. 53, 2012, pp. 118-125.

[61] B. Stevens, "How the Path to Wealth Leads to Death," at http://www.amerika.org/politics/how-the-path-to-wealth-leads-to-death/. "Most civilizations die young. Like people born with congenital diseases or doomed to die in battle, they rise to a level of promise and then seemingly vanish in the next stroke, not collapsing violently but fading away and leaving degraded versions of their old selves."

[62] S. P. Leonard, *Travels in Cultural Nihilism: Some Essays*, (Arktos, London, 2017).

[63] On this "great divide," see S. Baskerville, *The New Politics of Sex: The Sexual Revolution, Civil Liberties, and the Growth of Government Power*, (Angelico Press, Kettering, 2017).

[64] Tim Gamble, "The Three Existential Threats to America and Western Civilization," August 5, 2018, at https://www.timgamble.com/2018/08/the-three-existential-threats-to.html.

[65] B. Way, *Jobocalpyse: The End of Human Jobs and How Robots will Replace Them*, (CreateSpace, 2013); J. Barrat, *Our Final Invention: Artificial Intelligence and the End of the Human Era*, (St. Martin's Press, New York, 2013).

[66] Fiat currency (that solely declared by the government to be legal tender, not backed by a physical thing such as gold), has led to the collapse of almost every society using it: http://www.goldtelegraph.com/fiat-currency-always-ends-in-collapse/.

[67] D. Orlov, *The Five Stages of Collapse: Survivors' Toolkit*, (New Society Publishers, Gabriola Island, 2013); I. Wallerstein, "The Global Economy Won't Recover, Now or Ever," *Foreign Policy*, January/February, 2011, p. 76.

Depression, including impossible to pay global debt of $ US 164 trillion, almost 225 percent of world GDP;[68] the technical bankruptcy of countries such as the US and the end of the dollar.[69] Although the elites look forward to China rising as the world's dominant military and economic power, China has its economic problems based on the Communist party's desire to control all aspects of the economy, thus dampening growth, as well as unsustainable debt, a construction sector "financial time bomb," and other factors.[70] As noted previously, even mainstream sources are predicting coming hard times for countries like Australia, and recommend relearning lessons from the Great Depression.[71]

The next Global Financial Crisis will be devastating and will produce some of the effects predicted in this book, but the crisis to be considered here is deeper, and will be longer lasting, and will not be solved by a duct tape solution to the economy. The crisis to be described in this book transcends conventional politics, for it is a crisis of the very survival of that which is natural.[72]

The Era of Hyper-Violence

Peter Turchin, in his book *Ages of Discord* (2016),[73] predicts that the collapse of civilization is likely to occur in the 2020s due to political

[68] https://www.bloomberg.com/news/articles/2018-04-18/world-debt-hits-record-164-trillion-as-crisis-hangover-lingers.

[69] https://www.bsl-lausanne.ch/myret-zaki-la-fin-du-dollar-the-end-of-the-dollar/.

[70] A. Dupont, "China on the Road to a Big Crash," November 10, at https://www.theaustralian.com.au/news/inquirer/china-on-road-to-a-big-crash/news-story/821d095fda7c091ecb43937b5d57849b.

[71] On the coming economic crash see entries at http://theeconomiccollapseblog.com/; http://thegreatrecession.info/blog/tag/economic-collapse/; https://www.zerohedge.com/.

[72] P. Linkola, *Can Life Prevail?* (Arktos, London, 2011).

[73] P. Turchin, *Ages of Discord: A Structural-Demographic Analysis of American History*, (Beresta Books, Chaplin, 2016); M. Papenfuss, "Society Could Collapse in a Decade, Predicts Math Historian," January 7, 2017, at http://www.huffingtonpost.com.au/entry/peter-turchin-cliodynamics-society-collapse_us_586f1e22e4b02b5f85882988.

turmoil, which is part of regular cycles of violence in human history, seen in the West since ancient Rome and in China.[74] There are numerous factors leading to this collapse, from inflation and falling real wages, a food crisis caused by overpopulation, and violent riots.[75] Out of control bureaucracy, and military over-stretch leads to "state bankruptcy and consequent loss of military control; elite movements of regional and national rebellion; and a combination of elite-mobilized and popular uprisings that expose the breakdown of central authority."[76] Birth rates crash as social and economic insanity grips the country.[77] This same "impending demographic-structural crisis"[78] is now faced by the West, and may spell its doom, just as other civilizations collapsed.[79] What should be noted here, is that the effects of social conflict and environmental factors other than population increase are not considered in this cycle of violence, but once these factors are bracketed into the equation, things become critical.

The United States has cities which resemble war zones in various parts – in Chicago, and Baltimore, gang violence leads to blood flowing freely on the streets, as the corpses and body parts pile up. Here, for example, is a slice of an editorial from the *Chicago Tribune* about this "blood in the streets":

> The death and injury total from Friday night to Monday morning numbed the senses: At least 74 people were shot, 12 of them killed, according to a tally by Tribune reporters. Those are figures from a war zone; they shouldn't reflect the reality of an August weekend in an American city. Chicago is the nation's bleak outlier, where a culture of violence and bloodshed devastates some areas. Over the course of one hour early Sunday, there were at least

---

[74] Ibid., (*Ages of Discord*), p. 7.

[75] Ibid., p. 11.

[76] Ibid.

[77] Ibid.; P. Turchin and S. Nefedov, *Secular Cycles*, (Princeton University Press, Princeton, 2009).

[78] Ibid., (*Age of Discord*), p. 248; P. Turchin, "Dynamics of Political Instability in the United States, 1780-2010," *Journal of Peace Research*, vol. 49, 2012, pp. 577-591.

[79] http://www.bbc.com/future/story/20190218-are-we-on-the-road-to-civilisation-collapse.

two incidents in which four people were shot - a drive-by shooting in West Humboldt Park and a shooting at a block party in Lawndale. Then in Gresham at around 12:40 a.m., shots were fired into a crowd of people who had attended a funeral repast: eight people were struck with bullets, including a 14-year-old girl. At one point, Mount Sinai Hospital was so busy it briefly stopped accepting new emergency room patients. Mass shootings in Chicago often involve gang members targeting rivals. Summer weather brings more people outside, which creates more opportunities for mayhem. Fred Waller, Chicago Police Department's chief of patrol, told reporters a bad guy with a gun may be aiming at one person but will give zero thought to others in the field of fire. "You shoot aimlessly like that, you are shooting into a crowd," he said … A lack of job opportunities contributes to hopelessness. Families are fractured, creating a shortage of positive role models. Soon, another generation coming of age is lost. "We need parents to be parents," police Superintendent Eddie Johnson said at a news conference Monday. "We need neighborhoods to be neighborhoods," he said, asking for help identifying suspects. "You all know who these individuals are, they come into your homes every day, sleep with you every night. Grandparents, parents, siblings, significant others - you know who they are.[80]

In short, parts of Chicago, and large parts at that, are experiencing anarchy, openly described by the mainstream media as "war zones."[81]

Baltimore is even more murderous than Chicago,[82] having the highest homicide rate out of the USA's 50 largest cities, of nearly 56 murders per 100,00 people, recently breaking the murder record of the century,[83] and according to FBI statistics, the second-highest overall crime rate.[84] The standard response to this is that such crime is a response to economic inequality, historical injustice, and/or institutional racism. If so, the problem will not be solved but will only intensify once economic and ecological collapse comes.

---

[80] https://www.chicagotribune.com/news/opinion/editorials/ct-edit-violence-chicago-gangs-police-20180806-story.html.

[81] https://www.chicagotribune.com/news/columnists/kass/ct-met-chicago-violence-kass-0509-story.html.

[82] https://www.theguardian.com/us-news/2017/nov/02/baltimore-murder-rate-homicides-ceasefire.

[83] https://baltimore.cbslocal.com/2018/02/19/baltimore-named-nations-most-dangerous-city-by-usa-today/.

[84] https://www.usatoday.com/story/news/2018/09/25/baltimore-homicide-murder-rate-fbi-statistics-death-crime-killings/1426739002/.

As interesting as the US situation is, Europe, in many respects, is committing national suicide much quicker, for the entire place seems as if it could go up in flames at any moment. In fact, in November/December 2018/2019, this is exactly what was witnessed in France with what began as a grassroots protest by the Yellow Vests Movement (*Mouvement des gilets jaunes*) on November 17, 2018, against rising fuel prices, but which soon evolved into a wider-based protest against globalism, continuing the ritual of burning France to the ground.[85] France was subject to the most violent protests seen since the golden days of cultural Marxist revolutionism in May 1968.[86] Of note was the evolution of the *gilets jaune* to burning a newspaper office and apparent targeting of media outlets, along with the late December 2018 unsuccessful attempt by about 40 *gilets jaune* to storm the presidential retreat of the medieval Fort de Bregancon in Bormes-les-Mimosas.[87]

Mainstream journalist John Lichfield, who observed the violent clashes and fire-bombings, describes the protests as an "insurrection":

> The rivers of destruction which spread down the avenues radiating from around the Arc de Triomphe at the Place de L'Etoile were fed not just by social anger but by a kind of self-righteous hatred. A hatred of Emmanuel Macron. A hatred of the police. A hatred of the state. And a hatred of Paris as a symbol of the unshared wealth and success of Metropolitan France. Six buildings were set alight, dozens of restaurants and shops sacked and pillaged and over 100 cars burned, including every car along one section of the Avenue Kléber. The Arc de Triomphe, symbol of French Republican pride, was vandalised and tagged with insulting graffiti. Many, many yellow vests are decent, frustrated, suffering people. They no longer believe that any of the mainstream political movements – or even Marine Le Pen's Far Right or Jean-Luc Mélenchon Hard Left – will do anything to help them. They talk of a new "movement of the people and for the people" but have declined so far to choose recognised leaders or to put forward a united programme. When eight gilets jaunes

---

[85]   G. Guilluy, *Twilight of the Elites: Prosperity, the Periphery, and the Future of France*, (Yale University Press, New Haven, 2019); https://www.theguardian.com/commentisfree/2018/dec/02/france-is-deeply-fractured-gilets-jeunes-just-a-symptom.

[86]   https://www.nytimes.com/2018/05/05/world/europe/france-may-1968-revolution.html.

[87]   https://www.independent.co.uk/news/world/europe/yellow-vests-protest-macron-holiday-home-fort-de-bregancon-france-gilets-jaunes-a8702281.html.

"spokesmen and women" were chosen last week, they were immediately repudiated by other parts of the movement. Six of the spokespeople refused to attend a meeting with the Prime Minister Edouard Philippe after receiving violent threats from other gilets jaunes. In other words, this instant, anti-political, political movement not only detests the young technocratic President who was elected only last year. It detests anyone from within its own ranks who "put themselves forward as above the rest." As a result, the gilets jaunes risk falling into the clutches of a destructive, know-nothing and anti-democratic fringe – not a fringe of "entryist" political thugs but a fringe of desperate and unthinking people from within the movement itself. A pacifying dialogue may yet emerge. I fear, however, that the insurrectional thugs who laid waste to Paris on Saturday have no interest in dialogue. They simply want to vent their anger—and, yes, their hatred—on a "bourgeois," successful Metropolitan France which has ignored them for decades.[88]

Lichfield does not mention though, that whereas in America, only 51 percent of people have faith in "democracy" (37 percent, having lost faith),[89] in France, 70 percent of French voters believe that democracy does not work, 40 percent of French people maintain that a full-on revolution is the only answer to France's Great Mess, and 63 percent of young voters are ready for large-scale revolt.[90] Hence, a social blow-up was inevitable, with the French riot police by January 2019, arming themselves with quality Heckler and Koch G36 5.56 x 45 mm assault rifles (a fantastic gun), just to be safe against unarmed civilians.[91]

Further, the potential exists for much worse than this to occur right throughout Europe, and every riot has the potential to be a STHF trigger event.[92] This is especially so when protestors get their hands blown off by police percussion grenades, or journalists having

[88] https://www.thelocal.fr/20181202/analysis-the-savage-violence-in-paris-was-not-a-protest-it-was-insurrection.

[89] https://www.axios.com/poll-americans-faith-in-democracy-2e94a938-4365-4e80-9fb6-d9743d817710.html.

[90] https://www.bloomberg.com/opinion/articles/2017-04-26/social-unrest-is-france-s-biggest-risk.

[91] https://www.dailymail.co.uk/news/article-6586991/French-riot-police-using-semi-automatic-weapons-against-Yellow-Vest-protestors.html.

[92] http://www.shtfplan.com/headline-news/selco-on-the-riots-in-france-false-news-and-manipulated-rage-every-riot-can-be-the-start-of-shtf_12072018.

their faces pulped by tear gas grenades,[93] are shot in the chest and head by rubber bullets "like rabbits," when high school students are forced by riot police to kneel with hands behind their heads in Mafia-execution-style, and combat ready armored vehicles stand ready to be used against unarmed French protestors, demonstrating against this authoritarianism, producing appallingly inflammatory optics.

The nation state, as it has been known, is ceasing to exist, being fast replaced by pre-modern tribalism, within the framework of a decaying techno-modernist infrastructure, which in turn will disintegrate, since the social capital needed to sustain it will no longer exist.

The Ugly Face of Collapse

What will the early stages of collapse be like, on the ground? What is one likely to experience? Although there have been a number of books written by alleged survivors of socio-economic collapse, in my opinion, the one which best captures the level of violence and degradation that people will experience is Selco Begovic, *The Dark Secrets of SHTF Survival*.[94] This excellent book describes Selco's experiences in a city under siege during the Balkan War of the 1990s. As he says in the book, he had failed to read the signs and bug out, and thus was trapped in a nightmarish world where there was a struggle to obtain resources to exist, including food and water, as well as hyper-violence, that being that violence had become a way of life. Thus, gardening and most daylight activities were dangerous because of snipers. There was the constant threat of exploding shells, rifle fire, and invading gangs. People were tortured for amusement, burnt alive, and private prisons were established to allow torture and rape.

---

[93] "French Police Use 'Weapons of War' Against Protesters: Journalist Tells RT how Tear Gas Grenade Exploded in His Face," November 20, 2019, at https://www.rt.com/news/473838-yellow-vests-paris-journalist-grenade/.

[94] S. Begovic, *The Dark Secrets of SHTF Survival: The Brutal Truth about Violence, Death, and Mayhem that You Must Know to Survive*, (Daisy Luther Media, 2018).

The economic breakdown in Venezuela is another example of what happens when civilized order breaks down. Shortages of food, medicine and almost all resources, a product of an economically mismanaged socialist society imploding through hyperinflation,[95] has led to gangs of children fighting for "quality garbage" with machetes,[96] and females as young as fourteen selling sex, something common in collapse situations for unprepared women.[97] Power blackouts have added to the general level of chaos and daily threats to existence.[98]

The NGO Human Rights Watch has found that malnutrition is widespread in Venezuela, now beyond the World Health Organization's crisis limit, with 80 percent of households not having adequate food.[99] People struggle on a daily basis to get enough food to survive and relatively "safe" water to drink.[100]

The medical system has broken down, with almost all diseases at crisis point, and hospitals short of all resources. Often, X-ray machines do not work, due to power blackouts, and if they do, the X-ray films need to be examined outside in the sun, when the next power blackout occurs. Women have given birth in hospital corridors, lacking even a bed.[101] According to the Pharmaceutical Federation of Venezuela, the country has an 85 percent shortage of medicines, and a 90 percent shortage of medicines used to treat severe diseases such as cancer.[102] Emergency rooms have become a

[95] https://www.bbc.com/news/world-latin-america-36319877.

[96] https://www.miamiherald.com/news/nation-world/world/americas/venezuela/article206950449.html.

[97] https://www.reuters.com/article/us-venezuela-migrants-trafficking/venezuelas-crisis-boosts-trafficking-risk-for-women-children-experts-idUSKCN1LF1XG.

[98] https://www.theorganicprepper.com/blackout-chaos-venezuela/.

[99] https://www.hrw.org/es/video-photos/interactive/2018/11/14/los-exiliados-un-viaje-la-frontera-expone-la-crisis-humanitaria.

[100] https://www.theorganicprepper.com/surviving-in-a-venezuelan-city/.

[101] http://www.internationalhealthpolicies.org/the-alarming-collapse-of-the-venezuelan-healthcare-system/.

[102] https://www.npr.org/2018/02/01/582469305/venezuelas-health-care-system-ready-to-

medical emergency of themselves, with 70 percent having failures, and 22 percent being out of service.[103] The collapse of Venezuela's healthcare system has led to "medical refugees" seeking hospital treatment in other South American countries such as Colombia, which has placed a severe strain upon their health care systems.[104]

The country is also experiencing a collapse of most of its institutions, infrastructure, and public services, and collapsing infrastructure has now led to the country's oil production going into freefall.[105] Essential products and resources are in scarce supply, which has led to a spiral of violence and home invasions, especially attacks to obtain food:

> There have been reports on the roads to the East of the country (Cumana city for example) where 20 or 25 people gangs stop the cars and take whatever they want. LEOs will take whatever food you happen to carry, without bothering in giving you something else other than a warning that you are lucky to not be going to jail. This is something to be expected in such a situation, and it can't be more dangerous. However, it will not develop itself from one day to another; once things start to get bad and dope starts to be scarce ... the hunger will make the beast leap out. The predators will go after the easier preys first. Or whatever they believe these preys are. It is a hard compromise, but you can't look helpless and unable to defend. There are a lot of psychos here that will shoot innocent people in the head just because they can, and they know that no one is going to come after them. If you could see some of the videos that have been uploaded about what the gangs are able to do ... you would understand why I am so freaked out. Hands chopped. Picks used to drill someone´s head while a woman laughs as she is recording the footage. Jeez.[106]

The country is heading in the direction of the end of the rule of law, with ultraviolent gangs thriving, often targeting entire buildings and

collapse-amid-economic-crisis.

[103]   https://www.journalducameroun.com/en/report-highlights-deepening-venezuela-health-crisis/.

[104]   https://nypost.com/2018/03/08/sick-venezuelans-flee-to-colombia-in-growing-refugee-crisis/.

[105]   https://www.breitbart.com/national-security/2018/11/25/world-view-socialist-venezuela-oil-production-in-freefall-as-infrastructure-collapses/.

[106]   http://time.com/longform/hunger-crime-violence-venezuela/.

systematically looting and raping, with sex slavery rings existing.[107] It has now become rule of the warlords, with each neighborhood having its own hoods and "street lords."[108]

In 2017, the homicide rate was 26,616, averaging at present 73 dead a day, making Venezuela the second most dangerous place next to the rapists' paradise, El Salvador, where there is not a conventional war, although there is 4 GW asymmetrical warfare, as seen throughout South America: "Official numbers show just 239 women and girls among the murdered so far this year, about a tenth the number of men, with an additional 201 reported missing. Through August, 361 rapes were reported, two-thirds of them against minors. But the statistics don't begin to tell the story. Worldwide, women generally report only 20 percent of rapes, according to the World Health Organization, and that percentage is likely lower in El Salvador. The missing and dead also may be underreported. "We have cases in which the mother knows how her daughter died, but she cannot talk because the gangsters who raped and killed her have come to the wake to offer condolences for their girlfriend," said Silvia Juarez, a lawyer with the Gender Violence Observatory. "In this context, the state is incapable of offering protection."[109]

Violent gangs in Venezuela have something of a passion for dismemberment, slicing off victim's limbs, genitalia, and heads.[110] The return of piracy, in Venezuela, along with an epidemic of lynching by crazed mobs, people being set on fire, are other examples of the descent into savagery in a compact case study of what is to come for all of us.[111] And, while all of this occurs, the socialist regime of dictator Maduro performs in classic anarcho-tyranny fashion, ruling

[107] https://www.reuters.com/article/us-venezuela-gangs-idUSKCN1162AJ.

[108] https://www.prepperwebsite.com/10-survival-rules/?utm_source=feedburner&utm_medium=feed&utm_campaign=Feed%3A+PrepperWebsite+%28Prepper+Website%29.

[109] "El Salvador's Horrifying Culture of Gang Rape," November 6, 2014, at https://nypost.com/2014/11/06/the-youth-are-theirs-el-salvadors-horrifying-culture-of-gang-rape/.

[110] http://www.jamaicaobserver.com/news/dismemberment-latest-gory-trend-in-venezuela-crime.

[111] https://www.smh.com.au/world/central-america/pirates-of-the-caribbean-a-grim-reality-as-venezuela-disintegrates-20180813-p4zx79.html.

through terror, with beatings, rapes, torture and electrocution of anyone who may be a threat to his good times. That will be the West in a few years given present trends, as reviewed in the discussion above.[112]

Mexico is another South American country in free fall to collapse and chaos.[113] It is a country which saw 133 politicians murdered in the run-up to the 2018 elections.[114] Mexico is up there in the murder hit parade, with 2,599 homicide cases opened in July 2018 by the Ministry of Public Security, an average of 84 murders a day. The previous record of 2,894 was set in May 2018. In the first seven months of 2018, there were 16,399 homicide cases opened. Of course, much of this is fuelled by the drug cartels, where America's insatiable thirst for drugs creates an irresistible market.[115] There are also common headlines such as: "Brutal Mexican Zetas Leader Chopped Up Girl, 6, with an Axe While She was Still Alive In Front of Parents So They Would 'Remember' Him;"[116] and then there are the hyperviolent activities of gangs such as MS-13, who stabbed one victim 100 times, decapitated him, and ripped out his heart.[117]

In Tijuana, over 2,000 homicides occurred in 2018, up to the end of October. The imagery here is distinctively post-apocalyptic, where people can be torn apart, much as zombies do in TV shows such as *The Walking Dead*. However, the killers here are much more dangerous, having access to firepower to obliterate their victims, rather than mere rotting, disease-ridden teeth.

---

[112]   http://caslainstitute.org/informe-2018-sobre-tortura-sistematica-en-venezuela/.

[113]   S. Culper, "What Could "Collapse" Look Like? Let's Look at a Country Currently in Free Fall," July 6, 2018, at https://forwardobserver.com/what-could-collapse-look-like-lets-look-at-a-country-currently-in-free-fall/.

[114]   https://www.dailysabah.com/americas/2018/06/28/133-politicians-murdered-in-run-up-to-mexicos-elections-report.

[115]   https://www.zerohedge.com/news/2018-08-25/murderous-mexico-july-most-violent-ever-country-descends-chaos.

[116]   https://www.thesun.co.uk/news/3916896/zetas-mexican-cartel-lead-chopped-girl-axe/.

[117]   https://www.foxnews.com/us/ms-13-victim-was-stabbed-100-times-decapitated-had-heart-ripped-out-police-say.

Violence is so bad in Brazil that President Jair Bolsonaro, has moved to liberalize the country's strict gun laws to give ordinary citizens a fighting chance against gangs. However, in early January 2019, in response to such measures, gangs in the northern state of Ceará, unleashed waves of violence, attempting to destroy the city to teach Bolsonaro a lesson.[118]

Come the collapse of civilization, feral violent people just like these described above, will arise in every city, and down every street, to become the new war lords, or just vermin, of the world. We have seen this happen throughout history and across countries. There is simply no reason to suppose, as the academic Left does, that in such disaster situations, we will see the best of human nature. On the contrary, we do see civilized people helping others in situations such as natural disasters, but the premise is always, that order exists, and will soon be restored. But, we are contemplating the end of such order. What we have seen in this discussion is hyper-violence generated primarily from socio-economic decline. However, as theorists have argued, we have not seen anything yet because the socio-ecological-economic catastrophe will put this matter in a whole new light, or is it darkness? At present, there are abundant resources for the average person to survive, even if it means dumpster diving and living off charity. But, what happens when there is no such largess, purely from population competition? Humans will be just like any other species in plague conditions, experiencing overshoot and collapse. All that has saved the modern West so far has been technology, but that too depends upon a stable society, because technicians need resources to live, and are unfortunately not bullet proof.

Thus, see the collapse of the West as inevitable, given present political conditions. It is possible that some miracle could occur, but I would not bet on it. So, let us prepare for the worst-case scenario. Civilization will decompose. What then can individuals, families, and tribal groups do now in preparation for this end of endings? For one thing, we need to rise to the challenge that will confront us, and that I will now show will require becoming a barbarian in a world

---

[118] https://www.breitbart.com/national-security/2019/01/08/ceara-brazil-violence-gangs-bolsonaro/.

where civilization has collapsed anyway. What other choice is there other than to be tortured, die, and rot?

2.

After Ragnarok: Lo, the Neo-Barbarian

The strong must ever rule the weak,
is grim Primordial Law.
On earth's broad racial threshing floor,
the meek are beaten straw.
- *Ragnar Redbeard*[119]

Over-sentimentality, over-softness, in fact, washiness and mushiness, are great dangers of this age and of this people. Unless we keep the barbarian virtues, gaining the civilized one will be little avail. - *Theodore Roosevelt (1899)*[120]

British empiricist philosopher David Hume (1711-1776) was surely right in saying: "It is well known, that every government must come to a period, and that death is unavoidable to the political, as well as the animal body."[121] These remarks apply to techno-industrial society as well. There is, among other things, a collision between the unending economic growth of global capitalism/techno-industrial society and the ecological limits to growth.[122] In terms of ecological footprint analysis, with anticipated

---

[119]   Ragnar Redbeard, *Might is Right or Survival of the Fittest*, (Ostara Publications, 2013), p. 178.

[120]   Theodore Roosevelt, cited from Frank Miniter, *The Ultimate Man's Survival Guide: Recovering the Lost Art of Manhood*, (Regnery Publishing, Washington DC, 2009), p. 45.

[121]   David Hume, *The Philosophy of David Hume*, (Four Volumes), (Adam Black and William Tait, London, 1826), volume 3, p. 55.

[122]   K. Higgs, *Collision Course: Endless Growth on a Finite Planet*, (MIT Press, Cambridge MA, 2014).

and expected rises to existing standards of living, to produce something resembling global equity with standards higher than the existing average American, will require by the 2050s 20 Earth's, which is impossible. Attempts to avert this "collision course" by "sustainable development" are likely to be crushed by the tsunami of economic growth now crashing onto the shores of modernity. This, as has been detailed by many, is producing "peak everything" and a civilizational catastrophe, leading to a collapse of the world as we have known it, by 2030, and most likely, even sooner. Interestingly enough, as we saw earlier, hedge fund managers are presently buying remote farms in places like New Zealand as "secret boltholes," complete with landing strips in the event of civil uprisings. Some would escape to another planet if they could, and nuke us from orbit – just to be sure.

The collapse of techno-industrial society may be preceded by the collapse of its ideological underpinnings. Julius Evola is right in seeing mankind as being in a "Dark Age" or *Kali Yuga*, an age of dissolution.[123] This is an order where values have collapsed, or at least traditional values, and especially those that in the past had defined men and masculinity. Evola said: "There no longer exist the organizations and institutions that, in a traditional civilization and society, would have allowed him to realise himself wholly, to order his own existence in a clear and unambiguous way, and to defend and apply creatively in his own environment the principal values that he recognizes within himself."[124]

The moral and philosophical underpinnings of classical liberalism and its universalism are untenable. It is seldom discussed in contemporary political discourse, which begins with the assumption that egalitarianism, individualism, and universalism are the only rational games in the shanty town of philosophy. But this is not so.

---

[123] Julius Evola, *Revolt Against the Modern World*, (Inner Traditions, Rochester, Vermont, 1995).

[124] Julius Evola, *Ride the Tiger: A Survival Manual for Aristocrats of the Soul*, (Inner Traditions, Rochester, 2003), pp. 3-4.

To begin: assuming that traditional morality is at least cognately coherent, there is a long-term unsolved problem of *why* an individual should be moral at all, especially given the assumption of radical individualism.[125] This question grants that there may be "right" and "wrong," but asks: why do "right" and not "wrong," why move beyond self-interest? Kai Nielsen, who has investigated this question in depth, has concluded: "there can be no rational considerations showing us that we must, on pain of simply being irrational, be moral."[126]

If that is not challenging enough, the moralist then has the problem of refuting *moral skepticism* (moral statements are not knowable because they are either not true (or have no truth value) and/or are not rationally justifiable) and *moral nihilism* (moral statements making substantive positive claims are not statements of objective fact, and are either not true or have no truth value). Arguments for moral nihilism include the claim that morality exhibits ontological "queerness," or the strangeness of postulated moral facts, so that by Occam's razor (do not multiply entries in one's ontology beyond necessity), there are no moral facts.[127] And, even if one makes metaphysical sense of moral reference, there is the further problem of rationally justifying moral claims. Non-cognitivist positions such as "expressivism" (moral statements are not true or false statements, but express emotions and feelings on moral issues),[128] may be of little help to the moralist when confronted by the intractable nature of moral disagreements, which Mackie rightly saw "reflect adherence to and participation in different ways of life."[129]

[125] Kai Nielsen, *Why Be Moral?* (Prometheus Press, Amherst, 1989).

[126] Kai Nielsen, "Why Should I Be Moral? Revisited," *American Philosophical Quarterly*, vol. 21, 1984, pp. 89-91.

[127] Richard Joyce and Simon Kirchin (eds), *A World Without Values: Essays on John Mackie's Moral Error Theory*, (Springer, New York, 2010).

[128] R. S Landau, *The Foundations of Ethics*, (Oxford University Press, Oxford, 2010), p. 292.

[129] J. L. Mackie, *Ethics: Inventing Right and Wrong*, (Penguin, London, 1977), p. 36.

At the end of the dark rainbow is the super-ultimate problem of justification: that a moral standard M requires for its rational justification either a (vicious) infinite regression of other moral standards or meta-moral standards, M_1, M_2, M_3... or of rational principles, or an arbitrary stopping point (dogmatism) or the question-begging assertion of the rightness of the standard (the problem of the criterion).[130] Philosophers seldom face this Medusa reality, preferring epistemological comfort.

The rejection of orthodox morality and the resultant acceptance of moral nihilism does not imply that all values and evaluative norms are, therefore, to be rejected. A moral nihilist can still say that it is better than not for humans to maximize their flourishing according to their natures and constitutive powers (e.g., that all other things being equal, it is better to be physically stronger than weaker, and healthy rather than sick), as it would ultimately lead to the elimination of human beings if they had no interest in satisfying their functioning. Moral nihilists can accept that there are "valid" (if only pragmatically justified) norms of rational judgment and instrumental reasoning. There can still be useful instrumental and other values even if *morality* is an incoherent assembly of conceptual bits and pieces as Alasdair MacInyre argues in *After Virtue*.[131] The ancient Greeks did not have our moral preoccupations, although they still had values, as Bernard Williams argues in *Ethics and the Limit of Philosophy*.[132] Derek Browne also puts this point well:

> Morality adopts the universal point of view: that is what is most striking about this peculiarly modern phenomenon. The most useful way to view this feature of morality is to say that morality is ruled by the metaethical principle that the universal point of view has supreme authority over all other points of view. From the universal point of view, my own interests and those of my friends are impartially and neutrally weighed along with the interests of all significant others. The practical thinking that I undertake from the moral point of view

---

[130]   On the problem of the criterion see R. P. Amico, *The Problem of the Criterion*, (Rowman and Littlefield, Lanham, 1993).

[131]   Alasdair MacIntyre, *After Virtue*, 3rd edition, (University of Notre Dame Press, Notre Dame, 2007).

[132]   Bernard Williams, *Ethics and the Limits of Philosophy*, (Harvard University Press, Cambridge, 1985).

does not disregard my own well-being. But it relegates my own self to the status of one of the others with whom morality is impartially concerned, and my friends retreat to the distance of strangers. From the universal point of view, the local concerns of the self stand in need of moral justification, they are suspect unless they can be endorsed morally... According to utilitarianism—a theory which very clearly expresses the universalist thrust or moral thinking—it could happen that local concerns turn out to be morally indefensible. If that is so, then we ought—morally ought—to give them up. [...]

This conclusion is repugnant because it contradicts the way we are. A morality which lacks any plausible grounding in human psychology surrenders its claim to the allegiance of human beings. Universalist morality threats constantly to break the connection which ethics has with the goodness of a human life – human goodness, not moral goodness. Yet any plausible account of human goodness will be grounded in the facts of real human motivation. [...]

The self and its local concerns stands at the center of Greek ethics. The self and its local concerns are banished to the distance of strangers by morality. The suspicion that this is an unhealthy attitude is the major reason for thinking that we might be better off without morality. [133]

Some have held that moral notions such as the concepts of obligation, duty, right and wrong, are incoherent without a notion of divine law and its associated concepts of guilt and punishment for transgression. On this "law conception of ethics," G. E. M. Anscombe said in 1958, it "is not possible to have unless you believe in God as a lawgiver."[134] Thus, let us now turn to a consideration of the merits of Judeo-Christianity, the leading contender in our culture for not only supplying a "law conception of morality," but also supplying possible survival ethics for a post-apocalyptic world. Further to this, as Larry Siedentop has cogently argued in *Inventing the Individual*,[135] Christianity has provided the moral assumptions leading to liberal thought, with its belief that humans have freewill and its belief in moral equity, and manic cosmopolitan justice.

---

[133]   Derek Browne, "Ethics without Morality," *Australasian Journal of Philosophy*, vol. 68, 1990, pp. 395-412, cited pp. 408-409.

[134]   G. E. M. Anscombe, "Modern Moral Philosophy," *Philosophy*, vol. 33, 1958, pp. 1-19.

[135]   Larry Siedentop, *Inventing the Individual: The Origins of Western Liberalism*, (Allen Lane, London, 2014).

New Testament passages advocating universalism are ubiquitous: "There is neither Jew nor Gentile, neither slave nor free, nor is there male and female, for you are all one in Christ Jesus," Galatians 3:28. The Greeks (and arguably most Asian cultures), had no conception of the individual as distinct from social wholes, such as the polis and the community, and did not believe in freewill. And, they were much better off for it, as well.

Christinsanity

A search of a contemporary book site Amazon.com yields an enormous critical literature dealing with Christianity, ranging from works arguing that the Bible is riddled with numerous inconsistencies, absurdities, and immoralities,[136] to arguments that Jesus did not exist at all.[137] But, of course, not much of this is new, with the attack on Christianity beginning with Jewish, Greek and Roman thinkers in antiquity.

Porphyry of Tyre (234-305 AD), in his *Adversus Christianos* (*Against the Christians*), presented a critique which was one of the works burnt by Theodosius II in AD 435 and 448.[138] The work was devoted to attacking the historicity of Judeo-Christianity, such as the prophecy of Daniel (9:27; 11:31; 12:11), showing that Christ himself was wrong in accepting this, as in Matthew 24:15, although the verse referring to the "abomination that causes desolation" is so vague as to be virtually irrefutable. In any case, the passage is missing from

---

[136] D. Barker, *God: The Most Unpleasant Character in all Fiction*, (Sterling, New York, 2016); William Henry Burr, *Self-Contradictions of the Bible*, (Prometheus Books, Amherst, 1987); Bart D. Ehrman, *Jesus Interrupted: Revealing the Hidden Contradictions in the Bible (and Why We Don't Know about Them)*, (HarperCollins, New York, 2009); R. W. Hinton, *Arsenal for Skeptics*, (A. S. Barnes, New York, 1961).

[137] See for example, G. A. Wells, *Did Jesus Exist?* Revised edition, (Pemberton, London, 1986); R. Lataster and R. Carrier, *Jesus Did Not Exist*, (CreateSpace, 2015); Richard Carrier, *Why I am Not a Christian: Four Conclusive Reasons to Reject the Faith*, (Philosophy Press, 2011); D. M. Murdock, *The Origins of Christianity*, (Stellar House, Publishing, 2011); https://www.creatingchrist.com/.

[138] *Porphyry's Against the Christians: The Literary Remains*, translated by R. Joseph Hoffman, (Prometheus Books, Amherst, 1994).

the *Codex Sinaiticus* (the 4th century hand-written copy of the Bible in Greek).

Numerous Jewish theologians commented on aspects of the Christian doctrine, such as the Christian interpretation of Isaiah 7:14, that an *almah* (a young woman of marriageable age), will give birth to a child whose name will be Immanuel. The Greek translation rendered *almah* as *parthenos*, a virgin. The alleged virgin birth of Jesus Christ is stated to have occurred in the gospels of Matthew and Luke, but does not occur in Mark and John, and there is no mention of this in any of Paul's writings. Jewish critics referred to Jesus's father as "Panthera" (panther), a pun on the Greek word for "virgin," *parthenos*.[139] Celsus, a 2nd century Greek critic of Christianity, was well aware of such problems, which Christians met with ad hoc hypotheses and "just so" explanations, and he compared the Christian sects of his time to "a cluster of bats or ants escaping a nest, a bunch of frogs holding council in a swamp, or a clutch of worms assembling in the muck."[140] Although he used various scatological metaphors to depict Christians, his favorite one appears to be that of the worm, a metaphor also favored by Friedrich Nietzsche (1844-1900), who said: "Christianity is a revolt of everything that crawls along the ground directed against that which is *elevated*: the gospel of the 'lowly' *makes* low."[141] More on this below.

Biblicists maintain inerrancy insofar as the scriptures are taken to express truths about the nature of God. They tend to be dismissive of quibbles over conflicts about differences of, say, numbers of soldiers in armies, or mathematical inaccuracies (e.g., 2 Chronicles 4:2 which gets the circumference of a bowl wrong) and may deny theologian Charles Ryrie's argument that even minor translational issues would open the Bible to further suspicion of error.[142]

---

[139] See *Celsus: On the True Doctrine: A Discourse Against the Christians*, translated by R. Joseph Hoffman, (Oxford University Press, Oxford, 1987), p. 129.

[140] As above, p. 79.

[141] F. Nietzsche, *Twilight of the Idols and The Anti-Christ*, translated by R. J. Hollingdale, (Viking/Penguin, New York, 1985), p. 157.

[142] C. Ryrie, *Basic Theology*, (Moody Publishers, 1999), p. 77; C. D. McKinsey, *The Encyclopedia of Biblical Errancy*, (Prometheus Books, Amherst, 1995), p. 122; Lee Strobal,

Nevertheless, there is a tradition of critique running from Celsus though to d'Holbach[143] to Thomas Paine's *The Age of Reason* (1794, 1795, 1807),[144] to the liberal John Shelby Spong's *The Sins of Scripture* (2005),[145] which sees the genocide, massacres and ethnic cleansings of the Old Testament, as contrary to any basic moral code. Forgetting the physical absurdities of collecting all of the vast species of animals, including elusive platypuses from Australia, and putting them in an ark, what moral god would drown the whole human race except Noah and his family, including indigenous people from Australia?[146] If it is argued that humanity at the time was evil (with original sin, what else do you expect?), then an all-knowing God should have known about the inevitable consequences of "free will" and not made humans at all. No humans, no evil from them. At cosmic tort law, God would be a negligent creator. So, sue Him. Or, His representatives, the Church see (*The Man Who Sued God* (2001)).[147]

Every critic of Christianity has his/her favorite horror story from the "good" book, but as I have used the zombie metaphor previously, I personally favor these:

Leviticus 26: 29: "You will eat the flesh of your sons and the flesh of your daughters."

Deuteronomy 28: 53: "Then you shall eat the offspring of your own body, the flesh of your sons and of your daughters whom the LORD your God has given

---

The Case for Christ, (Zondervan, Grand Rapids, 2016), p. 317.

[143]   Baron d'Holbach, *The System of Nature*, (1770), (Burt Franklin, New York, 1970), "Of the Confused and Contradictory Ideas of Theology," pp. 191-202.

[144]   Thomas Paine, *The Age of Reason*, in *The Complete Writings of Thomas Paine*, edited by P. Foner, (New York, 1945).

[145]   J. S. Spong, *The Sins of Scripture*, (HarperSanFrancisco, New York, 2005).

[146]   R. D. Bradley, "A Moral Argument for Atheism," in M. Martin and R. Monnier (eds), *The Impossibility of God*, (Prometheus Books, Amherst, 2003), pp. 129-146, cited p. 134.

[147]   See also Michael Martin, *Atheism: A Philosophical Justification*, (Temple University Press, Philadelphia, 1990), where he argues that in terms of tort law, God is strictly liable for the evil actions of beings that he has created, just like farmers are responsible for rampaging animals, and humans are the most dangerous animals on Earth (pp. 386-388).

you, during the siege and the distress by which your enemy will oppress you."

2 Kings 6: 29: "So we boiled my son and ate him; and I said to her on the next day, 'Give your son, that we may eat him'; but she has hidden her son." Can you blame her?

Jeremiah 19:9: "I will make them eat the flesh of their sons and the flesh of their daughters, and they will eat one another's flesh in the siege and in the distress with which their enemies and those who seek their life will distress them.'"

Lamentations 4:10: "The hands of compassionate women boiled their own children; they became food for them because of the destruction of the daughter of my people."

Ezekiel 5:10: Therefore, fathers will eat their sons among you, and sons will eat their fathers; for I will execute judgments on you and scatter all your remnant to every wind.

Here is a doctrine of zombies, of the flesh eaters. And, this is not merely a product of the frantic imaginations of the Old Testament writers; Revelation 14: 10-11 says that unbelievers "will be tormented with fire and brimstone in the presence of the holy angels and in the presence of the Lamb." Presumably, they will have a few tinnies of beer while watching the BBQ.

Let us not forget about Matthew 27:51-53, where after the alleged crucifixion of Jesus, the bodies of the saints were allegedly resurrected and ran into the city, revealing themselves to many. This is surely the greatest miracle described in the New Testament, but there is absolutely no reliable historical evidence for this; the account is missing as well in the gospels of Mark, Luke and John.[148] But that is just water off a duck's back for the Christian.

To explain this, first we need to look at the idea of a meme, a cultural package of inheritance. The meme theme was advanced by Richard Dawkins in *The Selfish Gene* [149] and developed further in his Voltaire Lecture, delivered at the Conway Hall Humanist Centre, London, November 6, 1992.[150] There, Dawkins viewed

---

[148] H. L. Mencken, *Treatise on the Gods*, (Alfred A. Knopf, New York, 1930), p. 305.

[149] R. Dawkins, *The Selfish Gene*, (Oxford University Press, Oxford, 1976 and 2006).

[150] R. Dawkins, "Viruses of the Mind," in B. Dahlbom (ed.), *Dennett and His Critics:*

religion as spread by a memetic virus, and saw religious beliefs as "mind parasites." He showed that religious beliefs followed an epidemiology mode of transmission by infection/indoctrination beginning with parental socialization and later reinforced by religious institutions. As a leading atheist, he saw this as primarily a disease mode of transmission of an ideological pathogen, that ultimately had deleterious effects upon its host, as most parasites, unlike symbiotes, do.[151] These ideas have been expanded by others.[152] We should note that there is nothing preventing this argument being used back against atheism, liberalism and humanism, doctrines which are often as crazed and fanatical as Christianity. That *tu quoque*, however, does not save Christianity. Nor does arguing that there are other religions even more toxic. Perhaps there is a plague on *all* houses?

Susan Blackmore, who previously accepted the idea that religion was a virus of the mind, abandoned the idea when she heard a paper by Michael Blume at a conference.[153] The core argument was that the religious tend to have more children than the non-religious, so there is a Darwinian advantage to religious belief, in terms of survival value.[154] However, this demographic statistic is true primarily for traditional religious positions, with more liberal versions of Christianity being basically forms of humanism and liberalism. Cutting to the core, if the religion stresses traditional roles for women, a traditional nuclear family structure, and is critical of artificial contraception (something the Catholic Church well understood), then women, if they take it all seriously/or have to, as in the case of fundamentalist Islam, will have babies, all becoming

---

Demystifying Mind, (Blackwell, Oxford, 1993), pp. 13-27.

[151]   R. Dawkins, *The God Delusion*, (Mariner, Boston, 2008).

[152]   R. Brodie, *Viruses of the Mind: The New Science of the Meme*, (Hay House, Carlsbad, 1996); S. Blackmore, *The Meme Machine*, (Oxford University Press, Oxford, 1999).

[153]   S. Blackmore, "Why I No Longer Believe Religion is a Virus of the Mind," September 17, 2000, at https://www.theguardian.com/commentisfree/belief/2010/sept/16/why-no-longer-believe-religion-virus-mind.

[154]   E. Kaufmann, *Shall the Religious Inherit the Earth? Demography and Politics in the Twenty-First Century*, (Profile Books, London, 2011).

part of what Jack Donovan has called the "Empire of Nothing."[155]

Further, even if religious people do have more children than secular humanists, which is not saying much anyway given the below-net reproduction levels for most European populations, Christianity could still be a "slow virus," having a long thousand-year incubation period, but ultimately leading to a diseased state, and death, just as secular humanism does. In the case of biological diseases, retro-virus HTLV2, causing the disease Atypical Hairy Cell Leukemia, has a typical latency of 10-30 years.[156]

In her book, *Scatter, Adapt, and Remember,*[157] Annalee Newitz discusses the Jewish survival strategy of "scattering in the face of adversity."[158] This is illustrated by the First Diaspora, described in Exodus, of the Jewish flight from ancient Egypt, where they were allegedly held as slaves. It is a remarkable story, well portrayed by Charlton Heston as Moses in *The Ten Commandments* (1956). However, the story is not "true," even without the plagues of blood and slaying of the firstborn non-Jewish sons or the parting of the seas to destroy the Egyptian solders. Newitz says, "there's no evidence that the Jews or even their Asiatic ancestors were in Egypt during the time described in Exodus – roughly during the reign of Rameses in the late second millennium BCE."[159]

Early Christians such as Origen (185-254 AD), doubted that all of the Scriptures could be understood as historical truths because their point was to present moral teachings, not record history. Origen put it as follows: "The Scriptures contain many things which never come to pass, interwoven with the history, and he must be dull indeed who does not of his own accord observe that much which the

---

[155]   See the remarks at www.vhemt.org/religionbabieshr.htm; J. Donovan, *Becoming a Barbarian*, (Dissonant Hum, Milwaukie, 2016).

[156]   A. Jaswai and J. P. Singh, "Review of Virus Diseases in the Nervous System," *International Archives of Integrated Medicine*, vol. 2, 2015, pp. 125-130.

[157]   Annalee Newitz, *Scatter, Adapt, and Remember: How Humans Will Survive a Mass Extinction*, (Anchor Books, New York, 2014).

[158]   As above, p. 117.

[159]   As above, p. 120.

Scriptures represent as having happened never actually happened."[160] The Church used force to crush such thought until its power began to decline, to be replaced by new tyrannies of decadent liberalism.

In the 17th and 18th centuries, the Old and New Testament began to be subjected to a searching examination and criticism by rationalist and Enlightenment thinkers. Baruch Spinoza (1632-1677) undertook a critical deconstruction of the Old Testament in his *Theological-Political Treatise*[161] and Edward Gibbon in *The Decline and Fall of the Roman Empire*,[162] while also recognizing the mythical basis of Christianity, famously proposed that Christianity was one of the causes of the fall of the Roman Empire.

Hermann Samuel Reimarus (1694-1768) and David Friedrich Strauss (1808-1874) both regarded the scriptures as non-historical and mythopoetic, rejecting the alleged divinity of Christ.[163] These thinkers would influence the "Higher Criticism," a German hermeneutic school which would further the deconstructive critique.[164]

Godfrey Higgins (1771-1834), Gerald Massey (1872-1908), and Alvin Boyd Kuhn (1881-1963) argued that Judeo-Christianity had its origins in earlier Egyptian beliefs.[165] The omnipotent, omniscient God-creator, Ra, is similar to Yahweh of the Old Testament and the Hermetic Books of Egypt, such as *The Seventh Book of Hermes, His*

---

[160] Quoted from D. F. Strauss, *The Life of Jesus Critically Examined*, (SCM Press, London, 1973).

[161] Baruch Spinoza, *Theological-Political Treatise*, (*Tractatus Theologico-Politicus*), (Cambridge University Press, Cambridge, 2007).

[162] Edward Gibbon, *The Decline and Fall of the Roman Empire*, (Modern Library, New York, 1995), p. 502.

[163] D. Christie-Murray, *A History of Hersey*, (Oxford University Press, Oxford, 1989).

[164] V. A. Harvey, "New Testament Scholarship and Christian Belief," in R. J. Hoffman and G. A. Larue (eds), *Jesus in History and Myth*, (Prometheus Books, New York, 1986), pp. 193-200.

[165] G. Higgins, *Anacalypsis: An Inquiry into the Origin of Languages, Nations and Religions* (1833), (Kessinger Publishing, Kila MT, 1997); G. Massey, *Ancient Egypt, The Light of the World: A Work of Reclamation and Restitution in Twelve Volumes*, (Kessinger Publishing, Kila MT, 2001); A. B. Kuhn, *The Lost Light: An Interpretation of Ancient Scriptures* (1940), (Kessinger Publishing, Kila MT, 1997).

Secret Sermon on the Mount of Regeneration, has striking parallels with the (much later) sayings of Jesus.[166] Tom Haripur, who synthesized the works of Higgins, Massey and Kuhn, has concluded that "the entire Christian Bible, Creation legend, the descent into and exodus from Egypt, ark and flood allegory, Israelite "history," Hebrew prophecy and poetry, and the imagery of the Gospels, the Epistles, and Revelation, are now proven to have been transmitted from ancient Egypt's scrolls and papyri into the hands of later generations who didn't know their true origin or their fathomless meanings."[167]

Others have seen the same sort of "remarkable parallels" between the Mesopotamian god Marduk and Yahweh of the Old Testament, both as Lord of all gods and creators of the universe.[168] Noah's ark and the flood narrative borrows from the earlier *The Epic of Gilgamesh*;[169] earlier flood myths are found in the Sumerian epic of Ziusudra (ca. 2600 BCE) and the Akkadin epic of Attrahasis (ca. 1900 BCE), which even has the hero build an ark![170]

There is a considerable literature detailing historical precedents of much of the Old and New Testaments.[171] Apologists generally accept that the parallels exist, but deny that the Bible is a social construction, arguing (circularly) that because it is true, the earlier episodes are just anticipations of the main event, given by Judeo-Christianity. Against this, it has been argued that seeing the Bible as a cultural product, rather than being ghost written by "God," gives

[166] T. Harpur, *The Pagan Christ: Is Blind Faith Killing Christianity?* (Allen and Unwin, Crows Nest, 2004), p. 34.

[167] As above, p. 11.

[168] Edward T. Babinski, "The Cosmology of the Bible," in John W. Loftus (ed.), *The Christian Delusion: Why Faith Fails,* (Prometheus Books, Amherst, 2010), pp. 109-147, cited pp. 117-118.

[169] C. Gorden and G. Rendsburg, *The Bible and the Ancient Near East,* (Norton, New York, 1997).

[170] Paul Tobin, "The Bible and Modern Scholarship," in John W. Loftus (ed.), *The Christian Delusion: Why Faith Fails,* (Prometheus Books, Amherst, 2010), pp. 148-180, cited p. 174.

[171] Jaco Gericke, "Can God Exist if Yahweh Doesn't?" In John W. Loftus (ed.), *The End of Christianity*, (Prometheus Books, Amherst, 2011), pp.131-154.

a parsimonious explication of Biblical contradictions and errors which presumably an all-knowing God would not make.[172]

Biblical scholar and archaeologist, Roland de Vaux has said: "if the historical faith of Israel is not founded in history, such faith is erroneous, and therefore, our faith is also."[173] Gregory Alan Thornbury, writing in *Christianity Today* would agree: "No Jews in Egypt means no Exodus. No Exodus means the foundations of Judaism is a myth. And for Christians, it means that Jesus Christ and the writers of the New Testament got it wrong because they all accepted the reality of Moses and the Exodus and built their teachings on them."[174] According to John 5:46-47 (New International Version), Jesus said: "If you believed Moses, you would believe me, for he wrote about me. But since you do not believe what he wrote, how are you going to believe what I say?" A good question Jesus, now answered in the negative. We should not believe you, if you existed at all.

Consider the humble camel. Camels are mentioned 20 times in Genesis, which presupposes domestication. However, based on the radiocarbon dating of camel bones, camels were not used as beasts of burden in the ancient Near East until after 1000 BCE.[175] This was centuries *after* the time of Abraham, if he existed, and the alleged kingdom of David. Hence, the Biblical accounts were compiled long after the events they describe.

---

[172]   B. Ehrman, *Jesus Interrupted: Revealing the Hidden Contradictions in the Bible*, (Harper One, New York, 2009).

[173]   Roland de Vaux, quoted by Neil Asher Silberman and Israel Finkelstein, *The Bible Unearthed: Archaeology's New Vision of Ancient Israel and the Origin of its Sacred Texts*, (Free Press, New York, 2001), p.42; Daniel Lazare, "False Testament: Archaeology Refutes the Bible's Claim to History – Criticism," *Harper's Magazine*, March 2002, at http://www.yorku.ca/dcarveth/false_testament .

[174]   Gregory Alan Thornbury, "Why it Matters the Exodus Really Happened," February 3, 2015, at http://www.christianitytoday.com/ct/2015/february-web-only/why-it-matters-that-exodus-really-happened.html.

[175]   Lidar Sapir-Hen and Erez Ben-Yosef, "The Introduction of Domestic Camels to the Southern Levant: Evidence from Aravah Valley," *Tel Aviv*, vol. 40, 2013, pp. 277-285.

Exodus, as we have seen, is not an historical account, but a reworking of myths and folk tales to serve an ideological aim.[176] Amihai Mazur writes: "the Exodus story, one of the most prominent traditions in Israelite common memory cannot be accepted as an historical event and must be defined as a national saga. We cannot perceive a whole nation wandering through the desert for forty years under the leadership of Moses, as presented in the biblical tradition."[177] Supporting 600,000 warriors and three million people in a desert environment for 40 years is not possible in terms of water and resource use, and of course, would require regular miracles.[178] Excavations and surveys of the region, such as the camp at Kadesh Barnea, described in Numbers 33, a campsite allegedly for 38 years, yields no trace.[179] There is no trace at Ezion-Geber, and both of these places can be reliably identified. The late Bronze Age places such as Arad (Numbers 21:1-3) and the city of Heshbon (Numbers 21:21-25) and the states of Edom and Ammon, did not exist.

The conquest of Canaan, according to the book of Joshua, was done by an army in rags, women, children, the aged and sick. Yahweh tossed stones from heaven (Joshua 10:11). Not content with this, Joshua asked God to make the sun stand still (commitment to a geocentric universe) so that the complete extermination of Canaanites could be done (Joshua 10:13-14). Needless to say, there is no independent historical record of the Earth standing still (the geo-physical effects, to say the least, would be noticeable) and no record of any of these events in Egyptian Amarna tablets. Canaan cities were small, with no city walls for fortifications, so there were no walls of Jericho to blow down. Egyptian records have no mention of Israelites conquering any city; the only mention of them is "suffering a crushing defeat."

---

[176] Israel Finkelstein, "Patriarch, Exodus, Conquest: Fact or Fiction?" In B. B. Schmidt (ed.), *The Quest for the Historical Israel: Debating Archaeology and the History of Early Israel*, (Society of Biblical Literature, Atlanta, 2007), pp. 41-55.

[177] Amihai Mazur, "The Patriarchs, Exodus, and Conquest Narratives in the Light of Archaeology," in B. B. Schmidt (ed.), as above, pp. 57-65, cited p. 60.

[178] Shlomo Sand, *The Invention of the Jewish People*, (Verso, London, 2009), p. 118.

[179] Israel Finkelstein and Neil Asher Silberman, *The Bible Unearthed*, as above, p. 63.

The Kingdom of David and Solomon are myths, ideological constructions by the priests. There is no mention of either David or Solomon in any Egyptian or Mesopotamian text, and no evidence exists for Solomon's temple. There is indeed the "House of David" artefact discovered in 1993, written in Aramaic, describing the invasion of Israel by an unnamed Aramean king who boasts of ruining their towns and lands. This king had allegedly killed the "King of Israel." According to Finkelstein and Silberman: "the cities assumed to have been conquered by David were still centers of Canaanite culture throughout the time of his presumed reign in Jerusalem. And the monuments that have traditionally been attributed to Solomon and seen as symbols of the greatness of his state were in fact, built by the kings of the Omride Dynasty of the northern kingdom of Israel, who ruled in the first half of the nineth century BCE."[180]

Archeology and hermeneutics combine to produce the conclusion of Lemche that "the Israelite nation as explained by the biblical writers has little in the way of an historical background. It is a highly ideological construct created by ancient scholars of Jewish tradition in order to legitimize their own religion, community and its religio-political claims on land and religious exclusivity."[181] It is possible that the Bible has some "historical kernels," but the stories of the patriarchs, Exodus, the alleged conquest of Canaan, and the alleged monarchies of David and Solomon are "the creative expressions of a powerful religious reform movement that flourished in the kingdom of Judah in the late Iron Age." Thus, seeing the Bible as mythological makes sense of standard contradictions. (1) The five books of Moses are allegedly written by him even though Deuteronomy describes his death. He didn't write them and probably didn't even exist. (2) The two conflicting versions of creation in Genesis (1:1-2,3 and 2:4-25 are a reworking of two different creation myths. (3) The two different

---

[180]   Israel Finkelstein and Neil Asher Silberman, *David and Solomon: In Search of the Bible's Sacred Kings and the Roots of the Western Tradition*, (Free Press, New York, 2006), p.281.

[181]   Niels Peter Lemche, *The Israelites in History and Tradition*, (Westminster John Knox, Louisville, 1998), pp.165-166.

genealogies of Adam's offspring (Genesis 4:17-26 and 5:1-28) indicate that there was no "Adam." (3) The flood story (Genesis 6:5 9) is a reworking of past flood stories, and is not true, or refers to a local flood, not the engulfing of the entire planet, in a "Genesis flood."

There are also doublets and triplets of the same event. This is thought by Biblical scholars to be due to the putting together of two sources, written at different times and places; a "J" or Yahwist source (which used *YHWH*) and an "E" or Elohist source (which used *Elohim* or *El*). The J text was written in Jerusalem around 970-930 BCE and the E text written in the north, sometime from 930-720 BCE. Other books are viewed independently of the J and E traditions, such as Deuteronomy ("D"), and there is other material of a "priestly" source called "P." Although there are debates about the dates and authorship of these works, there is a general agreement that the first five books of the Bible are "not a single, seamless composition, but a patchwork of different sources, each written under different historical circumstances to express different religious or political viewpoints." In other words, a literary construction, not a dictation from god.

The New Testament itself falls apart, as an alleged factual document, when subjected to hermeneutic deconstruction, tempered with historical investigation.[182] Thus Matthew 2:16 has King Herod commanding the slaughter of all baby boys less than two years of age in and around Bethlehem. There is no New Testament-independent source for this; it is not mentioned by Josephus (37-100 AD) in his *Jewish Antiquities,* and he extensively documented Herod's crimes, including his lesser ones, so if this genocide happened, Josephus would have known about it.[183] The aim of the story is to present a parallel story to Moses in Exodus 1:22, where the pharaoh ordered the killing of baby boys, and thus Matthew is an *aggadic midrash* reworking of the older story. Nothing is wrong with that as far as literature goes, but it is not history.

---

[182] T. L. Thompson, *The Mythic Past: Biblical Archaeology and the Myth of Israel,* (Basic Books, New York, 2000) ("We can now say with considerable confidence that the Bible is not a history of anyone's past." (p. xv)).

[183] Paul Tobin, "The Bible and Modern Scholarship," in Loftus (ed.), as above, pp.148-180, cited p. 159.

Likewise, Luke 2:1 has Joseph and Mary travelling from Nazareth to Bethlehem because of a census called by Quirinius. This census is generally accepted to be in 6 CE. However, Jesus, if he existed, was allegedly born during the time of Herod (Matthew 2:1; Luke 1:5). Herod died in 4 BCE. There is no evidence of any Roman census in Judea before 6 CE. This creates an enormous problem for fundamentalists who have spilt much ink attempting to deal with this and many other such foundational difficulties. But, the simplest most economical explanation of this and other biblical "difficulties" and "contradictions" is to follow the conclusions reached on the Old Testament: that it is mythical and not a description of historical fact and truth.[184]

Therefore, even if Jesus did exist, he is not the son of God, since he believed falsehoods, a "false testament." Hence, there is no good reason to believe that his eschatology, or that of Judaism, is the view of the "world to come" (*Olam Ha-Ba*), as expressed in the Torah, Tanakh, and Talmud. Most importantly, the idea that during end times an "anointed king" *(mashiach)* from the House of David, a messiah who will overcome darkness and chaos and ring in an era of justice and peace, will appear, is also mythical. The predictions of doom and gloom in the last days made in both the Old and New Testaments – of plagues, pestilence, war, mega-death, societal corruption and decay, as also found in old Greek and Teutonic/Norse legends (more below) – are accurate. But, there will be no savior to rescue, at the 11th hour, humanity from the logical conclusion of its hubris, the zombie apocalypse. A Jewish, or any other type of messiah, is not going to come. Jesus is not going to come again if he even existed in the first place. And, what point is there waiting for Godot if Godot is just a mere historical construction? While Judeo-Christianity may give comfort and warm and fuzzy feelings to the converted, the true-believers (who would not be disturbed by any amount of evidence against their "faith"), this doctrine offers nothing by way of a survival philosophy, or even a philosophy of boldly facing inevitable or

---

[184] Keith W. Whitelam, *The Invention of Ancient Israel*, (Routledge, London and New York, 1996).

painful death. Christian beliefs may help some individuals who would otherwise collapse, but Christianity does not offer a genuine survivalist philosophy, because it is *false*. We need something based on cold, hard reality, not mythology.

Conservatives, especially American red-white-and-bluers, may lament that a rejection of Judeo-Christianity entails a rejection of that which gave us the Enlightenment values of liberalism and pluralism. It is granted that the metaphysics of Christianity did lead to the "invention of the individual," as Siedentop has argued. However, there was more to Enlightenment values than simply individualism and universalism, and "Western values" involve freedoms and lifestyle choices which conflict fundamentally with Christianity.

Christianity, as well, has exaggerated importance in the conservative world view in supposedly giving us cultural entities such as the common law system. But, this too is not so. In 1066 AD, the Norman legal system was imposed on Anglo Saxon England by William the Conqueror. English judges considered cases on the basis of the jurisprudence of the Norse, Germanics, Greeks and Romans, substantially drawing upon pagan sources. The claim that Judeo-Christianity is the foundation of Anglo-American law is an exaggeration: it is but one major influence. *Njals Saga*, a story dating from 960-1020 in pagan Norse Iceland, details the Norse legal system. The court system was a prototype of our own with aspects such as process servers summoning defendants to court; the possibility of an appeal to a higher court, the Althing for review; representation by lawyers; witnesses called for evidence; probate law; divorce law and specific penalties for criminal offences. US courts have frequently considered whether rights have existed in history, sometimes going back to consider Viking and Roman law. In *State v Delgado*, 692 P.2d 610 (1984), the Oregon Supreme Court held that there is a right to carry knives, noting that knives have provided protection since Viking times.

Finally, the untold destruction, despotism and terror unleashed by Christianity, the destruction of the literature of classical antiquity, the torture and murder of great pagan thinkers such as Hypatia (c.370-415 CE), and "heretical' Christian cosmologists such as Giordana Bruno (1548-1600), need not be discussed here.[185]

Thus Spake Nietzsche:

Nietzsche in the Apocalypse

Force rules the world still,
Has ruled it, shall rule it;
Meekness is weakness,
Strength is triumphant,
Over the whole earth
Still is it Thor's-Day!

Thou art a God too,
O Galilean!
And thus singled-handed
Unto the combat,
Gauntlet or Gospel,
Here I defy thee!

- Henry Wadsworth Longfellow, The Challenge of Thor

Much has been written in recent times about the warrior mindset and mental toughness for combat troops, applying the psychology of performance to combat training.[186] This paradigm has rejected the idea that mental toughness emerges from physical training alone, without specific psychological training. Thus, Giduck writing in *SWAT Digest* says: "If someone has great technique, but lacks these essential mental weapons, he will be defeated by an unskilled fighter who has them. That is why so many black belts get wiped out by street

---

[185]   Catherine Nixey, *The Darkening Age: The Christian Destruction of the Classical World,* (Houghton Mifflin Harcourt, New York, 2018).

[186]   D. Grossman, *On Killing: The Psychological Cost of Learning to Kill in War and Society,* (Little, Brown and Company, New York, 1995); D. Grossman, *On Combat: The Psychology and Physiology of Deadly Conflict in War and Peace,* (PPCT Research Publications, Millstadt, 2004).

punks in alley ways."[187] According to Nowicki, elite performance in sport or combat requires "self-regulation of arousal, intense focus of concentration, a positive focus on the event, being in control without forcing it and possessing determination and commitment."[188] This is done by holistic combat training, integrating emotional, psychological and physical abilities, over-training on *both* physical and mental skills, with stress exposure training, scenario-based training and tactical performance imagery, among other things.[189]

The individual warrior needs to acquire the survival attributes discussed in Jeff Cooper's classic text, *Principles of Personal Defense.*[190] These qualities are: (1) *alertness*, being in a state of ever-ready relaxed vigilance, because the world is a dangerous place; (2) *decisiveness*, having the ability to attack without hesitation; (3) *aggressiveness*, when attacking, to do so with an "explosive response," concentrating "utterly upon the destruction of your enemy;" (4), *speed*, doing to others as they would do to you, *first*; (5) *coolness*, doing all the above, with cold blooded self-control, with fear being kept at bay; (6) *ruthlessness*, not being constrained by "considerations of forbearance;" (7) *surprise*, hitting the opponent with the effective-unexpected, including even mounting a violent counter-attack. To be able to think in this way requires a profound philosophical reorientation. One needs to appreciate the depths of human savagery and depravity, not in all people, all of the time, but in most people, most of the time, as Hobbes observed.

It is clear that an important part of the warrior mindset relates to the philosophy of life that a fighter holds. A warrior needs some sort of ethico-philosophical, and possibly "religious" position (even an "anti-philosophy" and "anti-religion") to become more than just

---

[187] J. Giduck, "The Reality of Hand to Hand Combat II: Psychological Aspect and Benefit," *SWAT Digest*, 1ˢᵗ edition, 2008, pp. 34-38.

[188] D. Nowicki, *Gold Medal Mental Workout for Combat Sports*, (Stadion, Island Pond, 1994), p. xiii.

[189] A. Williams (et al.), "Research on Expertise in Sport: Implications for the Military," *Military Psychology*, vol. 20 (Suppl.), 2008, pp. S123-S145.

[190] Jeff Cooper, *Principles of Personal Defense*, (Paladin Press, Boulder, Colorado, 2006).

a killer. Your unfriendly neighborhood psycho can do that: kill. The warrior fights for some sort of "higher purpose" and does not kill for the sake of killing itself. That being so, and having rejected Judeo-Christianity, what should our, or rather, *my* philosophy/ "religion" of life, or death, be?

Those who leave the charnel house of Christianity may become secular humanists/materialists, equally as barren, or they may end up on the doorstep of Friedrich Nietzsche (1844-1900). Nietzsche famously proclaimed that god was dead, meaning that the transcendent (and associated values) have ceased to play a decisive role in a life that had become secularized and rationalized. Christianity for Nietzsche had "taken the side of everything, weak, base, ill-constituted, [and it had] made an ideal out of *opposition* to the preservative instincts of the strong life."[191]

Nietzsche saw the Christian church as "the most malicious false-coinage there is for the purpose of *disvaluing* nature and natural values."[192] He was astonished that the Northern Europeans had accepted Christianity, although in *The Anti-Christ* he did not explore the historical reasons why: "that the strong races of northern Europe have not repudiated the Christian god certainly reflects no credit on their talent for religion – not to speak of their taste. They ought to have felt compelled to have done away with such a sickly and decrepit product of decadence."[193] Nietzsche should have reflected upon the example of Charlemagne (742-814 AD), and as Charles I, Holy Roman Emperor (800-814 AD), who spread Christianity in northern Europe by ethnic cleansing and the genocide of tens of thousands of people of Norse-Germanic stock, including Frisians and Saxons in the north and pagan German and Slavic people in the East. Although Charlemagne fought back the Muslim invaders, he destroyed about two thirds of the Saxon population.[194] It has been

[191] Friedrich Nietzsche, *The Anti-Christ*, (Penguin Books, London, 2003), p. 129.

[192] As above, p. 162.

[193] As above, pp. 140-141.

[194] Osred, *Odinism: Present, Past and Future*, (Renewal Publications, Melbourne, 2010), p. 95.

argued that the Viking attacks on Saxon Christian monasteries such as Lindisfarne, constituted an Odinist revenge, since while the early raids were motivated by plunder, raids on monasteries kept coming even after riches were removed and hidden. The *Anglo-Saxon Chronicles* stress that the Vikings, especially in their destruction of Lindisfarne, were vicious and sacrilegious, indicating a pagan revenge.[195] Good for them; more on this below.

In full flight Nietzsche proclaimed: "I *condemn* Christianity. I bring against the Christian church the most terrible charge any prosecutor has even uttered. To me, it is the extremist thinkable form of corruption, it has had the will to the ultimate corruption conceivably possible. The Christian church has left nothing untouched by its depravity, it has made every value a disvalue, of every truth a lie, of every kind of integrity a vileness of soul."[196] He flirted with something of a crude conspiracy theory, running the implausible line that St Paul may have deliberately propagated Christianity as a psychological warfare weapon to pay back the Romans for the destruction of Jerusalem and the Second temple in 70 AD.[197] It is Nietzsche's weakest argument, for the chances of one disgruntled writer sitting down and dreaming up a new religion to bring Rome down, is astronomically small. That this did happen is not due to conspiracy, but more to the coming together of a number of factors, a perfect storm, that together enabled this faith to grow and ultimately contribute to the destruction of Rome, and arguably, to the destruction of European and other peoples (e.g., indigenous cultures) as well.

Nietzsche's stronger attack on Christianity was that it degrades healthy instinctual values; Christianity's fictional world is based upon a hatred of the natural and of strength. Weak, sickly people will have a god like that of the New Testament, a document that represents *slave* morality, which eliminates manly warrior virtues of strength, courage, bravery, pride, and honor. Thus, Christianity

---

[195] As above, p. 98; Robert Ferguson, *The Vikings: A History*, (Penguin, New York, 2009).

[196] Nietzsche, *The Anti-Christ*, as above, p. 198.

[197] See Oscar Levy (ed.), *The Complete Works of Friedrich Nietzsche*, volume 13, *The Genealogy of Morals*, (T. N. Foulis, Edinburgh, n.d.), pp. 54-55.

amounts to a "declaration of war" against the will to live and the will to power and constitutes mankind's greatest misfortune, until recently. Of course, its secular mutant offspring, malignant liberalism, in its present pathological form, has taken disease, decay and decadence to a terminal stage.[198]

By contrast to the slave morality of Christianity, Nietzsche, in works such as *Thus Spake Zarathustra*,[199] gave an account of the post-Christian human condition in terms of "self-over coming" or self-transcendence. Christianity and received philosophy held to, and still hold to, fixed generalist and universalist standards and principles, but Nietzsche sees all of this as life-suppressing. An authentic individual is required to seek to transcend all such standards.

In this respect, Nietzsche has advanced a position on life similar to the one which Bruce Lee proposed on the martial arts.[200] As far as I am aware, Bruce Lee, although having been an undergraduate philosophy student, did not refer to the work of Friedrich Nietzsche, although Lee's creative and free martial artist, drenched in a sea of training, is, within that limited sphere of reality, an "overman"/Übermensch, one who "overcomes" oneself through a process of physical and spiritual struggle. The Übermensch is not a fixed being, but rather is one who constantly engages in the process of overcoming, fighting against limitations, pushing boundaries and striving to overcome both himself and his enemies.[201] Pain, suffering and the struggle for life – beatings on the anvil of existence – are welcomed by the Übermensch, so that he can become stronger and crush pity and weakness, pity and weakness being sure signs of degeneracy.

---

[198] See Osred, as above.

[199] Friedrich Nietzsche, *Thus Spake Zarathrustra*, (Random House, New York, 1995).

[200] Michael Monahan, "The Practice of Self-Overcoming: Nietzschean Reflections on the Martial Arts," *Journal of the Philosophy of Sport*, vol. 43, 2007, pp. 38-51.

[201] O. Schutte, *Beyond Nihilism: Nietzsche without Masks*, (University of Chicago Press, Chicago, 1984).

Writing the year before poor Fred's death, and before the age of stifling, degenerate political correctness, H. Goebel and E. Antrim wrote of the Übermensch:

> ...the Übermensch is a sort of beast of prey: he sees in life nothing more or little more, than appropriating, robbing, overcoming, and destroying. In a word, the Übermensch is a sovereign individual, who, possessed of boundless power, sacrifices the world on the altar of self. Christ sought to deny self, and sacrificed self that others might live; the Übermensch seeks to elevate self and to sacrifice others. Christ sought peace; the Übermensch seeks strife. He is supremely happy when he can rise on the dead and wounded bodies of the weak; this strengthens his feeling of cruelty. Christ despised this life, because it is only a probationary period, and reward follows. The Übermensch honors this life because he knows no other; to him it may be the means to the highest development, the source of the greatest pleasure.[202]

Moral codes do not bind the Übermensch as these codes are merely the habits and customs of the "sheep". The only "God" is the "God" of life and overcoming: "God is to him that which serves life and the regnant will; evil is that which hinders life in its highest development and prevents the free action of regnant will."[203] The "good," the human good, not the "moral good" of analytic philosophy, is that which elevates the will to power, to strength and overcoming; the "bad" is all that grounded upon weakness.

H. L. Mencken in *The Philosophy of Friedrich Nietzsche*,[204] also gave us a vision of the "raw" Nietzsche before the deconstructionist intellectuals got their dirty talons into his work. On the Übermensch Mencken says:

> He will be rid of all delusions that hamper and oppress the will to power. He will be perfect in body and mind. He will know everything worth knowing and have strength and skill and cunning to defend himself against any conceivable foe. Because the prospect of victory will feed his will to power he will delight in combat, and his increasing capacity for combat will decrease

---

[202]   H. Goebel and E. Antrim, "Friedrich Nietzsche's Uebermensch," *The Monist*, vol.9, 1899, pp. 563-557, cited p. 570. Spelling consistent with the present text has been employed.

[203]   As above, p. 569.

[204]   H. L Mencken, *The Philosophy of Friedrich Nietzsche*, 3rd edition, (Kennikat Press, Port Washington, 1967).

his sensitiveness to pain. … He will be scornful, merciless and supremely fit. He will be set free from man's fear of gods and laws.[205]

Thus, the Übermensch in the "struggle for existence, asks and gives no quarter. He believes that it is the destiny of sentient beings to progress upward, and he is willing to sacrifice himself that his race may do so."[206] The Übermensch will be a "badass"[207] in the spirit of tough guy warriors that span time, cultures and races: giants like Shaka Zulu, Miyamoto Musashi, Attila the Hun, Genghis Khan, Eirik Bloodaxe and the great Quanah (?1845 or 1852 to 1911)[208] to name but a few.

The Übermensch, the "great blond beast,"[209] as Nietzsche at times referred to him, is unafraid of even metaphysical monstrosities such as eternal occurrence, the idea that history will ultimately be repeated exactly as it occurred in endless cycles, much like the playing of a cosmic DVD. For Nietzsche, the Übermensch does not find horror or boredom in this idea but embraces it. Nietzsche thought that the Newtonian physics of his time led to such an idea, although he later saw no ground for it in natural science, and cooled off from it. Mencken is right in my opinion in saying that the idea of eternal recurrence is not original, "and it would have been better for his philosophy and his reputation as an intelligent thinker had he never sought to elucidate it."[210] The logical problem with eternal recurrence is that the Übermensch does not experience each "movie of life" with knowledge of what happens next, such as the pains ahead. Each episode is experienced afresh, so there

---

[205]   As above, pp. 109-110.

[206]   As above, p. 111.

[207]   Ben Thompson, *Badass: A Relentless Onslaught of the Toughest Warlords, Vikings, Samurai, Pirates, Gunfighters, and Military Commanders to Ever Live*, (William Morrow, New York, 2009).

[208]   S. C. Gwyne, *Empire of the Summer Moon: Quanah Parker and the Rise and Fall of the Comanches, the Most Powerful Indian Tribe in American History*, (Scribner, New York, 2011).

[209]   Mencken as above, pp. 97, 112.

[210]   As above, p. 118.

is really nothing to overcome here. Nietzsche should have given a thought experiment of a being not being daunted by a repeat of the sufferings of life; perhaps he could have used the idea of time travel, of a person's consciousness/mind being transported back into time into one's past body, to re-live bad times, repeatedly (*Ground Hog Day* (1993), but with memory). Someone who welcomed even this would truly be a "superman."

The post-apocalyptic Übermensch will not be restrained by guilt, a product of sucking on the tit of conventional morality.[211] Decisions would be made not by reflection on some abstract standard of universalistic morality, such as appeals to human rights, the right to life, and other notions, but on pragmatic, tribal-based survival grounds. This is what one generally finds in the comments sections of blogs dealing with morality in the apocalypse.[212] In one such blog, a version of the philosopher's "trolley problem"[213] is given: you are in the basement of a relatively unsecured building (zombies can break in) with masses of zombies outside. If they don't hear any human-made sounds, they will pass by. But, there is a baby in the group which is about to cry. The noise will eventually attract the zombies leading them to overwhelm the group. What should one do? Should one knock the baby off? Generally, those into the zombie apocalypse culture respond pragmatically. Usually, a baby can be prevented from crying by satisfying its need – for food/ suckling (even a finger or nipple may stop it from crying) or a nappy change. A baby is a human resource in a world where the human population has been decimated and is thus valuable. If, after absolutely everything fails, in the limited time available, it may be necessary to put something over the baby's mouth, even if it kills it. Such is life – and death.

---

[211]   C. Cristofari and M. J. Guitton. "Surviving at Any Cost: Guilt Expression Following Extreme Ethical Conflicts in a Virtual Setting," *PLOS ONE*, vol. 9, 2014, p. e101711.

[212]   "Morality in the Zombie Apocalypse," at http://www.zombiesarecoming. com/2012/05/26/morality-in-the-zombie-apocalypse/.

[213]   J. J. Thomson, "The Trolley Problem," *Yale Law Journal*, vol. 94, 1985, pp. 1395-1415.

Lo, the Neo-Barbarian

Nietzsche's Übermensch is the ultimate expression of manliness.[214] He saw that barbarian culture produced more "complete beasts," better endowed with the warrior virtues.[215] However, Nietzsche's Übermensch needs a little fine-tuning to deal with something like the collapse of civilization and the zombie apocalypse. Nietzsche never contemplated the possibly of near-term human extinction, although he did consider that in the longer term, we "clever animals" may face extinction.[216] The overcoming and self-developing Übermensch was seen in a cultural context that still permitted some sort of "self-development." But, what about facing the likelihood not of eternal recurrence, but of mega-death, not merely the "death of God," but the "death of almost everything"? The apocalyptic Übermensch must be willing to do what is necessary for his tribe, perhaps of only 10, or even two, to survive, but if survival is not possible, he must go down fighting.

Hermann the Cherusci (Arminius, 18/17 BC – AD 21), should be given bad ass pride of place in Valhalla, for preventing the destruction of *Germani* by the decadent Old World order of the Roman military machine, led by the likes of Varus. Hermann had served in the Roman military but became aware of Rome's plan for the final conquering of the German tribes. He organized the previously disunited tribes, and at the Battle of the Teutoburg Forest (9 AD), fighting on forest ground that negated the usual advantages of Roman combat, the barbarians destroyed Varus' three legions. These had been the pick of Rome's army, and this crushing defeat broke the back of Rome's aggression east of the Rhine. As E. S. Creasy put it, "that victory secured at once and forever the independence of the Teutonic race." Well, not quite; there is the final battle yet.[217]

---

[214]   H. C. Mansfield, *Manliness*, (Yale University Press, New Haven, 2006).

[215]   H. J. Ausmus, "Nietzsche and Eschatology," *Journal of Religion*, vol. 58, 1978, pp. 347-364, cited p. 354.

[216]   Friedrich Nietzsche, "On Truth and Lie in an Extra-Moral Sense," in *The Portable Nietzsche*, (Viking, New York, 1976).

[217]   E. S. Creasy, *Fifteen Decisive Battles of the World from Marathon to Waterloo*, (Didactic

There is a brief historical mention in *The Anglo-Saxon Chronicles*[218] of an unnamed Viking at the battle of Stamford Bridge on September 25, 1066, a battle between the English under King Harold Godwinson and the invading Vikings under King Harald Hardrada and the English king's brother Tostig Godwinson. The battle had gone badly for the Vikings, and those not slain fled across a bridge. There is controversy among scholars about whether or not the bridge existed, but since the Anglo-Saxons recorded the incident, it is probably true, as they had no reason to lie. The bridge represented a choke-point, so that only one man at a time could pass. A giant Viking asked the king for permission to die on the bridge and enter Valhalla. Armed perhaps with a Dane axe, he held up the entire Anglo-Saxon army and chopped down 40 Anglo-Saxon soldiers. The Anglo-Saxons eventually killed him when a sneaky Anglo-Saxon soldier floated under the bridge in a half-barrel and speared him, perhaps through the ball sack, which no doubt was a huge target.[219] Shades of *300!*

The barbarian Übermensch need not necessarily go down with the ship in a heroic last stand but may survive against the odds, at least for a time. Jim Bowie (March 10, 1796-March 6, 1836), did make a last stand at the Alamo (1836), but he first became famous for surviving the Vidalia Sandbar fight of September 19th in 1827, outside of Natchez, Mississippi. In the aftermath of a duel between two men who had both missed each other, in a secondary melee, Bowie was shot in the hip by a pistol, then struck so hard over the head by that then empty pistol, that it broke. He was then stabbed by a sword cane, which was deflected by his sternum from his heart, and then, with an early version of his famous knife, he stabbed to death one opponent. He was shot again, and stabbed, then shot in the arm. However, Bowie then managed to cut off part of one attacker's forearm and entered badass history.[220]

Press, 2017).

[218] Michael Swanton (editor and translator), *The Anglo-Saxon Chronicle,* (J. M. Dent, London, 1996), p. 198.

[219] "Battle at Stamford Bridge," at https://en.wikipedia.org/wiki/Battle_of_Stamford_ Bridge; http://www.badassoftheweek.com/stamfordbridge.html.

[220] C. Hopewell, *James Bowie: Texas Fighting Man,* (Eakin Press, Austin, 1994). John

Bowie, though, was outdone in the badass stakes by John Jeremiah "Liver-Eating" Johnson (1824-1900), a mountain man who conducted a one-man war against the Crow Indians for the murder in 1847 of his pregnant wife, a member of the Flathead Indian tribe. Legend has it that he killed over 300 Crow Indians and ate their livers in revenge, as the Crow believed that an uneaten liver was necessary to enter the afterlife. It was alleged that he was once captured by Blackfoot warriors, who intended to sell him to the Crow. However, he managed to escape at night, killing his guard, scalping him with his own knife, and hacking off his leg. He ate the leg on his journey of 320 km/200 miles to the cabin of his trading partner. It all could be lies because some accounts have him only becoming a mountain man in 1862. In any case, the 1972 movie, starring Robert Redford, *Jeremiah Johnson*, is a moderately good portrayal of his life and mythos. For warriors-to-be, probably eating bodily parts of one's enemies is not advisable, due to the toxins likely to be found in contemporary livers, let alone viruses. But, here, Uncle Vlad has some alternatives.

Vlad III, Prince of Wallachia (1431-1476?/1477?), also known to his friends as Vlad the Impaler, and Vlad Dracula (Dragulea), served as the basis for Bram Stoker's *Dracula* (1897), but Vlad is regarded as a folk hero in Romania and Bulgaria for his stand against the Ottoman Empire. It seems that impalement – usually inserting a pointed stake into the unhappy victim's rectum and then using the body's momentum to carry the stake through to the head – was his favorite method of execution. In 1462 Mehmed II, who had conquered Constantinople, witnessed the "forest of the impaled:" 20,000 rotting impaled corpses of Ottoman prisoners of war impaled on stakes in a forest of the tortured dead outside the city of Tâgovişte. This ultimately convinced him to retreat. According to Professor Florin Curta of the University of Florida, impalement "was used as a *form of terror* – to terrorize the enemy coming to invade one's country. He had to do a lot of things with

Wesley Hardin (1853-1895) can be added as another iconic American bad ass neo-barbarian, who after killing his first man in self defense at age 15 years, went on to an outlaw career, allegedly killing at least 21 men; some claim an unlikely 42: John Wesley Hardin, *The Life of John Wesley Hardin: As Written by Himself*, (University of Oklahoma Press, Norman, 1973).

very limited resources. He used efficient methods to fight against his enemy without having that many men at his disposal."[221] Expect to see impalement-a-plenty in the post-apocalyptic world. Townships may greet outsiders with this friendly "welcome to our community" greeting.

These illustrations are both entitled The Forest of the Impaled, from Dracole Wayda, Ambr. Huber, Nürnberg, 1499 (right), and Dracola Wayda, Matth. Hupfuff, Strassburg, 1500 (left).[222]

The post-apocalyptic Übermensch should be a barbarian in the classic sense of being an outsider, even in his "own" society. Barbarians were not necessarily without a complex culture, but were "on the outside looking in."[223] Barbarians though, were usually poor and aggressive towards states and hence were likely to have been raiders. Although some argue that it was corruption that brought down the Western Roman Empire, the Eastern Roman Empire was just as corrupt; hence after the weakening effects of factors such as

---

[221]   E. Palermo, "Vlad the Impaler: The Real Dracula's Dark Secrets," October 30, 2014, at http://www.livescience.com/48536-vlad-the-impaler-dark-secrets.html/.

[222]   Source: "Vlad the Impaler," at https://en.wikipedia.org/wiki/vlad_the_Impaler.

[223]   Bennett Bronson, "The Role of Barbarians in the Fall of States," in N. Yoffee and G. L. Cowgill (eds), *The Collapse of Ancient States and Civilizations*, (University of Arizona Press, Tucson, 1988), pp. 196-218, cited p. 200.

Christianity and mass migration, barbarian attacks may have finally destroyed the Western Roman Empire.[224]

Jack Donovan, in his article "Becoming the New Barbarians,"[225] points out that men who follow the "way of men" and its tribalism will take on the role of modern barbarians or outsiders in our present world. Men alienated from the system should accept this label with pride and not care at all.[226] Neo-barbarians should strive to break the black magic spell of the oppressive state apparatus by measures such as: (1) separate "us" from "them," think tribally and expose the hidden tribalism and special interests of the cosmopolitans; (2) accept that things are not going to work and that "our" culture is in terminal decline; (3) de-universalize morality (discussed previously); (4) become independent from the state but interdependent between members of your tribe and (5) maintain a tribal identity by building up tribal links with your kind of people and creating communities like migrant communities, "exclusive, insular and interdependent."

British philosopher John Gray in his *The Silence of Animals*,[227] has said that barbarism is a disease of civilization.[228] It is a strange thesis to be advanced by a generally pessimistic thinker, one almost as pessimistic as myself. After all, Gray rightly sees humans as *Homo rapiens*, nasty, aggressive, violent, rapacious primates – and that's on a good day![229] Man is the "naked" killer primate. This view of human nature, one once commonly held in the ancient world, makes nonsense of liberal dreams such as a world governed by universal

---

[224]   A. H. M. Jones, "Comparison of the Processes of Decline in the Eastern and Western Parts of the Roman Empire," in S. N. Eisenstadt (ed.), *The Decline of Empires*, (Prentice-Hall, Englewood Cliffs, 1955), pp. 159-164; P. Heather, *The Fall of the Roman Empire: A New History of Rome and the Barbarians*, (Oxford University Press, Oxford, 2005).

[225]   Jack Donavan, "Becoming the New Barbarians," *A Sky Without Eagles: Selected Essays and Speeches, 2010-2014*, (Dissonant Hum, Milwaukie, 2014), pp. 129-143.

[226]   Jack Donovan, at http://www.jack-donovan.com/axis/2018/06/i-dont-care/.

[227]   John Gray, *The Silence of Animals: On Progress and Other Modern Myths*, (Allan Lane, London, 2013).

[228]   See Peter Conrad, "The Silence of Animals by John Gray – Review," March 3, 2013, at http://www.theguardian.com/books/2013/mar/03/silence-animals-john-gray-review.

[229]   David M. Buss, *The Murderer Next Door: Why the Mind is Designed to Kill*, (Penguin, New York, 2005).

human rights and "love, love, love." Confronted by the conclusion that progress in *civilization* (as distinct from technological advancement) is a myth, that is, that cumulative moral advances such as the abolition of slavery, torture, women's rights etc. can be quickly swept away, Gray at the end of his treatise can only offer us the option of taking up bird watching, ornithology. Ironically, the heroes of Gray's book are peregrine falcons. Ignoring grace, elegance and dazzling speed, they are bird-eating raptors, predators that have been used by humans for killing prey for over 3,000 years.[230]

Barbarism, on the contrary, is not a disease of civilization – it is civilization itself, which is the unnatural, unstable state. Robert E. Howard (1906-1936), the creator of *Conan the Barbarian*, was right in saying: "Barbarism is the natural state of mankind, civilization is unnatural. It is a whim of circumstance. And barbarism must always ultimately triumph."[231] The reason for this has already been provided in this book: the term "civilization" is usually defined as human society at an advanced level of technological, political, economic, social and cultural development (including arts, sciences and general learning), with complexity in both the social structure and culture. Barbarism is the negation of this. Maintaining this ordered structure requires dedication, commitment, energy and resources, but allowing it to wither on the vine is the easiest thing in the world and requires only that "good" men do nothing, which is what they do best. Hence, as Will Durant has put it: "From barbarism to civilization requires a century; from civilization to barbarism needs but a day."[232] Barbarism is the natural outcome of social entropy. As it is coming our way, fast and inevitably, we may as well embrace it.

The transition from civilization to neo-barbarism is seen in AMC's *The Walking Dead*, which illustrates many of the themes and doctrines discussed here, even though, of course, this is not the intention of the script writers. Throughout the ten seasons to date

---

[230]   J. A. Baker, *The Peregrine*, (New York Review of Books Classics, New York, 2004).

[231]   Robert E. Howard, "Beyond the Black River," in *Weird Tales* (1935).

[232]   Will Durant, *The Reformation: The Story of Civilization*, vol.6, (Simon and Schuster, New York, 1957), p. 190.

(2010-2019, 2020), the characters get into trouble through acting on good principals, when they exhibit trust of "aliens" or outsiders and act on a belief in human goodness.

The character Rick frequently speaks of his team as "family," and his men as "brothers," and he is correct in doing so. Thus, perhaps contrary to the intentions of the writers, *The Walking Dead* can be seen as an experiment in tribalism, where ecological scarcity means that almost all tribes will be warring. Indeed, the zombie apocalypse well illustrates Jack Donovan's insight that "[e]ssentially, tribal identity is everything that matters."[233]

In his book *Becoming a Barbarian*, Jack offers common sense arguments against universalism, and the interlocking networks of globalism (the "Empire of Nothing"), that includes multiculturalism and Christianity, because globalism and universalism are in essence impossible for humans to practice in any sustainable fashion because of our evolutionary past which has wired us to be tribal. Those who are not sufficiently wired, ultimately perish in a Darwinian sense, especially in a collapse situation. The abandonment of moral universalism means that we are all, and not just special groups, open to holding to the maxim: "Not my people, not my problem."

My Tribe: The Way of the Neo-Viking

The death of the gods of modernity and post-modernity, associated with Judeo-Christianity may lead many to seek to regain the world that has been lost, seeking pagan roots for a sense of ecological wholeness.[234] Other thinkers concerned with identitarianism or the search for tribal identity, such as Alain de Benoist,[235] have seen the return to paganism as a necessary part of the revolt against the "slave religions" of Christianity and liberalism, in a world

---

[233] Jack Donovan, *Becoming a Barbarian*, (dissonant Hum, Milwaukie, 2016).

[234] Lynn White, "The Historic Roots of our Ecologic Crisis," *Science*, vol.155, 1967, pp. 1203-1207.

[235] Alain de Benoist, *On Being a Pagan*, (Ultra, Atlanta, 2004).

"where everything is collapsing into the sunset."[236] De Benoist sees Christianity as an alien and revolutionary "anthropology," possessing a "*universalist and totalitarian* character,"[237] with concepts of absolute good versus absolute evil, where the enemies of the Christians are evil and must be destroyed. Christianity, De Benoist believes, laid the philosophical foundation for totalitarianism, although today radical Islam and jihadism carries such totalitarian thought even further. The Christian idea of the equality of all souls, the universalist mania of spreading the Gospel to all people, affirms universalism and egalitarianism on a "higher plane": "the absolute value of the individual soul receives from its filial relationship with God...shared by all humanity."[238]

Rejecting these ideologies, thinkers seek, as Thomas Molnar puts it a "rehabilitated paganism," which aims to "restore to the peoples their genuine identity that existed before monotheist corruption."[239] Michael O' Meara says in *New Culture, New Right*, that Christianity "emerged not as an organic offshoot of the European spirit, but as a plebeian encroachment of Rome's "cosmopolitan and disarticulated masses," and that its "Oriental essence seemed perverse, for notions of original sin, pacifism, self-abnegation, guilt, and monotheism could not but repulse those valuing strength and honor, loyalty and courage, balance, restraint, and respect for life's multiplicity."[240] By way of summary:

This nuanced understanding of truth rests on the most quintessential of pagan principles: that life has no purpose other than itself. As Homer, Hesiod, and Heraclitus portray it, life is struggle, nothing more. It is neither good nor bad. In a world without inherent purpose, the weak perish, while the

---

[236] As above, p. 4.

[237] Tomislav Sunic, *Against Democracy and Equality: The European New Right*, 2nd edition, (Noontide Press, Newport Beach, 2004), p. 94.

[238] Alain de Benoist, "Critique de l'idéolgie libérale," in his *Critiques-Théoriques*, (L'Age d'Homme, Lausanne, Suisse, 2002), pp. 13-29.

[239] Cited from Sunic, as above.

[240] Michael O' Meara, *New Culture, New Right*, (1st Books, Bloomington, 2004), p. 96; Pierre Krebs, *Fighting for the Essence*, (Arktos, London, 2012).

strong forge their values into a body of life-affirming principles – and thrive. Those who put their fate in the hands of others (whether those of a heavenly patriarch or of the liberal's nanny state) are easily thrown down and crushed. Believing life has no aim other than to complete itself, the ancients thought life concealed no higher meaning: man alone creates it. Every human form— individual or communal—unconsciously seeks a higher level of being. This is nature's law. In Homer's world, there were, for instance, heroes fated to die young (like Achilles) and others who could enjoy a long, eventful existence (such as Odysseus). Unlike Judeo-Christians, Europe's greatest poet made no moral distinction between them. In the face of an impersonal reality, it is not right or wrong, good or evil, long life or short that counts, but honor and dishonor, beauty and ugliness, courage and cowardice. Only those imposing themselves and their style on the primordial chaos, drawing the sublime from the setbacks and triumphs that inevitably accompany their struggles, survive and achieve a meaningful life. In affirming the innocence of being and the inevitable normative influences at work in every human community, the tragic, heroic spirit of pagan Europe endeavoured, then, to shape existence according to its forms. This made paganism a religion of works, not faith.

By contrast, the monotheistic truths of the Abrahamic tradition, like those of liberal rationalism, are universal, grasping the world in form applicable to everyone, everywhere, at every time. Infused with an intolerance and rigidity ... the early church hoped to reorganize the world on the basis of its indisputable truths. Liberalism later sought the same, only with a secular concept of logos. In either case logos was addressed through the individual's spirit or reason, not the community's destining project. Pagans, by contrast, felt no compulsion to dismiss the immediate real for an allegedly higher reality, even though they, unlike modern men, felt the eternal presence of the transcendent. The sacred—that which is greater than man—was indeed thought to envelope the profane, giving it meaning and significance. As the old Nordic adage describes it: "The divine sleeps in the rock, breathes in the plant, dreams in the animal, and wakes in man." This notion made the divine integral to the pagans' world, part of the continuum linking man, being and cosmos. They thus identified with its particularisms – rather than retreat from them, like Christians, or incessantly reform them, like liberals.[241]

Northern Christianity came about because the Holy See had "convinced their "long hair kings" of the diplomatic advantage of doing so,"[242] but mostly by genocide, such as that committed by Charlemagne (742-814 AD), king of the Franks (768-814 AD) and as

---

[241] As above, pp. 100-101.

[242] As above, p. 97.

Charles I, Holy Roman Emperor (800-814 AD), against the Saxons (772-804 AD). As has been said earlier, evil Charlie's slaughter, plundering, and burning, led to the destruction of about two thirds of the Saxon population. In 782 AD he forbade the celebration of Odinist rites on pain of death, and then proceeded, as tyrants do, to divide up Saxony into a series of counties to be run by local puppet Saxon traitors who had accepted evil Chuck's rule in exchange for their "30 pieces of silver." One may perhaps fantasize about having a time machine and taking back in time a few thousand men heavily armed with 21st century weaponry to teach them a lesson, but as already pointed out, as Osred argues in *Odinism*, Viking raids on Anglo-Saxon monasteries may have involved more than just obtaining easy treasure.[243] Christians soon removed treasure from the monasteries but: "Over and over, the Vikings hammered the Christian sites that had played a role in the chain of events leading to the destruction of the continental Saxons ... The fact that the raids on the centers of Christian evangelism kept coming indicates beyond reasonable doubt the religious aspect of Viking aggression."[244] *The Anglo-Saxon Chronicle* well-recognized the sacrilegious nature of the Viking attacks, especially on Lindisfarne or Holy Island, an island of the north east coast of Northumberland, attacked by Vikings in 793 AD. Ferguson has said: "With an indifference to the humanity of their Christian victims as complete as that of Charlemagne's towards the Saxons, a psychopathic rage directed at the Christian 'other' was unleashed, expressing itself in infantile orgies of transgressive behaviour that offered the same satisfactions whether the taboos transgressed were their own or those of their victims."[245] One example is the drowning of monks as a "travesty"

---

[243]   Osred, *Odinism: Present, Past and Future* (Renewal Publications, Melbourne, 2010), pp. 97-98.

[244]   As above.

[245]   Robert Ferguson, *The Vikings: A History,* (Viking Adult, New York, 2009), p. 56; R. I. Page, *Chronicles of the Vikings: Records, Memorials and Myths,* (British Museum, London, 1995); Philip Parker, *The Northmen's Fury: A History of the Viking World,* (Jonathan Cape, London, 2014); Philip Lane, *The Vikings and Their Enemies: Warfare in Northern Europe, 750-1100,* (Pen & Sword Military, Barnsley, 2014); Ben Hubbard, *The Viking Warrior: The Norse Raiders Who Terrorised Medieval Europe,* (Amber Books, London, 2015).

of baptism. Christians immediately saw the 793 raid as part of a religious war, and it was. Hence the need to destroy the Vikings.

Thus, many thinkers reject Judeo-Christian values of humility, fear of god and all that jazz, and instead turn to the pagan values of courage, honor and Faustian self-surpassing, striving to transcend the limits of the human condition.[246] Oswald Spengler, writing at a time before the regime of political correctness, saw northern Europeans as "hard races," hammered by a harsh climate to become "beasts of prey whose inner forces struggle fruitlessly to break the superiority of thought, of organized artificial living, over the blood."[247] Such "Vikingism" faces the reality as Osred, a leading Odinist puts it, that most people in the West today are "[a]pathetic, docile, immature, uninformed, crassly materialistic, consumed by consumerism, suicidal, addicted to the cult of personality"[248] and about as far away from Nietzsche's "blond beast" as they could be. Not to worry; nothing here that the apocalypse and natural selection's struggle for existence can't fix, with the magic of the coming struggle for life.

Be that as it may, the remnants of my tribe—all ten of them if we are optimistic—(other tribes having gone their own epistemological ways), surviving the apocalypse for however long, may choose to enter Valhalla, if it exists, as a real entity or alternatively as a manifestation of Germanic-Norse collective unconsciousness,[249] through embracing past pagan belief systems such as Odinism/ Asatru, as their philosophy of death.

---

[246] On Faustian nature see Ricardo Duchesne, *The Uniqueness of Western Civilization*, (Brill, Leiden and Boston, 2011) and *Faustian Man in a Multicultural Age*, (Arktos, London, 2017); H. F. K. Günther, *The Religious Attitude of the Indo-Europeans*, (Clair Press, London, 1966).

[247] Oswald Spengler, *Man and Technics: A Contribution to a Philosophy of Life*, (George Allen and Unwin, London 1932), pp. 78-79.

[248] Osred, *Odinism,* as above, p. 2.

[249] Carl Gustav Jung, "Wotan," *Neue Schweizer Rundschau*, n.s. 5., no.111, March 1936, pp. 657-669, and *Civilization in Transition*, (Routledge and Kegan Paul, London, 1964), pp. 179-193. Jung notes that Nietzsche had no knowledge of Germanic literature, p. 182.

John Stanley Martin, in *Ragnarok: An Investigation into Old Norse Concepts of the Fate of the Gods*, says, regarding myths for the Norsemen: "*A myth is a narrative which involves supernatural persons: gods, giants, dwarfs, and elves. Such a narrative does not refer to any real or perceptible event but consists of a series of images which exist independently of observed phenomena in the physical world.*" Nevertheless, myths are to the believer no less real than phenomena perceived through senses; they are built on culturally imbedded symbols and are not pure fantasy or individual invention; they are the *raison d'être* of a particular human group, and ratify and make effectual its communal activities." [250]

Odinism/Asatru has been defined as "the organic spiritual beliefs and religion of the indigenous peoples of northern Europe as embodied in the Eddas and as they have found expression in the wisdom and in the historic expression of these peoples."[251] In particular, the nine noble virtues rise to central importance in one's life: courage, truth, honor, fidelity, discipline, hospitality, self-reliance, industriousness, and perseverance. These "virtues" are not to be understood as comprising some sort of "morality," as understood by Christian-influenced analytic philosophy, articulating a decision procedure for action. Rather, those values, as Odinist Stephen McNallen puts it are the "distilled experience of a specific biological and cultural group from its very beginning, and as a folk-based religion, offer strong survival values for the group: continuation of the people in question becomes a religious imperative. It creates a strong in-group, encourages healthy families, elevates a heroic ethos, and teaches the hard virtues of loyalty, courage, and honor."[252] Further, the values in question are warrior

---

[250] John Stanley Martin, *Ragnarok: An Investigation into Old Norse Concepts of the Fate of the Gods*, (Van Gorcum, Assen, 1972), p. 9.

[251] Osred, *Odinism*, as above, p. 3, quoting from the Constitution of the Odinic Rite of Australia, 1995. See also Stephen McNallen, *Asatru: A Native European Spirituality*, (Runestone Press, Nevada City, 2015).

[252] Stephen McNallen, "Why I'm a Pagan," November 17, 2013, at http://pagan-place. blogspot.com/2010/03/why-im-pagan-by-stephen-mcnallen.html; H. M. Chadwick, *The Cult of Othin: An Essay in the Ancient Religion of the North*, (C. J. Clay and sons, London, 1899).

values, traditionally associated with manhood, and the philosophy of strength and toughness.[253]

Jack Donovan, in his essay "CROM!"[254] gives, I believe a "correct" idea about how the neo-barbarian and/or neo-Viking should view the Gods, even if they exist as "real" entities. Crom is the god of Conan the Barbarian, the character created by Robert E. Howard (1906-1936), perhaps based on the ancient Celtic deity Crom Cruach/Crom Dubh, possibly a fertility or solar god, to whom human sacrifices may have been made.[255] But, today Crom is best known from John Milius' 1982 film *Conan the Barbarian,* starring Arnie Swarzenegger at his muscle-ripping best, before his descent into the abyss of liberalism. *Conan the Barbarian* introduced Norse elements, making Crom more like Odin. Odin/Crom requires a warrior to be able to answer "the Riddle of Steel." Which is more powerful, steel (as in weapons) or flesh? Answer: neither; it is the flesh of a steel-wielding Übermensch with an indomitable spirit, all acting in unity, which is strongest. The warrior who cannot correctly answer the Riddle of Steel is cast out of Valhalla and laughed at by Odin/Crom.[256]

Odin/Crom is grim and generally uncaring about petty and puny humans, but does at birth breathe "power to strive and slay into a man's soul."[257] Odin/Crom is concerned with *valor*, heroic courage in the face of overwhelming odds, with the threat of death and destruction hovering overhead. This is what Conan faced in the 1982 movie, and in a memorable scene, Conan addresses Crom while waiting for the bad guys to come for a showdown, Conan

[253] Stephen McNallen, *Thunder from the North,* (Asatru Folk Assembly, Nevada City, 1993).

[254] Jack Donovan, "CROM!" In his *A Sky Without Eagles: Essays and Speeches, 2010-2014,* (Dissonant Hum, Cascadia, 2014), pp. 145-152.

[255] "Crom", at https://en.wikipedia.org/wiki/Crom_(fictional_deity).

[256] "The Riddle of Steel," at http://aahabershaw.com/2012/07/12/the-riddle-of-steel/. Donovan compares Crom to Odin at, Nathan Leonard, "Action is Key: An Interview with Jack Donovan," at http://heathenharvest.org/2014/08/10/action-is-key-an-interview-with-jack-donovan/.

[257] As above.

being armed with his iconic Atlantean sword and a huge battle axe. He says: "Valor pleases you, Crom... so grant me one request. Grant me revenge! And if you do not listen, then to hell with you!" Whether Crom came to Conan's aid is irrelevant; what matters is that Conan got his revenge and cut down his enemies. Odin/Crom is an appropriate anti-god for those of us believing with Nietzsche that "god is dead" and pretty much everything else.

Howard's Conan also has the right badass attitude towards the gods and fate as well: "I have known many gods. He who denies them is as blind as he who trusts them too deeply. I seek not beyond death. It may be the blackness averred by the Nemedian skeptics, or Crom's realm of ice and cloud, or the snowy plains and vaulted halls of the Nordheimer's Valhalla. I know not, nor do I care. Let me live deep while I live; let me know the rich juices of red meat and stinging wine on my palate, the hot embrace of white arms, the mad exultation of battle when the blue blades flame and crimson, and I am content. Let teachers and priests and philosophers brood over questions of reality and illusion. I know this: if life is an illusion, then I am no less an illusion, and being thus, the illusion is real to me. I live, I burn with life, I love, I slay, and am content."[258]

Along the same lines H. R. Ellis Davidson has said:

Men knew that the gods whom they served could not give them freedom from danger and calamity, and they did not demand that they should. We find in the myths no sense of bitterness at the harshness and unfairness of life, but rather a spirit of heroic resignation: humanity is born to trouble, but courage, adventure, and the wonders of life are matters for thankfulness, to be enjoyed while life is still granted to us. The great gifts of the gods were readiness to face the world as it was, the luck that sustains men in tight places, and the opportunity to win that glory which alone can survive death.[259]

[258] Robert E. Howard, "Queen of the Black Coast," at http://gutenberg.net.au/ebooks06/0600961h.html, originally in Weird Tales, May 1934.

[259] H. R. Ellis Davidson, Gods and Myths of Northern Europe, (Penguin, Harmondsworth, 1964), p. 218.

How then does one reach the old Gods of war?[260] Colin Cleary is right in saying that "our hope lies in Ragnarök ... the complete destruction of the modern world and memory of it."[261] The collapse of materialist consumerism, grounded upon runaway scientific rationalism, will leave a vacuum that will be filled, and that vacancy will naturally be filled by that which existed before the rise of modernity.[262] The old ways and beliefs will return, because they never really left us, being covered up by the unnaturalness and unsustainability of techno-industrial civilization.[263] As Icelandic pagan Jörmunder Ingi has said, "We maintain that the Viking mentality and old beliefs never left the Icelanders. Some people believe that Christianity never did take hold here. It was like a patina on top of the culture."[264]

Post Apocalyptica will be a ceaseless battle for survival, with the prospects of a painful death, ever-present. One could do worse in such a world than embracing the cult of the berserker, especially with regards to melee weapons and battles. The berserker can give one a battle-ready exemplar, with some common-sense modifications. Berserkers feature extensively in Norse literature, in both *Eddas*, in numerous Sagas, historical works, and skaldic verses.[265] The berserker is best known for his battle fury and savagery, an out-of-control "Hulk smash" explosion of violence.[266] They were linked to totem animals such as a bear or a wolf; hence *berserkir* ("bear-shirts") and *úlfheðnar* ("wolf-hides"). The wolf skin is itself a symbol

[260] Osred, "Odinism and Green Science," *Renewal*, vol. 1, no. 1, 1994, p. 7.

[261] Colin Cleary, *What is a Rune? And Other Essays*, (Counter-Currents, San Francisco, 2015), and *Summoning the Gods: Essays on Paganism in a God-Forsaken World*, (Counter-Currents, San Francisco, 2011).

[262] Brian Regan, "Shamanism for Survival," The Runestone, Summer, 1996, pp. 8-11.

[263] Derrick Jensen, *Endgame Volume 1: The Problem of Civilization*, (Seven Stories Press, New York, 2006).

[264] P. J. Vesilind, "In Search of Vikings," *National Geographic*, vol. 197, May, 2000, pp. 2-27.

[265] B. Blaney, *The Berserker: His Origin and Development in Old Norse Literature*, (PhD Thesis, University of Colorado, 1972); B. Blaney, "The Berserker Suitor: The Literary Application of a Stereotyped Theme," *Scandinavian Studies*, vol. 54, 1982, pp. 279-294.

[266] H. R. E. Davidson, *Shape Changing in Old Norse Sagas*, (Rowman and Littlefield, Totowa, 1978).

of Odin, and Odin was regarded as inspiring the battle fury and rage in them. Further, the wearer was regarded as having abandoned humanity and to have become a "divine predator."[267] In the *Ynglinga Saga*, the berserkers are described as becoming so crazed that they chew on their shield rims in their frenzy. Berserkers were often a danger to fellow warriors, killing everything within swiping range. This would be an obvious liability in the apocalypse so it would be wise to tone down this rage a little. While it could be argued that the entire notion of the berserker is a Christian fabrication to paint the Vikings in a bad light, and this may be applicable to some of the more extravagant shield-biting descriptions, it is clear to anyone who has ever fought for their life, that one can enter a state of battle rage, fuelled by adrenal, and the berserker was probably an extreme example of this. How, then, could they *not* exist in some shape or form in a culture like the pagan Vikings?[268] And, if the berserkers did not exist, then they should in the future post-apocalyptic wastelands.

The state of *berserkergang* has been thought to be due to the consumption of the fly agaric amantia mushroom, *Amanita muscaria*, an idea first proposed by Samuel Ödmann in 1784, and taken up by H.D. Fabing in 1956.[269] A better known discussion of the use of these mushrooms was made by John Allegro in his much-criticized book, *The Sacred Mushroom and the Cross*,[270] where he argued that Jesus in the Gospels was a code word for *Amantia muscaria* and that Christianity was essentially a dope cult. There is even less reason to believe that the action of the Viking berserkers was due to this dope, as the main active chemicals in the mushrooms muscimol (3 hydroxy-5-aminomethylisoxizol acid and ibotenic acid), typically do not produce aggressive attitudes, but rather hallucinatory effects,

[267] "Berserkers and other Shamanic Warriors", at http://norse-mythology.org/gods-and-creatures/others/berserkers-and-other-shamanic-warriors/.

[268] Osred, "Odinist Myth Busting 1. Berserkers: A Christian Fantasy?" *Renewal*, September, 2016, p. 5.

[269] H. D. Fabing, "On Going Berserk: A Neurochemical Inquiry," *American Journal of Psychiatry*, vol. 113, 1956, pp. 409-415.

[270] John Allegro, *The Sacred Mushroom and the Cross*, (Hodder and Stoughton, London, 1970).

central nervous systems dysfunction and intoxicated sleep.[271] Hence, it is likely that the state of berserkergang is self-induced, produced by flooding the body with adrenaline, and thus can be controlled to some degree, or at least switched on. This would be particularly useful in melee battles to come in the apocalypse.[272]

And in the end... there is Ragnarok. There was a prediction made by the Jorvik Viking Centre that Ragnorok, the twilight of the Gods and end of the World was going to occur on February 22, 2014, as the ancient horn Gjallerhorn was thought to have been heard on the "roofs of York" in November 2013.[273] Sadly, not so. Norse myths do not put a date on Ragnarok.[274] The Ragnorok myth could well be, as Martin puts it, an "eschatological motif... devolved from traditional seasonal ritual for the re-invigoration and sustenance of the natural order."[275] Alternatively, it could be an attempt by snotty-nosed Christian scribes such as Snorri Sturluson (1179-1241) to put an end to the old Gods.

Snorri in *The Prose Edda* has it that after Ragnarök, the world begins again, and people will be rewarded with the coming of the "mighty god from on high, who is ruler of all," thus working in Christianity, as to be expected. Thorskegga Thorn, "Thor and the Midgard Serpent,"[276] argued that Ragnarök was a Christian invention. Thor had dealt with the Midgard Serpent (Jormundgand) pre-Ragnarok, so that at Ragnarok Thor would have come to Odin's

[271] D. Michelot and L. M. Melendez-Howell, "*Amanita Muscaria*: Chemistry, Biology, Toxicology, and Ethnomycology," *Mycological Research*, vol. 107, 2003, pp.131-146. For further criticisms of the dope theory of berserkergang, see: "Berserkergang," at http://uppsalaonline.com/berserk.htm.

[272] See "The Berserkergang: Berserker Basics," at http://uppsalawayland.tripod.com/id3.html.

[273] Alex Co, "Ragnarok is Upon Us, Vikings Predict World Ending Today," February 23, 2014 at http://www.escapistmagazine.com/news/view/132434-Ragnarok-is-Upon-Us-Vikings-Predict-World-Ending-Today.

[274] "A Rant about 'Ragnarok 2014'", February 21, 2014, at http://aclerkofoxford.blogspot.com.au/2014/02/a-rant-about-ragnarok-2014.html.

[275] Martin, *Ragnarok*, as above.

[276] Thorskegga Thorn, "Thor and the Midgard Serpent," *Théod*, vol. 3, no. 4, 1996, pp. 32-36.

aid in fighting the Fenris Wolf and together they would have defeated him, thus being able to help the other Gods and together, all defeat Surtur, so the concept of the doom of the gods collapses. Ragnarök, apart from the Last Judgment, is consistent with the Bible. However, some regard this consistency as a mere accident, with Ragnarok believed to come from Indo-European eschatological sources rather than Christian influence.[277] However, even if the Gods do not perish, it seems that Ragnarök is an apt description of the fate of humanity, especially Northern Europeans, rushing head-on into oblivion. Still, Ragnarök is mythopoetically inspiring, and why not run with it, rather than from it, just remembering that we are the ones facing doom, not the gods?

Ragnarök, *Gotterdammerung*, the twilight/doom of the Gods and humanity in Norse mythology, involves a final apocalyptic battle occurring between the forces of "good" and the forces of "evil" and darkness. The Gods and heroes of Valhalla take a last stand. All are destroyed save for a few Gods and heroes such as the sons of Thor and Baldar who returns. One man, Lif and one woman, Lífþrasir, survive Ragnarök by taking refuge in the world tree of knowledge, Yggdrasil, so that the cycle of life can begin again.[278] According to Hans-Peter Hasenfratz in *Barbarian Rites*: "for us modern people, living in a world whose very existence has become fragile and fractured by foreseeable ecological and social catastrophes of incalculable dimensions, an existential gateway is also opened up to this type of mythology."[279]

If this is so, then it cannot be said that we should expect some sort of rebirth of nature from the polluted, radioactive wasteland that the forces of evil and darkness are almost certain to leave the world in. Rather, from the Norse eschatological tradition, we may

---

[277]   Hans-Peter Hasenfratz, *Barbarian Rites: The Spiritual World of the Vikings and Germanic Tribes*, (Inner Traditions, Rochester, 2011), p. 132.

[278]   Henning A. Klövekorn, *Asatru*, (The Author, 2013), p. 58; H. R. Ellis Davidson, *Pagan Scandinavia*, (Thames and Hudson, London, 1967), and *Scandinavian Mythology*, (Hamlyn Publishing, London, 1988); Viktor Rydberg, *Teutonic Mythology*, (Swan Sonnenschein & Co., London, 1891).

[279]   Hasenfratz, *Barbarian Rites*, as above, p. 133.

gain the courage to raise a "rude finger" and our battle axes, if only metaphysically, to the Midgard Serpents and Fenris Wolves of this world. We fight on to see them fall, even though ultimately, if poisoned like Thor (in snotty Snorri's *Prose Edda*), we stagger to our deaths, happy to rot, but glad that our enemies have perished before us.

PART II

Self-Defense in a Hostile World

3.

Becoming a Neo-Barbarian:
Martial Muscle in Post Apocalyptica

The biologist, who sees man as a balanced whole, and for whom muscles, bones, sinews, and veins are as important as brains, can only look on, upset as the destruction of all physical work and fitness continues. - *Pentti Linkola*[280]

This new law-table do I put over you, O my brothers: Become hard! -*Friedrich Nietzsche*[281]

From Martial Arts to Survival Combat

Fernando "Ferfal" Aguirre in *The Modern Survival Manual: Surviving the Economic Collapse,* is right in my opinion in recommending that anyone who wants to survive the coming collapse should acquire skill in self-defense including hand-to-hand fighting, firearms and melee weapons (non-projectile handheld weapons).[282] Hand-to-hand fighting will be considered in this chapter. Even though most personal fighting in the future, as I see it, will involve firearms and other projectile and explosive weapons, there may still be situations where opposing parties run out of

---

[280]   Pentti Linkola, *Can Life Prevail? A Radical Approach to the Environmental Crisis,* (Integral Tradition Publishing, 2004), p. 31.

[281]   Friedrich Nietzsche, *Twilight of the Idols: Or, How to Philosophize with a Hammer,* (Penguin Books, London, 2003), p. 122.

[282]   Fernando "Ferfal" Aguirre, *The Modern Survival Manual: Surviving the Economic Collapse,* (The Author, 2009), p. 98.

ammo. Then, as discussed in the next chapter, melee weapons such as fixed bayonets have, and may, be used. In more limited situations, where melee weapons are not available, for whatever reason, people must resort back to using the natural weapons of their bodies. That is the domain of the so-called "martial arts" and our present concern.

Survivalist literature, dominated by US writers, has a strong gun focus, with little attention devoted to personal self-defense in jurisdictions where gun control has disarmed the population. There is almost nothing written about self-defense in a more distant future world after the collapse, when either all presently commercial ammunition has been used up or where commercially produced smokeless powder supplies are depleted. If it is the case that guns may have a shelf life in a post-apocalyptic world (as depicted in the *Mad Max/Road Warrior* movies, where people frantically search for ammo), hand-to hand combat gains more relevance.

Hand-to-hand combat has long supplemented melee weapons fighting, and even firearms, being used when weapons have been dropped for one reason or another, or where a kick can be fitted in naturally. The Viking Sagas, as well as most medieval and Renaissance fight manuals, use striking and grappling methods in unity with melee weapons fighting.[283] Further, as argued in this chapter, hand-to-hand combat skills can have a "kick-on" effect, improving one's skill and power in the use of melee weapons.[284]

So, should one study a martial art now, if one has not done so, and if so, which one? That is the question. The opinion of Fernando Aguirre in *The Modern Survival Manual* is that the martial arts, as such, are full of "bullshit":

You find a healthy amount of BS in everything people do, but with martial arts it's a whole new level of BS. Right up there with fortune-telling and magic male enhancement pills. It's not just Hollywood that's always feeding testosterone candy to the public, its BS imported from the entire Eastern world. Jesus, the

---

[283]   William R. Short, *Viking Weapons and Combat Techniques*, (Westholme Publishing, Yardley, 2009).

[284]   T. Brown, *English Fighting Arts*, (Anglo-Saxon Books, Hockwold-cum-Wilton, Norfolk, 1997), p. 10.

amount of Oriental bullshit sold to the Western world regarding martial arts is just too much. We should sue the bastards.[285]

What Aguirre may have had in mind is *Asian classicism,* Japanese, Korean, and Chinese systems which have as a philosophical basis traditional Eastern religions, cosmologies, and metaphysical systems. Such systems make use of notions of Zen, yin and yang, Tao, *I-Ching* (the *Book of Changes*) and chi. These elements of Oriental philosophy could be either integrated into the physical activities of the martial art itself and/or part of the guiding philosophy of a spiritual warrior ethos, as in Bushido. As an example of the former, in Wing Chun, a kung fu style which is generally described as the most "non-classical" of the classical kung fu styles, in the first "Little Idea" form (*Siu Lim Tao*), a form which is performed stationary, the circling hand move (*huen fok sau*) is performed three times, said to be "three times worship the Buddha." The form is performed slowly in a pigeon-toed stance (*yee gee kim yeung ma/* "pinching goat stance) and *chi kung* ("life energy training") is undertaken.[286] Most Western practitioners do not know that in performing Wing Chun's first form, they are worshiping the Buddha.

For the Westerner, Wing Chun's centerline theory is thought to be based on physical principles of efficiency (the shortest distance between two points, is a straight line). But the Easterner also sees a Confucian basis in the *Chung Yong* principle, the idea of aligning action with the centerpoint of action, based on the idea of living in moderation and avoiding extreme points in living.[287] While this is arguably wise advice for living (also given in the West by numerous philosophers, from Aristotle onwards), there are sound biomechanical and strategic arguments for the center point action principle. Such elements, though, can be pruned from their Oriental

---

[285]   Aguirre, as above, pp. 100-101.

[286]   D. Chow and R. Spangler, *Kung Fu: History, Philosophy and Technique,* (Unique Publications, Burbank, 1982).

[287]   A. M. Simpkins and C.A. Simpkins, "Confucianism and Asian Martial Traditions," *Journal of Asian Martial Arts,* vol.16, no.1, 2007, pp. 50-57.

philosophical basis, and for most Western practitioners of Wing Chun, the movements have no religious significance.

The over-spiritualized conception of the Asian martial arts may itself be a recent "invented tradition," for 17th century Chinese Shaolin literature does not link the martial arts with "Buddhist enlightenment."[288]

The external Asian philosophies associated with the martial arts can be jettisoned as they are generally practiced in the West, because if these philosophies exist at all, they are only given lip service too, or indulged in as an academic pursuit. Judo, karate, and Tae Kwon Do can be practiced today in most cities with very little cultural baggage. So, Aguirre's skepticism should not be applied to them, although, as we shall see, there are still questions which can be raised about their combat effectiveness.

Aguirre's skepticism best applies to less regulated, and outrightly wild and woolly orientations such as some parts of Chinese kung fu. There one can easily find, with a few minutes' internet research, incredible claims about what chi can do. One kung fu book, to be unnamed, says that an advance kung fu practitioner pulled a stone roller weighing over 250 kg over his testicles (allegedly unharmed), and licked a red-hot iron shovel straight from the furnace (allegedly unharmed). This is just superstition and magic, used to extract training fees from gullible students. In the case of touching hot objects, briefly, use is deceptively made of physical principles such as the Leidenfrost effect, where the body is momentarily protected by water vapor. As another example of these cons, it is said that Bruce Lee was at a demonstration where a chi kung man was showing off his allegedly invincible stomach. He offered Lee a strike; Lee punched him in the head and knocked him out, a very *Jeet Kune Do* thing to do. The moral of the story is: what good is all of the chi in the world if *you* end up the one on the ground?

---

[288]   M. Shahar, "Ming-Period Evidence of Shaolin Martial Practice," *Harvard Journal of Asiatic Studies*, vol. 6, no.2, 2001, pp. 359-413.

"Bullshit," or what has been alternatively called "epistemic viciousness"[289] in the martial arts, especially kung fu, can be seen in many "sharp" practices, used to exploit students. It is one thing to expect students to be respectful and disciplined, but quite another to foster a cult-like/religious-gurus attitude, where sifu (teacher) becomes "god-like." For example, Bruce Lee (1940-1973) was a martial arts genius and innovator who had an immense impact on martial arts thought, but he was still a man with moral "faults" and physical flaws. He apparently had numerous extramarital affairs. Further, Lee apparently *ate* cannabis, which some felt, along with anabolic steroid abuse, may have contributed to his ill-health at the end of his tragic life. Seeing such a person as "god-like" degrades his truly stunning human performance and he himself repeatedly said that he was nothing special, the product of being driven to train and succeed.[290] Gods don't need to bust their asses striving for martial arts excellence.

Kung fu philosophy can also be manipulated to financially exploit students or commercially control them. For example, it was traditional to have "indoor" and "outdoor" students. The outdoor students waited outside of the teacher or sifu's house to train; the indoor students were taken in from the cold to train. Paying more money, the indoor students received the full teachings, allegedly, while the outdoor ones were taught less and not shown the "secret techniques." For example, in Wing Chun kung fu, the outdoor view of the *taun sao* (palm-up deflection) is that the fingers are straight; the indoor view holds that only the index finger is straight, the others are relaxed and held up, the wrist rotated, so the hand has a greater surface to "stick" in *chi sao* (sticking hands) to the opponent's arm. Indoor students generally went through a formal ceremony called *Bai Si*, a tea ceremony, to mark one's admission and where sifu was given money. Westerners prefer a more egalitarian approach to things.

---

[289]   Gillian Russell, "Epistemic Viciousness in the Martial Arts", in Graham Priest and Damon Young (eds), *Marital Arts and Philosophy: Beating and Nothingness,* (Open Court, Chicago and La Salle, 2010), pp.129-144.

[290]   "Leave sagehood behind and enter once more into ordinary humanity. After coming to understand the other side, come back and live on this side": Bruce Lee, *Tao of Jeet Kune Do,* (Expanded Edition), (Black Belt Books, Valencia, 2011), p. 212.

Kung fu and organized crime/Chinese triads have an intimate connection. The triads were secret societies originally formed to overthrow the Qin Dynasty, but which then morphed into crime gangs.[291] Triads exercise vast power in Hong Kong today and their world and part of the darker side of kung fu, blend into each other, perhaps symbolically as well as literally.

There are some other problematic aspects of traditional kung fu. One is the view that only one style is the "correct" one. Thus, for example, in Hong Kong Yip (Ip) Man Wing Chun, Bruce Lee's style (he studied for about two years with Yip (Ip) Man), there was in the 1980's various challenge fights issued in the martial arts magazines to prove who is the true Wing Chun master/champion, as Yip (Ip) Man apparently did not appoint one before dying. Buckler in his 2010 Ph.D. thesis on Wing Chun says: "the resulting 'farce' resembled a playground fight with no clear winner and indeed from video evidence, no explicit Wing Chun techniques were utilized."[292] No leader emerged from this "classical mess,"[293] and the conflict merely confirmed the remarks made by one practitioner on ewingchun. com: "The majority of Wing Chun people that I've come across are egotisic know-it-alls …. They've become a slave to their Wing Chun or their particular Wing Chun lineage."[294] Bruce Lee, if he lived, would have been ashamed to have seen this.

This master/slave dialectic was well illustrated by some of the Western Wing Chun schools' past denial or silence about Wing Chun in mainland China and South East Asia. Not true, and today other names and long-standing schools are recognized, such as Sum

---

[291] J. M. S. Ward and W. G. Sterling, *The Triads: The Hung Society or the Society of Heaven on Earth,* (Kegan Paul, New York, 2006).

[292] S. R. Buckler, *Sects and Violence: Development of an Inclusive Taxonomy to Hermeneutically Explore the Histo-Philosophical Motivators for the Inception and Development of the Martial Art, Wing Chun Kuen,* (PhD, Coventry University, 2010), p. 25.

[293] Leung Shiu Hung, "The Rise and Fall of the Wing Chun (Ving Tsun) Family?" November 5, 2010, at http://ewingchun.com/article/rise-and-fall-wing-chun-ving-tsun-family.

[294] "The Best Wing Chun," June 10, 2012, at http://www.ewingchun.com/article/best-wing-chun.

Nung, Pan Nam, Jiu Wan, Yuen Kay-San, Gu Lao, Pao Fa Lien, Jee Shim, Hung Suen and Pien Jan branches to name a few.[295]

Here are some vastly different Wing Chun systems, some of which can now be viewed on YouTube: (1) Gu Lao Wing Chun consists of 40 "tactics" instead of the familiar Yip (Ip) Man three forms; (2) Sun Nung's Yuen Kay-San style employs the method of striking with the head and shoulders (not in Yip (Ip) Man Wing Chun); (3) Pao Fa Lien Wing Chun from Qing Yuan, Guangdong, has 10 empty-hand sets, four wooden dummy sets, and a half-dozen weapons sets; (4) the Malaysian Wing Chun which Yip Kin brought to Malaysia in the 1930s has additional weapons such as the tiger trident and plum blossom spear and (5) the Vietnamese Wing Chun of Ngyen Te-Cong (Yen Chai-Wan), started in Hanoi in 1936, has a gim (sword) added. There is thus more diversity in Wing Chun kung fu than we older Western students have previously been led to believe. Indeed, even within the Yip (Ip) Man School, there are variants in techniques such as the wooden dummy form (*muk yan jong*), with some of Yip Man's students having 108 movements, some 116. Yes, people are willing to fight over such trivia.

Chinese kung fu systems also have an origins mythology; at its most extreme, techniques were given by gods or divine forces (meaning that the system is *that* good), or more humbly, arose from some sage observing an animal in battle. This inspired the development of the system, just in the nick of time to save the good guys. For example, to chain punch Wing Chun Kuen again, the classic origin story has a Buddhist nun Ng Mui developing the style about 250 years ago in the Siu Lum Monastery, after watching a snake battle a crane (itself, an unlikely event). After the Siu Lum Monastery was destroyed by an attack from Manchu troops, she fled to a village where she met a beautiful young woman Yim Wing Chun. Poor Yim was sexually harassed by the local bully who wanted to marry her. Ng Mui took pity on Yim and took her into the mountains to train her in the new style. She, in good *Karate Kid* style, learnt quickly, returned, and challenged said horny bully to a fight, which of course

[295]   Robert Chu (et al.), *Complete Wing Chun: The Definitive Guide to Wing Chun's History and Tradition,* (Tuttle Publishing, Tokyo, 1998).

she won. She then marries her one-true-love, Leung Bok Chau, in Siu Hing, Canton, and trains him. The subtext here is that this style is so good that even our women can beat you. The style was eventually passed on to Wong Wah Bo and a monk who had fled from the Siu Lam monastery, Chi Shin, both on the operatic Red Junk. There, Chi Shin taught the six-and-half pole techniques to both Wong Wah Bo and Leung Yee Tei, techniques with their big circle movements and horse stance, completely at variance with the rest of what we now know as Western Wing Chun. Leung Yee Tei taught Leung Jan, a herbal doctor in Foshan, who taught Chan Wah Shan, who taught Yip (Ip) Man. Yip (Ip) Man himself, seems to have accepted this basic romantic narrative.[296] There is no evidence for it and a moment of sober reflection would reveal that it is just romantic nonsense.

Yip Man's son, Yip (Ip) Chun, says that "Yim Wing Chun is only a storybook character" and that "Wing Chun was brought to Foshan from the North by a person called Tan-Sau Ng (Palm-up Arm Ng – a nickname).[297] Yip Chun also cited a book by Mak Siu Har, *A Study on the History of Cantonese Operas*, which records that Cheung Ng of Wu Pak, aka Tan-Sau Ng, went to Foshan and organized the Hung Fa Wui Koon for the development of opera. The book records that Cheung Ng was a highly skilled martial artist and his "*tan sau* (Wing Chun's defensive palm-up deflection) was peerless throughout the martial arts world." Wing Chun stances and techniques would be suitable for fighting on the unstable surfaces of boats, strengthening the Red Junk connection.

Pan Nam, a mainland China grandmaster, has a similar story.[298] Wing Chun was founded by a Buddhist monk Yat Chan Um Chu, who lived in a temple in Heng Shan (Mt Heng) of the Hunan Province. He taught actor Tan-Sau Ng who in turn, taught other actors, some of whom were revolutionaries, all on the Red Junk.

[296] IP (Yip) Man, "The Origin of Ving Tsun (Wing Chun)," at http://www.vingtsun. hk/Origin.htm.

[297] Yip Chun (with Danny Connor), *Wing Chun: Skill and Philosophy*, (Stanley Paul, London, 1992), p. 18.

[298] Pan Nam, "The History of Wing Chun," November 6, 2011, at http://www.ewingchun. com/wiki/history-wing-chun-pan-nam.

Academic S. R. Buckler also hypothesizes that Wing Chun arose on the Red Junks which were a hiding place for revolutionaries and that the name "Wing Chun" is not a woman's name but is linked to revolution, the words occurring in revolutionary slogans of the time to overthrow the Qing Dynasty.

The example of Wing Chun's tempestuous history does illustrate some of the extreme angst that comes from devotion to a traditional martial art with its quasi-religious commitment to the ego of "sifu," and where the art itself takes on aspects of the sacred. This was recognized by Bruce Lee (1940-1973), whose critique of classical martial arts will now be discussed.

Bruce Lee's Critique of the "Classical Mess"

The most powerful critique of Asian classicism was made by Bruce Lee. Lee in his early work was somewhat obedient to the philosophies and techniques of Chinese kung fu,[299] but he had come, at least at the time of his back injury (1970), when he wrote the notebooks that formed *Tao of Jeet Kune Do*[300] and *Bruce Lee: Jeet Kune Do*,[301] to reject Asian classicism. His article "Liberate Yourself from Classical Karate" (1971),[302] generated a storm of controversy. "All styles require adjustment, partiality, denials, condemnation, and a lot of self-justification. The solutions they purport to provide are the very cause of the problem because they limit and interfere with our natural growth and obstruct the way to genuine understanding."

Lee thus followed that other martial art giant, Miyamoto Musashi (1584-1645), who in *A Book of Five Rings* said: "I have lived without

---

[299] Bruce Lee, *Chinese Gung-Fu: The Philosophical Art of Self-Defense*, (Ohara Publications, Santa Clarita, 1963/1987).

[300] Bruce Lee, *Tao of Jeet Kune Do*, (expanded edition), (Black Belt Books, Valencia, 2011).

[301] John Little (ed.), *Bruce Lee: Jeet Kune Do: Bruce Lee's Commentaries on the Martial Way*, (Tuttle Publishing, Tokyo, 1997).

[302] Bruce Lee, "Liberate Yourself from Classical Karate," *Black Belt*, September 1971, pp. 25-27.

following any particular way. Thus with the virtue of strategy, I practice many arts and abilities – all things with no teacher."[303] It has been said that Lee was "prevented by Yip Man from learning the "entire" Wing Chun system" as Lee was Eurasian, and Yip (Ip) Man was a traditionalist who thought that Wing Chun was for the Chinese, not for someone who was going to take it to the West.[304] This may or may not have been so; whatever the reason, Lee sought to go beyond Wing Chun, which was one of the more liberated styles, "non-classical." He said:

> As a matter of fact, they [martial arts systems] each have their strong points and weak points. They all need self-evaluation and improvement. They are too narrow-minded. They can only see their strong points, but not their weak points and other's strong points. A man confirmed in thought and scope will not be able to speak freely. Therefore, if he wants to seek for truth, he should not be confined by the dead forms.[305]

Lee came to see Jeet Kune Do, as itself possibly limiting if it was frozen into a "style" or quasi-style.[306] The important thing is not names or abstract philosophies but "smashing the guy before he hits you, with any method available." [307] "Let your opponent graze your skin and you will smash into his flesh; let him smash into your flesh and you fracture his bones; let him fracture your bones and you take his life!"[308] The right stuff indeed!

Specifically, on the limitations of Wing Chun Lee said: "I've lost faith in the Chinese classical arts—though I still call mine Chinese—because basically all styles are products of dry-land swimming, even the Wing Chun School. So, my line of training is

[303]   Miyamoto Musashi, *A Book of Five Rings* (Axiom, 2006), p. 6.

[304]   Eric Oram, "Why Bruce Lee Left Wing Chun," *Inside Kung Fu*, at http://www.lawingchun.com/ikf_bruce_lee.html.

[305]   John Little (ed.), *Bruce Lee: Jeet Kune Do: Bruce Lee's Commentaries on the Martial Way,* (Tuttle Publishing, Tokyo, 1997), p. 21.

[306]   Dan Inosanto, *Jeet Kune Do: The Art and Philosophy of Bruce Lee,* (Know Now Publishing, Los Angeles, 1980), pp. 66-67.

[307]   John Little (ed.), *Bruce Lee: Jeet Kune Do,* as above, p. 59.

[308]   Bruce Lee, *Tao of Jeet Kune Do,* as above, p. 16.

more toward efficient street fighting with everything goes."[309] His reasons for not sticking to Wing Chun were that his style "has more to offer regarding efficiency." From Lee's perspective he could have gone much further in his criticism of Wing Chun limitations. While it does have some circular strikes (as in the *chum kil* form), its principal claim to fame is the centerline theory (attack and defense through the centerline) using generally linear attacks such as chain punching/running punch or fingertip strikes (*bil jee* form). The Wing Chun justification for this centerline-based theory is that attack and defense (and simultaneous attack/defence) protects most vital organs and is, all other things being equal, quicker, as the shortest distance between two points is a straight line. Granted, but this is the time for a bit of ying and a bit of yang. Straight attack can defeat circular attack, but circular attack, when used strategically, can defeat straight attack. Thus, a carefully used Muay Thai round house kick, either high or low, in a combination of brutal attacks may destroy the rhythm of the standard Wing Chun attacker. And, if some circular attacks have been allowed into Wing Chun, then why not a full array? While it makes combat sense to keep kicks low, why not allow in a low roundhouse kick which has proved so successful in Muay Thai? To even think this thought is heretical, according to the "wisdom" of the book reviewers of the classical school, and that, in a nutshell, is the limitation of the classical martial arts: fossilization.

Wing Chun in its Hong Kong, mainland Chinese, and South East Asian variants lacks ground-fighting, or at least sophisticated ground-fighting, to match systems such as Brazilian jiu jitsu. This is somewhat ironic since one of the main Wing Chun brawls in the "who's the king of the castle" quests involved rolling around on the ground. Supposedly, Wing Chun's *chi sao* (sticky hands) can be used to prevent a grappler getting a hold. Indeed, it can, and I have done it several times. But against really good, really strong opponents with hard-core wrestling experience, one's skill and luck may run out, and in "bouncing" (hotel security work) I have seen all matter of fancy martial arts techniques, all of which I could perform but would never use in a street fight, fail dramatically. I have seen black

---

[309] John Little (ed.), *Bruce Lee: Jeet Kune Do*, as above, p. 53.

belt hot shots who thought that the sun shone out of their martial arts anal hole, get dumped on their proud asses by tough guys such as bikers, who were immune to pain, due to them having consumed a mountain of drugs and an ocean of alcohol. Yet, the standard line in Wing Chun circles is not to add wrestling to Wing Chun: "We can only match a wrestler on the ground if we possess the requisite physical strength and talent and devote a disproportionate amount of time and effort to appropriate training." Contrary to this opinion, as I will argue shortly, acquiring grappling skills, while hardly a top priority in collapse training, should still be on the "to do" list.

Bruce Lee's core critique of the classical martial arts is that they are governed by tradition and culture rather than scientific principles and empirical testing. Seen in this light, a traditional rising block with the fist beginning at the hip, will be too slow to stop a punch from an equally as fast (or maybe even slightly slower) boxer, let alone the faster fighter.

Some more on the classical Asianist mindset. Patricia Petersen in her contribution to the classical minded edited volume by Graham Priest and Damon Young, *Marital Arts and Philosophy: Beating and Nothingness*, "Grrrrl in a Gi,"[310] described how training in karate-do improved her life and made her into a feminist, not just a university-produced one, but a *true* feminist, no longer emotionally dependent on men. She looks forward to a world where all women are feminists, trained in karate-do and where men will do their "own washing, clean the loo, and darn their own socks." Her feminist narrative is that men are abusers, especially in domestic violence, and that karate-do will help solve this. She rolls out statistics which do not conclusively support her position; for example, in the US, although 1.5 million women are allegedly raped and/or physically assaulted by an intimate partner annually in the United States, 834,700 men are also. This statistic relates to rapes and/or physical assaults by *intimate partners*. Petersen doesn't consider US statistics on the rape and/or physical assault of men, primarily white men by black men

---

[310] Patricia Petersen, "Grrrrl in a Gi," in Graham Priest and Damon Young (eds), *Marital Arts and Philosophy: Beating and Nothingness*, (Open Court, Chicago and LA Salle, 2010), pp. 93-103.

in US prisons. If sexual abuse in prisons is considered, more men are raped in the US than women. In 2008 it was estimated by the Department of Justice that 216,000 inmates were sexually assaulted while serving time in prison compared to 90,479 rapes outside of prison.[311] There are also incidents of female prison staff sexually assaulting male prisoners.

Many self-defense books have stories of women who have been raped and/or physically assaulted, who turned to karate, Tae Kwon Do or kung fu as an answer. Generally, the classical arts have helped in giving a sense of empowerment, which is good.[312] But many female black belts, after spending years doing katas and fighting the wind, have been raped and/or assaulted a second time because they froze up, or if they did fight, their techniques failed, and they were not able to put down the attacker.[313]

The remarks of Kevin Krein, a karate practitioner who contributed the essay before Peterson's paper in the Priest/Young volume, seems relevant here when he notes that for self-defense, "Karate seems a poor investment of my time and energy. Sure, I learn some combat skills, but spending decades refining techniques makes little sense, next to other self-defense options. For pure self-defense, a short course combined with carrying a practical self-defense weapon such as mace, would be a much better use of my time."[314]

[311]   "More Men are Raped in the US than Women, Figures on Prison Assaults Reveal," October 8, 2013, at http://www.dailymail.co.uk/news/article-2449454/More-men-raped-US-women-including-prison-sexual-abuse.html.

[312]   Sharon Guthrie, "Liberating the Amazon: Feminism and the Martial Arts," *Women and Therapy*, vol. 16, 1995, pp. 107-119.

[313]   John Perkins (et.al), *Attack Proof: The Ultimate Guide to Personal Protection*, 2nd edition, (Human Kinetics, Champaign, 2009), p. 36.

[314]   Kevin Krein, "Sparring with Emptiness," in Priest and Young, as above, pp. 81-91, p. 82.

The Heavy-Duty Combat Sports
Critique of Traditional Martial Arts

Muay Thai kickboxers defeated in professional fights Taiwanese kung fu fighters in numerous contests from 1959 to 1971. The kung fu fighters always whinged about having to wear gloves, arguing that their well-conditioned fists would destroy the Muay Thai fighters. In 1971 the kung fu men got their wish in matches with no gloves and were destroyed in less than two minutes of the first round.[315] Muay Thai fighter's fury was the product of both a simple but highly efficient system and barbarian training: kicking banana palms and conditioning the shins to become so tough (and to endure pain) that a coke bottle could be broken on them (although I have not personally seen this). Muay Thai has mean techniques that work, such as beating an opponent's bicep until the arm drops and an elbow smash to the head can be delivering, or in a clinch, violently shaking the opponent's head from side-to-side, so he doesn't know what the hell is happening, and pulling the head onto a series of knee attacks.[316] A simple system enables the techniques in the tool box to be grasped in a relatively short time. Compare: one Wing Chun school I have heard of said that one would take fifteen years to complete the system, that is, to learn the three forms, wooden dummy, associated skills, butterfly knives and six-and-half-pole! A lot of money there for fat, greedy sifu. By contrast, for combat sports like Muay Thai, that time could be spent in refining the techniques, training (conditioning, focus pad training, speed ball and heavy bag work) and full contact sparring. Melee weapons training could be done in European systems.

Bruce Lee is reputed to have said: "Someone with only a year of training in boxing and wrestling could easily defeat a traditional martial artist of twenty years' experience."[317] A wee exaggeration,

---

[315]   Don F. Warrener, *Full Contact Martial Arts,* (Paul H. Crompton Ltd, London, 1979), pp. 30-31.

[316]   Erich Krauss (et al.), *Muay Thai Unleashed,* (McGraw Hill, New York, 2006).

[317]   See www.jkdtalk.com/archive/index/t-3062.html.

but not too far from the mark. Good Western boxers have been observed to defeat martial artists in street fights (sensible ones have conditioned their hands and don't work out on the heavy bag with gloves). However, in Western boxing (generally with gloves on) vs. wrestling matches, the wrestlers generally win. Most of the time the boxer can't knock the wrestler out with one punch or a quick combination of punches, and they are gone. As illustrated dramatically in the *Rocky III* match between Rocky and Thunderlips (Hulk Hogan), wrestlers are just too tough for boxers. (Check out the clip on YouTube.) The eruption of Mixed Martial Arts onto the combat sports scene has taken these "what if" matches to a new level.[318]

Jigoro Kano (1860-1938) modified jiu-jitsu to form judo. One of Kano's first students was Mitsugo Maeda, who fought contests around the world. He finally settled in Brazil and taught Carlos Gracie. Carlos taught his brothers including Helio. Helio fought matches all over Brazil and eventually faced Masahiko Kimura, the leading Japanese jiu-jitsu fighter of the time, and defeated him. Helio then took up the invitation to fight and teach in Japan. He taught his sons Rickson, Royler, Royce, Relson and Rorion.[319] The Gracies defeated boxing, karate, Tae Kwon Do and kung fu fighters across Brazil. Rorion Gracie moved to the United States in 1978 but found that Americans were not interested in his style, with its focus on ground fighting. It was the era of spectacular kicks, generated by Bruce Lee's *Enter the Dragon* (1973). Rorion made a tape of Gracie fight matches, *Gracies in Action*, which he promoted.

In 1989 his three brothers Rickson, Royce, and Royler came to America and opened the Gracie Academy in Torrance California. Rorion, working with Art Davie, put together a proposal for pay-per-view companies for different martial arts styles fighting each other: the beginning of Ultimate Fighting Championship (UFC)

---

[318]   Royce Gracie, *Ultimate Fighting Techniques Vol.1 & 2: Fighting From the Bottom*, (Invisible Cities, Montpelier, 2005-2006).

[319]   Paul Hansford and Al McKillop, *Mixed Marital Arts: (The Last Word)*, (Germinal Press, 2011), p. 21.

and Mixed Martial Arts (MMA).[320] A match held in November 1993 at McNichols Sports Arena, Denver, saw a match similar to the Brazilian "vale tudo," no-holds bar matches that the Gracies fought in Brazil: no gloves, "no rules" (in principle no eye gouging) and no weight division, held in the octagon ("the cage"). Senator John McCain saw these matches as "human cockfighting," and his campaign led to a ban on "no holds barred" fights in 36 US states. This led to reform of the sport with gloves becoming mandatory and the official ban being lifted in November 2000. From then on MMA has had success after success and in the US betting revenues from MMA now exceed boxing. In one of the most remarkable sports business ventures of all time, MMA will probably lead to boxing withering away with the emergence of MMA as *the* global combat sport.

The business story of MMA, as impressive as that is, is overshadowed by the fact that MMA devastated traditional Asian martial arts fighters as well as straight boxers. In the first UFC match Royce Gracie "Without throwing a single worthy punch…defeated expert strikers and shattered the mysticism that surrounded the Eastern fighting styles." This performance was repeated in the second UFC contest in November 1994. Bruce Lee famously said: "I don't care what you've heard; there's no such thing as a 90-pound weakling tossing a 250-pound giant."[321] True, but the 180 lb Royce Gracie in 2008 defeated Sumo Grand Champion Akebono (486 lb) with a shoulder lock, so a smaller powerhouse can defeat the bigger guy, if he is a Gracie![322] In this battle of the titans, Royce delivered numerous punches to Akebono's head/ear in a ground 'n' pound, which did nothing but annoy the big guy.

The sports combat success of MMA resolves a long-standing issue about the alleged superiority of classical Asian systems over Western systems. Although Bruce Lee's theoretical work essentially provided the philosophical grounding for MMA, his film work

---

[320]   Jens Pulver (with Erich Krauss), *Little Evil: One Ultimate Fighter's Rise to the Top,* (ECW Press, Toronto, 2003), p. 137.

[321]   John Little (ed.), *Bruce Lee: The Tao of Gung Ku: A Study in the Way of Chinese Martial Arts,* (Tuttle Publishing, Tokyo, 1997), p. 175.

[322]   Paul Hansford and Al McKillop, *Mixed Martial Arts,* as above, p. 49.

promoted mysticism around spectacular high kicks. Sometimes a flying side kick or spinning back kick may work in a combination, but in the ring and on the street, it will often fail with disastrous results. MMA, on the other hand, takes us back to the heavy-duty combat sports of the West of pankration, practiced in ancient Greece and featured in the Olympic Games from 648-393 BC.[323] Only biting and eye gouging were forbidden and the Spartans allowed even that! The loser ended up either crippled or dead.[324]

In the "boxing" of ancient Rome, in its gladiator matches, the introduction of the *cestus* (weaponized gloves), meant that the loser was usually killed; certainly maimed.[325] These combative sports were real life and death struggles, perhaps tougher than any modern street fight. Before ancient Rome and Greece, wrestling, boxing, and probably kicking techniques were practiced in ancient Egypt, Babylonia and Assyria, at least 2,000 years before the birth of Christ (if he existed). Paintings in the Egyptian tomb of Beni Hasan (c.2050-1930 BCE, tomb 15) depict wrestling, incorporating both standing upright and ground wrestling.[326] Wrestling is even mentioned in the 22nd chapter of the book of Genesis. Accounts of wrestling matches are mentioned by Homer (c. 800 BCE) in the *Odyssey* and the *Iliad*; most of the heroes of Greek mythology were skilled wrestlers and philosophers such as Pythagoras, Plato and Aristotle, either wrestled or were knowledgeable about wrestling.

From the fall of Rome, through the Dark Ages and onto the scientific revolution, there was a significant concern with personal self-defense, although melee weapons such as swords and projectile weapons such as bows and arrows, and later guns, were more important than unarmed combat. Frank Docherty argues that the English martial arts, in particular, embodied skills used "to subdue"

[323] M. Poliakoff, *Combat Sports in the Ancient World: Competition, Violence, and Culture*, (Yale University Press, New Haven, 1987).

[324] E. N. Gardiner, *Athletics of the Ancient World*, (Clarendon Press, Oxford, 1940, reprinted 1970).

[325] J. Carcopino, *Daily Life in Ancient Rome*, (George Routledge and Sons, London, 1941).

[326] G. Kent, *A Pictorial History of Wrestling*, (Spring Books, Middlesex, 1968), pp. 9-10.

other cultures, including the East.[327] However, the use of firearms, which civilians up until recent times, could own, led to hand-to-hand combat and melee weapon fighting systems of Western "martial arts" being eclipsed and side-lined. The boxer rebellion of 1900 of nationalist Chinese kung fu fighters (and others) against British riflemen, which led to the slaughter of these Chinese warriors, proved the superiority of gunfire over chi. Nevertheless, pre-Marquis de Queensbury boxing did incorporate gouging, throws, grappling, head-butts, knee-strikes, and elbow attacks, and there was, unlike judo, no reliance on a gi for a takedown. Techniques could still prove useful in the age of the gun.

Today, MMA captures the barbarian spirit of the West's hand-to-hand fighting systems. MMA is, of course, a combat sport, because unlike the ancient Greeks and Romans, we like our fighters to last more than one match. Gloves have been added for hand protection, which you will not likely have in a survival situation and so have rules prohibiting such tactics as eye gouging, breaking the fingers, biting, flesh tearing and other great barbarian tactics. A combat survival version of MMA, as I see it, would go back to a pankration-style battle and incorporate all MMA foul techniques: everything goes.[328]

Without gloves, there is a perennial problem with punching of breaks to the small bones in the hand. If one has fists like hams, generally this is not a problem, but for lighter fellows, fists need to be conditioned by both building up the muscles in the hand through heavy weight training and good old traditional training methods from karate and the "iron hand" training of kung fu. One can, for example, workout on a heavy bag of sand or dried peas. (I have fond memories of skinning my knuckles as a kid doing this, so beware.) However, a greater variety of hand attacks beyond punching need to be added, including palm strikes, the hammer fist and chop, the fingertip strike (*bil jee*) to attack the throat and everything else in

---

[327] Frank Docherty, "English Marital Arts," *Journal of Western Marital Arts*, May 2003, at http://ejmas.com/jwma/articles/2003/jwmaart_docherty_0503.htm.

[328] Sammy Franco, *Out of the Cage: A Complete Guide to Beating a Mixed Martial Artist on the Street*, (Contemporary Fighting Arts, Kindle edition, 2014).

the classical styles, lifted, but practiced, with barbarian pankration spirit.

One of the MMA philosopher's controversies is the place of ground fighting in hand-to-hand combat situations. Professor Bradley J. Steiner has written a brilliant paper critiquing the myth of ground fighting supremacy in battles out of the ring.[329] We should note that even great ground fighters have been beaten in the octagon – Royce Gracie by Matt Hughes via punching, so no single technique is a master technique. The leaders in core hand-to-hand military combat such as W. E. Fairbairn and Rex Applegate, although excellent ground fighters, did not incorporate ground fighting into training soldiers because of its obvious dangers. MMA champion Forrest Griffin best sums this up when he wrote:

> If you want to be a MMA fighter, you absolutely must learn to grapple, but taking your opponent to the ground shouldn't be your first choice in an apocalyptic street fight. Unless the natural disaster that eliminated the majority of humanity somehow covered the surface of the earth with soft feathers, I would recommend doing everything in your power to keep a fight standing. Just think about all the rusty nails and jagged scrap metal that will be littered around.[330]

And just think about dealing with an opponent who will most certainly have pulled a knife that will probably end up in your guts. As well, even today, a street fight without weapons (now very rare) will usually involve a pack of punks beating up on you. Being on the ground is the last place one wants to be. But, if you have screwed up and for one reason or another, find yourself on the ground, do what you have to do, get up quick or expect to have your head kicked in or worse.

---

[329] Bradley J. Steiner, "The Great Myth of 'Ground Fighting Supremacy' in the Modern Combative Field," at https://guidedchaos.kartra.com/page/SteinerMythOfGrappling.

[330] Forrest Griffin (with Erich Kraus), *Be Ready When the Shit Goes Down: A Survival Guide to the Apocalypse*, (William Morrow, New York, 2010), p.48.

The Hard-Core Hand-to-Head Combat Tradition

Nevertheless, while MMA is an excellent conditioning and training source which I recommend as superior to styles like Wing Chun, there is a need to embrace the spirit of military self-defense systems with quick, dirty, simple, effective and violent moves to do the maximum damage to opponents in the shortest time.

There is a considerable literature on hand-to-hand fighting for commandos, the SAS and the general military, also geared for civilians in life-or-death situations including early works from World War II (Gordon E. Perrigard, *All Out Hand-to-Hand Fighting for Commandos, Military and Civilians* (1943)[331] and the classic texts by William E. Fairbairn (*All-in Fighting*[332] and *Get Tough*[333]) and Col. Rex Applegate (*Kill or Get Killed*)[334] along with contemporary street fighting versions.[335] The take home message form this genre of literature is that, as Mark Hatmaker well puts it, "Much of what is proffered in the realm of self-defense instruction is unadulterated bullshit."[336] There are no sure-fire methods of defeating predators, and there are no super-systems capable of enabling you to defeat a roomful of said ghouls, contrary to the email advertisements that I seem to get each week, and Hollywood martial arts movies (e.g., *Into the Badlands* (2015-2019)). At best, one needs to internalize a small set of brutally effective techniques that *you* can do under extreme stress situations and condition your body to become a neo-barbarian.

---

[331]	Gordon E. Perrigard, *All Out Hand-to-Hand Fighting for Commandos, Military and Civilians,* (Renouf Publishing, Montreal, 1943).

[332]	William E. Fairbairn, *All-in Fighting,* (Naval and Military Press, 2009).

[333]	William E. Fairbairn, *Get Tough: How to Win in Hand-to-Hand Combat,* (Paladin Press, Boulder, Colorado, 1996).

[334]	Rex Applegate, *Kill or Get Killed,* (Paladin Press, Boulder, Colorado, 1976).

[335]	Bradley J. Steiner, *The Tactical Skills of Hand to Hand Combat,* (Paladin Press, Boulder, Colorado, 2008).

[336]	Mark Hatmaker, *No Second Chance: A Reality-Based Guide to Self-Defense,* (Tracks Publishing, Chula Vista, 2009), p. 15.

Thus, if punching is your strong point and the hand issue is not a problem, then train relentlessly on it and make it "your thing." Grappling attacks may be dealt with by eye gouging, as was made an art in fights in the Virginia backcountry before the American Civil War,[337] or finger snapping. Effective finger snapping can be achieved by exercises which increase grip strength and the strength of one's hands. For example, one can practice quickly snapping small twigs and then thicker ones, working up to tearing up old books and ultimately phone books.

There are a number of books detailing the effects of adrenaline on motor activities in survival combat.[338] In general, while adrenaline gives short-term pain resistance, it also leads to auditory exclusion, tunnel vision and a sense that things are going in slow motion. As Mark Johnson has put it, in a life-or-death fight, "you'd be lucky to see any technique in the flurry of most real fights. As for discerning a specific style, the planets will have to be in the correct alignment before that happens."[339] Agreed: hence one needs to over-train on a technique or techniques that becomes "your thing," that you can do automatically, in the dark, whatever, wherever. Punching and the hammer fist are my thing. The hammer fist action fits in nicely with the use of weapons such as a sword, Viking axe and various types of "smashers" (as discussed in the next chapter). If possible (and legal), use a weapon. I explain further.

In 2019, on YouTube, there were a number of masters bitterly arguing amongst themselves about the "right" way of escaping a real naked choke. Some of them think that the technique is to cut off air, when in fact, the aim of a well-placed rear naked choke is to cut off the blood supply to the brain. If one is lucky, one has five or so seconds before a blackout. If the hold is maintained, then you die. So, most martial arts breaking techniques are probably not going to

---

[337]   Elliott J. Gorn, "'Gouge and Bite, Pull Hair and Scratch': The Social Significance of Fighting in the Southern Backcountry," *American Historical Review*, vol. 90, 1985, pp. 18-43.

[338]   Rory Miller (ed.), *Campfire Tales from Hell: Musing on Martial Arts, Survival, Bouncing, and General Thug Stuff*, (Marc MacYoung, 2012).

[339]   Michael Johnson, "Stage Fighting is Not Real Fighting," in Rory Miller (ed.), *Campfire Tales from Hell*, as above, pp. 29-34, cited p. 31.

work against an enraged attacker determined to wring your neck; I have in mind the classic smack to the nuts. But, in post-apocalyptic collapse combat, the response will be to fast draw a razor-sharp small dagger (e.g., Sheffield Knives Fairbairn Sykes Gen 3 blade), or a fixed blade karambit (with its nasty claw) and viciously drill it deep into the forearm, then rapidly carve the arm with deep furrows. It is generally accepted that short of being totally zapped on drugs, most humans let go quickly.

Manual labor, such as tree felling with an axe, or braking up rocks with a sledgehammer, can improve one's unarmed strikes, creating a strong neural circuit for such a mind brain-body interaction. Do it enough and it becomes second nature.

In the next chapter it will be convenient to discuss some of the appalling martial arts myths associated with knife fighting.

Strength, Muscle, and Toughness: The Return of Manual Labor

There is a story that those ultimate desk jockeys—philosophers—like to tell. Professor A. J. Ayer, of logical positivism fame, apparently liked the ladies, which in itself was somewhat odd for a philosopher, most being virgins (not incels though), even the married ones with children. Anyway, old Freddie was at a party where boxer Mike Tyson, then aged 21, was also present. Tyson was apparently forcing himself on model Naomi Campbell. Ayer, then aged 77, intervened. Tyson said: "Do you know who the fuck I am? I'm the heavyweight champion of the world. "To this Ayer said: "And I am the former Wykeham Professor of Logic. We are both pre-eminent in our field; I suggest that we talk about this like rational men." As they talked, Campbell exited.[340] A nice story, but it could have ended differently if Tyson had said, "No. Fuck you! Let's fight, you silly old bastard.

---

[340] E. Fitzgerald, "Philosophical Rumble: Mike Tyson vs A. J. Ayer," at http://www.eamonn.com/2012/10/08/philosophical_rumble_mike_tyso/.

Whack!" Talk carries us only so far; certain situations require martial muscle, something modern man is sadly lacking.

Peter McAllister in his paper "The Evaluation of the Inadequate Modern Male,"[341] estimates that the average Neanderthal women would have beaten Arnold Schwarzenegger (in his prime!) at arm wrestling (or if you like, barbell curls) and the average male could have picked him up and thrown him through the air. As for our fellow primates, chimpanzee muscles are about four times stronger than humans, as chimp fibers fire all at once, while human muscle fibers are staggered. This enables chimps to swing their relatively heavy bodies through the trees – and to literally tear humans apart. A few years back, one upset chimp tore a woman's face off. Don't even think about comparing humans to gorillas and bears in the muscle stakes.[342]

The Greek author Xenophon wrote in the 4th century BCE that an Athenian warship, powered by oars, was rowed 263 km in a day. The Athenian oarsman averaged 7-8 knots over the 12-16-hour trip. The description is likely to be true because Xenophon mentioned the trip casually, in passing, with no motive for boasting. It was nothing special. Modern rowers are only able to reach a speed of 6 knots for only an hour and could not reach the Vo_2 max of the Athenians. It is likely then that the average Greek oarsman was as fit as, or fitter than, modern Olympic athletes. And, to rub salt into the wound, nutrition in the Athenian navy consisted of barley, mixed with olive oil, washed down with wine.

McAllister rejects the hypothesis that there are significant genetic differences between the ancient Greeks and us moderns on the grounds that there is not enough time for such large changes to become established. The reason is lifestyle; life then involved high levels of exercise, and people lived tough lives with strenuous toil, doing hard labor from the age of three, onwards until death.

---

[341] Peter McAllister, "The Evolution of the Inadequate Modern Male," *Australasian Science,* May 2011, pp. 19-21.

[342] Peter McAllister, *Manthropology: The Science of the Inadequate Modern Male,* (Hachette Australia, Sydney, 2009).

Before bodybuilding was popular, and before anabolic steroids and growth hormone etc. were available, there were hyper-strongmen in the modern era who are likely to be a match for the strongest Spartans, Greek and Vikings. A shortlist of the mighty moderns include Eugen Sandow, Louis Cyr, Thomas Inch, George Hackenschmidt, Hermann Goerner, Arthur Saxon, Sig Klein, Otto Arco, Paul Anderson, Edward Aston, Mark Berry, Anthony Ditillo, John Grimek, John Jesse, George Jowett, Ed Jubinville, Charles McMahon, Reg Park, Harry Paschall, Bob Peoples, William Pullum, Peary Rader, Michael J. Salvati, David P. Willoughtby, Doug Hepburn, Tommy Kono, Steve Stanko, John Davis, William Boone, Alan Calvert, Martin Burns, Bobby Pandour, Edward Aston, Don Athaldo …[343] Outside a small circle of strength enthusiasts, these names and their books, documenting their Herculean quests to obtain super-strength, are forgotten. Arthur Saxon's bent-press (not bench press) of 371 pounds with one arm is not merely forgotten, but the lift itself is seldom performed.

Today, weight training largely involves some form of bodybuilding or body crafting, to create an esthetically desirable physique. For most gym mice, this involves getting six pack abs (abdominal muscles) and some sort of bulging biceps by training high repetitions on a machine. At the competitive level, bodybuilders do train with free weights, almost exclusively, but relative to strength athletes, power lifters and Olympic lifters, this involves light weights with high repetitions. An example would be looking at one's beautiful self in a mirror and doing biceps curls until one gets the "burn" and a "pump," better than an orgasm Arnie Schwarzenegger allegedly said. At a seminar in the 1980s, I stood next to a Mr. Olympia runner-up, who said that all one needed for biceps training was barbell curls with 50 lbs, which he proceeded to do. He then gave me the bar and asked if I could beat his reps, which I failed to do because I trained heavy. Although there is "natural" bodybuilding which is drug tested, lower level bodybuilding contests generally are not, and where there is drug testing in higher level contests,

---

[343] See Bill Hinbern's, www.superstrengthtraining.com; John Wood, http://www.functionalhandstrength.com; http://www.oldtimestrongman.com.

bodybuilders seek masking drugs to cover their use of anabolic steroids. In a collapse situation, one is not going to have such drugs and the low body fat of the bodybuilder is as dysfunctional in a survival situation as it would be exactly the opposite, grossly obese. The bodybuilder competing on stage, that "condom full of walnuts" as they have been described, is highly unhealthy, not only having been pickled in steroids, but also force-fed protein like a turkey, and subjected to a dehydration regime to deal with "water retention" to get ripped. As Mike Adams has rightly observed: "If an economic collapse were to occur the day before a bodybuilding competition, those participants would quite literally find themselves on the verge of death and need to take immediate action to rehydrate and intake mass quantities of salt and calories just to get back into functional shape again."[344] Bodybuilding is very much a sport of the well-fed, well-drugged, civilized world and will disappear the day after the collapse, if not earlier when the gyms close their doors forever.

Strength, obtained by hard progressive resistance training and sweat, has substantial health benefits for people of all ages, especially men; strength training improves heart and cardiovascular health and for men increases testosterone levels.[345] Low testosterone levels are associated with diseases such as diabetes, obesity, and metabolic syndrome, although it is not yet decided which comes first: low testosterone or poor health. It is known though that androgen deficiency is the most common hormone deficiency in males, affecting one in 200 men under 60 years of age, and one in 10 men aged over 60.[346]

Strongman George F. Jowett was right in saying: "[t]he word 'strength' fascinates me. It squares my shoulders and clenches the fist that drives me onward to a bigger purpose. Strength is Health.

---

[344] Mike Adams, "Health Alert: Why You Don't Want Ripped Abs if You Hope to Survive the Coming Economic Collapse," NaturalNews.com, October 14, 2012, at http://www. naturalnews.com/037536_body_fat_ripped_abs_survival.html.

[345] Lou Schuler, *The Testosterone Advantage Plan: A 9-Week Food and Fitness Breakthrough*, (Rodale, London, 2003).

[346] Thea O'Connor, "The Trouble with Men," June 17, 2013, at https://www.smh.com.au/lifestyle/health-and-wellness/the-trouble-with-men-20130614-2070x.html.

One cannot exist without the other. They are inseparable forces that bind the body to direct purpose. If you lack strength your body will collapse and double up like a jack knife."[347] Strength is part of what *should*, and *will* in the future, be what it means to be a man. It is of unquestionable value in a survival situation. But what is strength?

This question has been examined by sports scientists and has been answered.[348] While there is much technical literature that could be cited, Dr. Frederick C. Hatfield ("Dr. Squat"), who held for a time the world squat record, in his book *Power: A Scientific Approach*, gives a clear and precise account. There are various components to strength including: (1) concentric *absolute strength* (one repetition maximum in lifting a weight); (2) eccentric *absolute strength* (one repetition maximum involving controlled lowering of a weight); (3) *static strength* (at a given range of motion/position, the maximum holding strength); (4) *limit strength* (absolute strength under some extraordinary influence, extreme stress, hypnosis etc.); (5) *speed strength* ((a) starting strength – the capacity to bring into play the maximum number of muscle fibers simultaneously; (b) explosive strength: the capacity to maintain the firing of muscle fibers for a given activity; (6) *anaerobic power* (a) *local muscular endurance,* "your ability to continue submaximal force output over a long period;" (b) *strength endurance,* "your ability to put forth maximum muscular contractions time after time with no appreciable decline in the force output;" *speed endurance,* "your ability to maintain your maximum speed over distances less than 400 meters."

To train all strength components it is necessary to use the overload principle or principle of progressive resistance, to gradually increase the training load, or as John Jesse puts it in *Wrestling: Physical Conditioning Encyclopaedia*: "for skeletal muscles to increase in size, strength, and functional ability…they must be taxed to the limit of their present ability to respond."[349] There are some

---

[347] Logan Christopher, *Strongman Manifesto*, (www.legendarystrength.com, 2008).

[348] Frederick C. Hatfield, *Power: A Scientific Approach*, (Contemporary Books, Chicago, 1989).

[349] John Jesse, *Wrestling: Physical Conditioning Encyclopedia*, (The Athletic Press, Pasadena, 1978), p.35.

general principles relating to the training of each of the components of general strength which Dr. Hatfield has summarized:

1. Absolute and limit strength: heavy weights, over 80-85 percent of the maximum with each repletion (i.e., one performance of the act e.g. a barbell squat) with 3-8 reps per set.
2. Static strength: 2-3 reps for 6-10 seconds; the same for eccentric strength.
3. Starting strength: primarily ballistic training, performing rapid lifts.
4. Explosive strength: achieved by "compensatory acceleration:" "as you progress through a movement, you must attempt to accelerate the weight so that maximum force is being delivered throughout the movement."

In general, absolute and limit strength for a particular movement is optimally achieved through the use of free weights, primarily a barbell with adjustable plates, dumbbells and kettle bells for various lifts. Free weights permit a greater range of movements (machines eliminate ballistic movements), as well as the use of stabilizing muscles to balance the weight, as in the bench press. Having a bar loaded with plates generates a "fight or be crushed" psycho-endocrine challenge that "safe" machines don't deliver. Further, it would be relatively easy to make up a survival gym in the back woods with maybe a flat bench, a good power rack (easily built from purchased steel and concrete), a barbell, and mountains of steel plates. But, one doesn't even need that, and a power workout can be done in an iron junk yard just lifting scrap, or in nature, lifting logs and large stones.

Training for absolute and maximum strength, for one repetition, or even a few, has been comprehensively covered by the Olympic lifting and power lifting traditions. One can imagine survival situations where possessing great absolute strength could prove of survival value, but a more important form of strength for a post-collapse world is *strength endurance*. One of the greatest of all strongmen, Arthur Saxon famously said: "Genuine strength should include not only momentary strength as proved by the ability to life a heavy weight once but also the far more valuable kind of strength known as *strength endurance*. This means the ability, if a wrestler, to wrestle a hard bout for half an hour with a good man without rest, yet without becoming exhausted and reaching the limit of your strength."[350] And as an example, Gama (1878-1960), the famous Indian wrestler who destroyed his opponents across the world, and was undefeated in his 50 years + career, got out of bed at 3 am, did 4,000 deep knee bends, 700 of them jumping squats, before breakfast. After this "warm-up," in the afternoon, he did 2,000 one and two arm push ups, ran a minimum of four miles, and then had 3-4 hours of heavy-duty continuous wrestling. He also used free weights, such as a 95 kg doughnut-shaped exercise disc. Gama trained everyday harder than his opponents trained in their lives.

Contemporary strongman Steve Justa, the "Nebraskan Wildman," is very much what I imagine the post apocalyptical strength trainer would be like. Although he has done plenty of impressive conventional strength lifts – such as an old school hand and thigh lift/one-quarter deadlift of 2,050 pounds[351] and lifting a Ford F600 grain truck loaded with 3 tons of wood, much of his two excellent books, *Rock Iron, Steel* (1998) and *High Plains, Heavy Metal, Iron Master, Super Strength Bible*,[352] outline a wide range of exercises for developing global strength, including doing moderately heavy lifts for repetition; lifting barrels full of materials such as large rocks; pushing and pulling vehicles; carrying weights over long distances; performing heavy singles; isometric tension (e.g., pushing on an immovable object such as a giant tree), and heavy partial lifts and "negatives" for tendon, ligament and bone strengthening.

[350] Arthur Saxon, cited from Jesse, as above, p. 54.

[351] Steve Justa, *Rock, Iron, Steel; The Book of Strength*, (IronMind Enterprises, Nevada City, 1998), p. 5.

[352] Steve Justa, *High Plains, Heavy Metal, Iron Master, Super Strength Bible*, (Strongerman Productions, 2012).

Support for training with objects other than conventional barbells has been made by strongmen Bud Jeffries[353] and Brooks Kubik.[354] Kubik is the philosopher king of this field, and I think from the quality of his works, rightly so. In the bestselling classic *Dinosaur Training*, he lashed out at the modern commercial gym of chrome, ferns and glaring pop music, with rows of machines and circuits, and pencil neck clients being fitness-processed. Real strength cannot be developed in these basically "boy meets girl/girl meets girl/boy meets boy" social encounter rooms. Old style training along the lines of Arthur Saxon and all the other giants of muscle involves: (1) hard training whether one uses a bar or a huge rock or log; (2) the performance of basic compound exercises (squatting, lifting from floor, lifting overhead, walking with the weight etc.); (3) abbreviated training – short, infrequent workouts with a small number of challenging exercises, with low repetitions and a low number of sets because of the *intensity*, no more than three times a week; (4) heavy weights, be these barbells, thick pipe with improvised weights or huge logs/parts of a tree and (5) progression in poundage and intensity.

These principles hold for all lifters, but older lifters (>40 years) need to be especially careful of injuries, with increased warmups, very careful stretching (improper stretching can cause injuries as can no stretching), extreme care in proper form in lifting (as you age there is no room of mistakes as injury-wise your body is not forgiving) and a greater time between workouts to ensure recovery. The older lifter spends less time with maximum weights, partials and heavy negatives and needs to drop exercises causing pain, deadlifts often being one such exercise due to lumbar problems. Exercises with a reputation for causing injuries are typically those involving stretching with resistance and include bench presses with a bar allowing the hands to go below chest-level; barbell presses behind

---

[353] Bud Jeffries, "Twisted Conditioning: How to Combine Barbells, Strongman Training and Bodyweight Exercises for the Ultimate in Strength and Endurance," at http://www.strongerman.com/products/twisted-conditioning/.

[354] Brooks D. Kubik, *Dinosaur Training: Lost Secrets of Strength and Development* 5th edition, (The Author, Louisville, 2006).

the neck; barbell or dumbbell pullovers; the good morning exercise (which Bruce Lee injured his back performing); parallel or lower dips and others. These should be avoided. He notes that the old timers preferred plenty of overhead lifts to the bench press, leaving bench pressing as a secondary exercise. But, beginning in the 1950s, a bench press cult developed. The result of this has been shoulder problems in ageing lifters, as the bench press focuses primarily upon the front deltoids, unlike standing front overhead barbell presses, which work the entire shoulder area. Bench presses need to be part of a balanced shoulder/chest training routine for the entire area.

Even though at, say, 60 years of age you are not going to be the man you were at your prime, one's decline can be graceful, a gentle meander down a grassy hill, rather than an abrupt fall over a cliff onto life's jagged rocks. And, strong, fit and trained old guys have still beat the excreta out of punks who have tried to bully them just because they are old. Shades of "Epic Beard Man."[355]

The case for the importance of strength and strength endurance for the martial artist and unnamed combat practitioner has been strongly put by Bud Jeffries in his book, *Super Strength and Endurance for Martial Arts*.[356] This no-nonsense book advances the "caveman theory of fitness:" "regardless of what I look like, if I can out-fight, out-run, out-lift and out-work you, then I am fitter than you are." I fully agree. The book details 34 training routines involving conventional weights such as barbells, dumbbells, and kettlebells, but also old school training with sled dragging (or car pushing), truck tire flipping, stone lifting, barrel lifting, sledgehammer lifting and/or smashing (on say a thick tire) and so on. Logan Christopher has an excellent site with numerous books and routines, advancing holistic training, dealing with strengthening not only muscles, but also bones, tendons, ligaments and joints, as well as exercises to achieve overall physical and mental excellence.[357]

---

[355] "AC Transit Bus Fight," at https://en.wikipedia.org/wiki/AC_Transit_Bus_Fight.

[356] Bud Jeffries, *Super Strength and Endurance for Martial Arts*, (The Author, 2005).

[357] See www.legendarystrength.com.

Another useful book is John Little (ed.), *Bruce Lee: The Art of Expressing the Human body*[358] which details how Bruce Lee not only built up a physique which was admired by masters of the iron, such as Arnold Schwarzenegger, Lou Ferrigno, Flex Wheeler, Shawn Ray, Dorian Yates, and Lee Haney – but also increased his speed, endurance and flexibility.

Lee's strength routine was three times a week for 15-30 minutes and involved weights plus isometric exercises; too little in my opinion. Lee used primarily compound exercises such as squats, bent over rows, bench press, and shoulder presses, but he also did isolation work such as arm curls, wrist curls, and reverse wrist curls. For the 1960s, this approach was better than the fast food style workouts served up today in the "muscle comics" and the "get sexy fast" lifestyle magazines. Although Lee primarily trained with free weights, it seems that in training for his last film *Enter the Dragon* (1973), he used a multi-exercise weight machine, the Marcy Circuit Trainer, which had nine stations: bench press, lat. pull-down, two high pulleys, two low pulleys, an isometric rack, leg-raise, shoulder press, chin-up bar and leg press. Lee had been observed doing 50 *one-arm* chin-ups. Most weight lifters, let alone bodybuilders, can't even do one.

Strength and power training, however, are but one important part of overall physical fitness and toughness. Georges Hébert (1875-1957), a French physical educator, was appalled at the "weak and degenerate" nature of civilized man. He had long been impressed by the physical strength and agility of native peoples. In 1902, while an officer in the French Navy, he was stationed in the town of St. Pierre, Martinique, when a volcanic eruption occurred. He helped to coordinate the escape of several hundred people and the difficulty that people had escaping reinforced his belief in the need for practically useful physical fitness. As a physical instructor for the French marines in Lorient, he refined his exercises for his "Natural Method."

---

[358]   John Little (ed.), *Bruce Lee: The Art of Expressing the Human Body*, (Charles E. Tuttle, North Clarendon, 1998).

Hébert built upon the work of Francisco Amorós, a military man from Spain, who in 1819 in France organized the Normal Gymnastic Civil and Military School for the teaching and practice of practical movement skills such as jumping, carrying, throwing, climbing in real world environments. Amorós set out his philosophy of fitness in his treatises *A Guide to Physical, Gymnastic, and Moral Education* (1830) and *Nouveau Manuel Complet d'Education Physique Gymnastique et Morale* (1847). These works, in turn, built up the foundations of early gymnastics and calisthenics by Friedrich Jahn (1778-1852) in Germany. Jahn had developed outdoor exercise clubs called the *Turnenvereins* (gymnastics associations, with the *Turnplazt* being the actual open-air gyms). The training was conducted in exercising via vaulting, climbing, balancing, jumping, and running.

Rejecting competitive sport, Jahn, Amorós, and Hébert all maintained that the main purpose of physical training was to deal with the demands of life to promote physical prowess, muscular strength, speed, virility, courage and willpower. This philosophy of fitness has influenced the development of modern forms of athleticism such as *parkour*. Indeed, Hébert's system had an obstacle course called a "parcours."

Raymond Belle was born in Vietnam in 1939 and raised at a military orphanage. He trained intensely on the parcours. His son David Belle was born in 1973 in France and learnt "parcours" from his father. He then trained a small group, including relatives in free running, jumping, climbing, landing and rolling. The system was later called *parkour*. The opening of the James Bond film *Casino Royale* (2006) has a spectacular foot chase between Bond (played by Daniel Craig) and a terrorist (played by parkour master Sébastien Foucan) in a Madagascar construction site.[359]

All of these activities strive to create and preserve functional strength for survival. Le Corre has said: "Natural human movement is not an option. It has always been, still is, and will always be a biological necessity. In a world crowded with an increasing

---

[359] See David Belle, *Parkour*, (Intervista, 2009); Sébastien Foucan, *Free Running*, (Michael O'Mara, 2009).

number of disempowered men, the timeless endeavor of real-world preparedness is once again becoming a fundamental component of the art of manliness."

An associated movement is the "Centurion method" of Craig Fraser, which could be described as the fitness method for the "Post-Apocalyptic Hominid." The inspiration is from the training of the soldiers of ancient Rome and Sparta, who had hard, painful training designed to make them tough and used to hardship.[360] Craig Fraser has said of their workouts: "We are growing toward doing a lot of military preparedness workouts: can you outrun a pursuer, can you climb a tree at speed, can you jump over obstacles at speed, and can you bring an attacker down with one arm? All if this is molded around three basic systems, the Primal Training which is agility, speed and mobility; the Guerilla Training which is aggressiveness, power and strength and finally the English gangster method which is very, very simply the *Silent Killing* system devised by W.E. Fairbairn and used by the British armed forces in WW II. Centurion Method is whatever you want it to be, but whatever level you start at the aim is to develop you into a lean, mean hunting machine. The same hunting machine that has stalked the deserts, tundra, forests and plains of the planet for hundreds of thousands of years."[361] Natural, functional all-round super-fitness is obtained by training in natural environments: climbing trees or cliffs rather than doing chin-ups in a gym, lifting logs and carrying heavy rocks over a distance, or even hunting where there is a risk. While I haven't heard of Centurion followers doing it, I have heard of those following Germanic, Nordic and Viking ways, hunting wild boars with a spear (throwing spears and shorter thrusting spears, with back up "pig sticker" knives to stab and draw-slash the pig's throat).

CrossFit programs are another excellent way of developing universal holistic fitness, understood to be continuous improvements in cardiovascular/respiratory endurance, stamina, strength,

[360] Jack Donovan, "The Centurion Method," February 8, 2013, at http://www.jack-donovan.com/axis/2013/02/the-centurion-method/.

[361] "Centurion Method: Outdoor Fitness, Guerrilla Style," April 26, 2013, at http://www.healthgauge.com/read/outdoor-fitness-guerrilla-style.

flexibility, power, coordination, agility, balance, and accuracy. This requires more than just a traditional workout with free weights and encompasses interval training, gymnastics, stretching, and a wide range of outdoor physical activities such as rock climbing, resulting in a type of "paleo" survival style fitness, for a primal world.[362]

In all of this, one should not forget the role of hard manual labor. Every training method mentioned above is practiced to develop certain skills, but manual labor is performed to achieve an end. Much of that which has been described and referenced deals with workouts for urban people either in gyms or sheds or urban people going to rural and outback areas. One alternative to all of this, which I have taken, is to not live a "civilized" life at all but to embrace as much of the barbarian ways of my ancestors as possible. Start by not sleeping on a bed, but on the floor, using the bed only for sex, if and when you get any.

Manual labor, used as a foundation for building strength, has been long recognized. For example, Slim "The Hammerman" Farman has done incredible level lifts with a 24 lb and a 56-pound hammer: "He lifts it up until it is straight arm's length. Without moving his arm or bending an elbow, he lowers and touches it to his head, then brings it back to the vertical position." Farman in his late teens, worked in a rock quarry breaking rocks with sledgehammer up to 14 hours a day 6-7 days a week. In 1975, he did a world record hammer lift with a 56-pound hammer.

In Australia, wood chopping in the 19th century was not only necessary manual labor but was also a popular sport. In the early years of the 20th century, one Arthur Burgess, at the age of twelve, could cut with an axe seven tons of wood a day for the steam boilers in the Shuttleton mine at Cobar.[363]

Hard work is what survivors in Post Apocalyptica will face as the age of consumer softness comes to a grinding halt. For people

---

[362] "What is Fitness?" October 2002, at www.library.crossfit.com/free/pdf/CFJ_Trial_04_2012.pdf: https://www.facebook.com/iamkhanporter.

[363] Geoffrey Blainey, "When Muscles Were King," in *The Blainey View*, (ABC/Macmillan, Sydney and South Melbourne, 1982), pp. 67-79, cited p. 68. Thanks to my Aussie editor for this local reference, which impressed this wood-chopping son of the South.

who have a survival retreat, it will be the main form of exercise that they do. Time and energy permitting, other training must be fitted in around an arduous work schedule. A life devoted to hard labor and training will build toughness, the ability to withstand beatings on the anvil of life, building psycho-physical strength to face the coming storms of the wolf age to come.

Conclusion

In this chapter, I have examined whether classical martial arts systems will provide an adequate basis for hand-to-hand combat. Clearly, most personal fighting will involve firearms and when the ammo runs out other projectile weapons such as crossbows, compound, recurve, (maybe even longbows) and arrows. At closer ranges, melee weapons will prevail. But unarmed skills will still provide a backup in cases where a weapon is lost or dropped, and as well will increase physical prowess. It is concluded that the Mixed Martial Arts (MMA), given a more combat rather that sports orientation, would be a good basis for unarmed personal protection. From this basis, a study of the various military/ commando "silent killing" methods could be undertaken. If no schools are available in one's area, then with an MMA basic, it should still be possible to refine a small set of techniques that could be used on an automatic basis during combat situations when stress and an adrenaline surge typically destroy fine motor skills.

Always keep to the basics, not only with fighting techniques but with strength training and overall physical conditioning. Be like a Spartan or a Viking; take the hard path. In a rural environment, this is dead easy to do as there are always challenging jobs to do, many of which can be done by hand and/or with hand tools. Even in the city, one can avoid the traps of civilization, by riding a bike or walking rather than using a car. Seated work further lowers your fitness; maybe it is possible to work at a work station where you can stand to use a computer. Be creative. This is, after all, the apocalypse: martial muscle is survival.

So much then for martial muscle. We turn now to a philosophical consideration of the virtues of melee weapons.

4.

Melee Weapons:
Destroying Your Foe with a Bo or a Jo, Blade or a Spade

All fighting science boils down to calculated and applied brutality. When you are fighting for your life, your best chance for survival comes from prior training that has honed your instructive ability to be as calculating and brutal as possible. - *Fred Hutchinson*[364]

You should not have a favourite weapon. To become over familiar with one weapon is as much a fault as not knowing it sufficiently well. You should not copy others, but use weapons which you can handle properly. - *Miyamoto Musashi*[365]

The present-day interest in all things to do with the apocalypse and/or zombies has led to the publication of some generally sound books on melee weapons, non-projectile hand-held weapons. Melee weapons do not fire a projectile (ranged weapons, such as a crossbow with arrows do) and are usually used by hand, and thus do not include traps such as punji sticks (a spike trap in a pit, the spikes covered in human excrement for infection). While these books are typically concerned with hand-to-hand combat with

---

[364] Fred Hutchinson, *The Modern Swordsman: Realistic Training for Serious Self-Defense*, (Paladin Press, Boulder, Colorado, 1998), p. 66.

[365] Miyamoto Musashi, *A Book of Five Rings*, Axiom Publishing, 2004), p. 15.

"the walking dead," there is some concern with dealing with bandits and MZB (Mutant Zombie Bikers), the feral scum of the apocalypse.[366]

While guns would be the obvious choice for post-apocalyptic fighting for individuals against foes, melee weapons can provide a backup, or be used when ammunition runs out, and in jurisdictions where firearm ownership is already severely restricted. Further, as we are contemplating the end of human civilization in this book, guns, comprising moving parts, are subject to wear and tear and breakage. Quick 'n' dirty, guerrilla gun smithing can be done, but after many generations, such patch ups may no longer be possible. Ammunition will eventually run out. One can reload, but eventually, even over a century, stored gunpowder will begin to breakdown. Some people may be chemically aware and brave enough to make smokeless power, and others, black powder. (*Disclaimer*: for legal and safety reasons, not to be made now, but only in post-apocalyptic times, after the end of the present rule of law.)

Nevertheless, for many less innovative people in the time to come, guns and ammunition would have a use-by-date. Then, as mentioned, there are jurisdictions where private gun ownership is controlled, heavily restricted, or outrightly banned. People there will face the apocalypse with a usually limited range of projectile weapons (weapons such as crossbows are beginning to face the same restrictions as guns) and a limited range of melee weapons, given a slowly creeping range of legal restrictions in many jurisdictions, often prohibiting the traditional Okinawan weapons such as nunchakus and other weapons such as swords. For example, the state of Victoria, Australia, has prohibited the ownership of all swords (defined in the *Controlled Weapons Regulations 2011* (Victoria) Schedule 2 as "a thrusting, striking or cutting weapon with a long blade having one or two edges and a hilt or handle"), with only special exceptions. The definition is vague enough to encompass various garden tools, but would fail to capture *short* "swords" (e.g., the gladius), and some machetes escape the net.

---

[366] See for example Adam Alasdair, *Weapons and Warfare in the Zombie Apocalypse: How to Go to War with the Undead*, (The Author, 2012); Roger Ma, *The Zombie Combat Manual: A Guide to Fighting the Living Dead*, (Berkley Books, New York, 2010).

Another limitation of firearms is the issue of missing targets under the stress of combat. A study of New York police found that their hit rate at live targets from only nine feet away was 11 percent, and for a target greater than 20 feet, the hit rate was four percent, even though some officers had a 98 percent accuracy rate at the gun range on paper targets.[367] That statistic needs to be comprehended next to the "Tueller drill." It was shown by Sergeant Dennis Tueller of the Salt Lake City Utah Police Department, that a healthy attacker with a knife could cover 21 feet (6.4 meters) in about 1.5 seconds.[368] *Mythbusters,* in a 2012 episode "Dual Dilemmas," found that at under twenty feet, the knife-wielding attacker could stab before being shot. Thus, up-close a knifeman can be as deadly as a gunman.[369] Hence, one of the take-home messages of the Tueller drill is the need to improve accuracy in real combat,[370] but another is that when the fine motor skills necessary for accurate shooting collapse, perhaps against a knife-wielding opponent, one needs to use a more badass melee weapon.

At the turn of the 20th century, Moro guerrillas in the Southern Philippines attacked US army officers with a bladed weapon, the *kampilan,* well suited for beheading. These warriors were essentially on a suicide mission, having leather binding on their testicles to make them crazy with pain, combined possibly with narcotics, fanaticism and adrenaline and a fierce desire to kill or die – Asian berserkers in fact. They were able to soak up .38 Colt revolver rounds like an American kid soaks up drugs. The .45 Colt Peacemaker was brought back but did not solve the problem. Legend has it that the .45 ACP Colt M1911 was put into action to deal with them, which appears not to have occurred.[371] It probably wouldn't have worked either. In fact,

[367]   Matt Mogk, *Everything You Ever Wanted to Know about Zombies,* (Gallery Books, New York, 2011), p. 178.

[368]   Dennis Tueller, "How Close is Too Close? *SWAT Magazine,* March 1983, reproduced at http://www.theppsc.org/Staff_Views/Tueller/How.Close.htm.

[369]   Sam Sheridan, *The Disaster Diaries: One Man's Quest to Learn Everything Necessary to Survive the Apocalypse,* (Penguin Books, New York, 2013), p. 221.

[370]   Mark Greenman, *The Zombie Shooting Guide: Survival Training for the Worst-Case Scenario,* (Ooda Media Group, Los Angeles, 2013).

[371]   "History of the M1911 Pistol," at http://www.sightm1911.com/1911-History.htm.

Moro's often survived rounds from the Krag rifle (.30-40 Krag/.30 Army), long enough to kill, then die themselves. Nevertheless, the Moro would not have been able to do this beheading if he was beheaded first by an opponent with an even more badass weapon, such as a great sword, *zweihänder*, Dane axe, katana or any number of pole weapons such as the halberd, where he was chopped to pieces.

This chapter will give a concise review of the most plausible melee weapons that an ordinary person could acquire and realistically use in an apocalyptic environment. It is a convenient fiction to consider dealing with the "living dead," since weapons that stop them would easily stop normal human ghouls and predators. In AMC's *The Walking Dead*, characters frequently destroy walkers using knives and get zombie splatter on them. But, contact with such infected blood through skin cracks, sores, abrasions and with any mucous membranes would be likely to lead to infection.[372]

Melee weapons for the ordinary man should be durable, easy to use, readily available, and capable of taking down one's opponent. Standard movie weapons such as the chainsaw or even an angle grinder (e.g., *Wolf Creek 2*) should be discarded quickly from consideration, being heavy, noisy, hard to start at the best of times and requiring fuel/electricity, thus limiting mobility. Probably one could disable this Road Warrior weapon with a good whack on the blade with a thick steel reo rod or flat bar. Chain saws are relatively fragile tools when they come up against metal, even nails in trees, contrary to Hollywood slasher movies.

Likewise, discard the baseball bat and cricket bat (e.g., *Shaun of the Dead*), golf clubs and other household sporting items often featured in the lists of improvised weaponry. People have been killed with all of these items; for example, in February 2014 in Sydney, a cricket bat was used in a murder and golf clubs have been used in farmhouse invasions in South Africa. Our concern though is with a collapse of civilization situation requiring *sustainable* weaponry rather than just making do with some rigid body with mass for the odd close encounter.

---

[372] Jonathan Maberry, *Zombie CSU: The Forensics of the Living Dead*, (Citadel Press, New York, 2008).

A baseball bat is a reasonable weapon for certain melee combat encounters, though the narrow handle can break and aluminum bats can warp. But one can do much better. Various demolition and entry tools such as the Halligan tool (consisting of a claw, a blade/adze and a pick), the RatBar with a spike, the Dead On Annihilator (multi-purpose demolition hammer[373]) and other utility tools could be put to use as weapons, but they are designed for functions other than cracking skulls. Some utility tools which could be put to self-defence in a pinch, but ideally are best used for their demolition purposes, include the Stanley Fat Max Xtreme 55-120 Fu Bar III (a multi-purpose demolition tool combining a sledge hammer, ripping hook, nail puller, pry bar, hydrant wrench and gas shut off wrench); Innovation Factory IF-221, Trucker's Friend All-Purpose Survival Tool (can cut branches, chip hard-packed ice, has an axe, hammer, pry bar, lever, nail puller and spanner) and the Fulton Corporation TW48WB 48-ich Long Wrecker Pry Bar. These are tools all worth having on hand.

Thus, let us now consider melee weapons that can, and should, be secured for a coming apocalypse. There are, of course, an enormous number of possible weapons that could be used, such as exotic weapons like the katar, the Indian "punch dagger." However, our concern is with weapons that can be *readily* obtained, without undue cost, and concerns about quality. Thus, for example, the Shaolin Monk's spade (consisting of a spade-like blade, sharpened on three edges and at the other end, a crescent moon shaped blade) may be a good anti-zombie weapon, but the problem will be finding a good quality reasonably priced version of this weapon. In this brief review, we will start from the "inside" and work "out," from close-range melee weapons to longer-range ones, beginning with the knife.

---

[373] "Best Budget Zombie Weapon," at http://zombieresearchsociety.com/archives/6264.

Knives: Confronting Cold Steel at Close Range

As anyone will tell you who has been on the business end of a knife, or seen what damage a knife can do to the human body, at close range (defined as basically spit-in-the-face range of a few feet), a razor-sharp knife is a highly formidable weapon delivering devastating attacks where one can be carved to pieces. A knife does not need ammo and does not jam, and merely requires sharpening to be at its deadliest. Severed arteries from knife slashes, such as a cut carotid artery, one of the two principle arteries of the neck, lead to a bleed-out in seconds. Knives, especially tactical folders, are easily concealable on the body, making them favored urban weapons. Knifes are usually cheaper than the cheapest guns, making them a likely weapon people will have now, and a certain one to have in the zombie apocalypse.

As well, only after one has been stabbed and/or slashed does one appreciate the fear that a blade can produce in combat. Needless to say, it is a severe psychological disadvantage to be bleeding profusely while fighting. The psychological fear of a knife attack was demonstrated in late 2015 when there was a spate of "lone wolf" knife attacks by Palestinian youth upon Israelis, done primarily for the psycho-fear impact. Psychologist Shaul Kimhis said: "It [i.e., the knife] is an everyday object that everybody has at home or can readily obtain, which needs no training and is easily concealed. A knife attack is not primarily intended to kill but to spread fear and it achieves that goal." Of course, knife attacks can easily kill, as shown by the London 2019/2020 spree of knife attacks.

Stab wounds can be lethal, and even relatively shallow penetration can be fatal: 20 mm blade penetration gave a 41 percent probability of lung penetration, a 60 percent probability of liver or femoral artery rupture and a six percent chance of heart penetration, according to one study.[374] Forensic scientists have found from experiments on cadavers that a "low" force is needed to penetrate

---

[374] Sarah Hainsworth, "Cutting Crimes," *Ingenia*, no.37, December 2008, pp. 38-43 and "How Much Force?" In G. N. Rutty (ed.), *Essentials of Autopsy Practice*, (Springer-Verlag, London, 2013), pp. 151-170.

the skin with sharp blades, and even lower force to penetrate muscle and fat beneath the skin, with smaller tipped blades penetrating better. Sharp edges also allow continuous penetration. Even kitchen knives have penetrated deep into the human skull,[375] although thinner-bladed knives may break and knives, in general, may get stuck in the skull. In World War I this problem was solved by the use of the trench spike to punch through helmets and skulls, the spike having less surface area, with less pressure on the spike. Although a knife is not an ideal weapon for head strikes and brain destruction, it can be done, accepting the dangers of such close-range combat, and wear and tear on the knife.

In this context, there have been many excellent books written about the reality of knife fighting[376] – namely, that in a knife vs. knife match you are likely to be cut and stabbed multiple times, and you could die, and that unarmed against the knife, unless your opponent is a complete fucking idiot, or you luck out lottery-winning style, you are probably going to be killed. There is also much nonsense by those who should know better. For example, Bruce Lee said: "A man with a weapon is the one at a disadvantage ... the man who pulls a knife on you is at a disadvantage. He will clearly lose the fight. The reason is very simple. Psychologically, he has only one weapon. His thinking is therefore limited to the use of that single weapon."[377] Lee's idea here is that the knife fighter will focus on knife attacks, exclusively, while you can use all of your natural weapons.

The problem with Lee's argument is that it is based on a false premise. A "good" knife fighter may not even show you the knife; you may be stabbed in a surprise attack prison-style, or if it is an open confrontation, the knife may not lead (unless it is more sword-like), but be protected, while the attacker launches attacks with the

[375]   Sarah Hainsworth (et al.), "How Sharp is Sharp? Methods for Quantifying the Sharpness and Penetrability of Kitchen Knives Used in Stabbings," *International Journal of Legal Medicine*, vol. 122, 2008, pp. 281-291.

[376]   D. Pentecost, *Put 'Em Down, Take 'Em Out! Knife Fighting Techniques from Folsom Prison*, (Paladin Press, Boulder, Colorado, 1988); J. LaFond, *The Logic of Steel: A Fighter's View of Blade and Shank Encounters*, (Paladin Press, Boulder, Colorado, 2001).

[377]   John Little (ed), *Jeet Kune Do: Bruce Lee's Commentaries on the Martial Way*, (Tuttle Publishing, Tokyo, 1997), pp. 23-24.

other arm (perhaps feinting) and/or kicks. The skilled knife fighter will also be skilled at unarmed combat and will hit you with the full martial arts kitchen sink. Almost all of the standard knife disarms are unrealistic and ineffective and generally involve the attacker leading with a wild *Psycho* ice pick strike, and although that strike can be used effectively in limited circumstances, it is not used in the way many books and DVDs portray it, setting up a "straw man" knife fighter.[378] The US War Department has said: "Against a knife fighter who does not use overhand or underhand thrusts or slashes, but moves his weapon in swift arcs in all directions, disarming tactics are extremely difficult if not impossible."[379]

There are many debates in the wonderful world of knives about the "best" knife for self-defense, such as should your knife be a fixed blade or tactical folder, should it have a serrated edge, and how big should it be? Not all of these debates are relevant to the present discussion because we are only concerned with apocalyptic survival, rather than utility or self-defense uses in our present cucked urban world. Sure, have a folder with a serrated edge to cut the rope, or to flip out to cut a wedge of ham for your burger, but for fighting with a blade when the chips are down forever, a little more is required.

There are many firms making excellent quality blades to deal with the present, largely urban-based need for self-defense, from Aitor Knives to the legendary Cold Steel through to Zero Tolerance Knives, to go alphabetical, with thousands in between, especially if European knife makers are included (such as H. Roselli of Finland and Zlatoust Knives of Russia). There are also many thousands of knife craftsmen making knives across America, Canada, Europe and Australia, giving the consumer more choice than ever.

What is more important than the brand is the type of knife that should always be at your side during the apocalypse. I agree with Fernando "Ferfal" Aguirre, who discusses the issue of a survival/combat knife in his book *The Modern Survival Manual: Surviving*

---

[378]   G. L. Grossman and J. McCurry, "The Top Ten Errors of Martial Artists Defending Against a Blade," *Journal of Asian Martial Arts*, vol. 15, no. 4, 2006.

[379]   US War Department, *Basic Field Manual FM 23-25: Bayonet*, (Washington DC, September 7, 1943), p. 32.

the Economic Collapse.[380] Ferfal gives a fascinating account of the Argentinian Gauchos (similar to a cowboy, with a knife replacing a gun), who fight with a razor sharp *facón* knife, (the facón being a form of Criollo knife) their "love of their lives, " as Ferfal puts it. This knife is over 14 inches long and has a narrow tip for stabbing, but enough heft to allow moves such as *achazo* (a smash onto the top of the head cutting into the brain) and *bajar las tripas* (a deep slash across the abdomen so that the opponent's guts drop out).[381] The famous Argentinian knife fighter Juan Moreira (?-1874) had a facón knife with a two foot long blade and of such high quality that in his last stand battle with soldiers, he broke a soldier's saber while blocking with this magnificent piece of steel.[382]The apocalypse knife should resemble this, tapping into this badass spirit of the blade.

The "large knife" fighting school holds that, within reason, the larger the knife, the better. The "within reason" qualification is added because after about sixteen inches or so, the knife becomes a short sword. But if a knife is too big, a person may not wear it all the time, perhaps taking it off to do hard manual labor – and that will be when the knife is needed, quickly. Large knives with blades of impressive but not clumsy lengths include the Japanese tanto, the iconic Bowie,[383] and the kukri with its recurve blade.[384] One can also obtain reproductions of the Viking/Saxon fighting knife, the seax or scramasax, which have blades up to 76 cms (thirty inches) long; mine is a modest penis length of sixteen inches. All types of medieval daggers can be purchased online, including Rondel daggers with their distinctive rounded guards; Renaissance daggers aplenty and

[380] Fernando "Ferfal" Aguirre, *The Modern Survival Manual: Surviving the Economic Collapse*, (The Author, 2009), and *Street Survival Skills*, (the Author, 2019).

[381] As above, pp. 120-121; Mario A. López Osornio, *Esgrima Criolla*, (Hemisferio Sur, Buenos Aires, 2009, first published El Ateneo, 1942).

[382] "Gauchos and Knife Fighting," March 16, 2009, at http://ferfal.blogspot.com.au/2009/03/gauchos-and-knife-fighting.html; "The Knife History," at http://www.gauchoknives.com/the_knife_history.htm.

[383] Bill Bagwell, *Bowies, Big Knives, and the Best of Battle Blades*, (Paladin Press, Boulder, Colorado, 2000).

[384] See Everest Blade at https://everestblade.com/; The Khukuri House: https://www.thekhukurihouse.com/.

enough Scottish dirks to satisfy the most anal-retentive clansman. D guard Bowies, popular during the American Civil War with their characteristic D-shaped knuckle guard and blades of up to eighteen inches are available.

Having trained in Wing Chun Kung Fu and with Wing Chun's butterfly knives for much of my life, my *personal* preference would be for the *bart jarm dao*. Here we have essentially two short swords (the length of the weapon is the length of the practitioner's arm from the little knuckle on the clenched fist to the point of the elbow. In principle, armed with these two "knives," one could face a swordsman and have a fighting chance. I think the "two-onto-one" factor would definitely give the neo-Wing Chun fighter an advantage against other single knife fighters. My only reservation with the *bart jarm dao* is that they are usually choppers with only a thick edgefor stabbing. This is said to be because the Shaolin monks using them didn't want to have a lethal weapon. Kept razor sharp, these big blades could easily lop off heads (Bowies and kukris can do this anyway.) All of the traditional skills can be performed with the knife delivering more devastating stab wounds.

Those who agree that bigger is better could go the way of the short sword or machete, or even hybrid style weapons such as W.E. Fairbairn's "smatchet," a leaf-shaped short sword based on an ancient Celtic design (or at least that is as it appears).[385] The Welsh World War I trench sword similarly has an overall length of 24 inches with a blade of 17.5 inches, being three inches wide at its widest section. It was used to great effect by the Royal Welsh Fusiliers at the Battle of Messines Ridge on the Western Front in 1917 in trench warfare. It is battle-proven in close hand-to-hand fighting.

Len McDougall is one of the few survival writers to comment on the contemporary merits of a short sword: "a heavy short sword ... can slash through bone or stab through a ribcage with equal ease, and do either in the blink of an eye."[386] There is much to choose from,

---

[385] In W. E. Fairbairn, *Get Tough: How to Win in Hand-to-Hand Fighting, as Taught to the British Commandos and the U.S. Armed Forces*, (Paladin Press, Boulder, Colorado, 1974), p. 43.

[386] Len McDougall, *The Self-Reliance Manifesto: How to Survive Anything Anywhere*,

and all are excellent fighting weapons that have served humanity, some for over two thousand years: the Greek hoplite, parazonium, xiphos, and kopis; the Roman pugio and gladius; Sparta's lakonian; falchions (various types including Italian falchion); longer seaxs, longer kukris; falcata; the Russian kindjal and shasqua; Persian kard; various scimitars and the charay. The Japanese wakizashi would also serve one well. This is the short sword or *shōtō* worn with the longer katana (*daitō*) to form a sword pair (*daishō*) by the samurai, especially during the Edo period (1603-1867). The wakizashi has been overshadowed by the katana, but in many respects, for survivalists, it is a more convenient weapon, especially for bugging out, with its blade of about 60 centimetres in length.

The only disadvantage of short swords is that very good ones (such as a very good wakizashi) can be a burden on the budget when one needs to purchase guns, guns, and more guns, plus ammo to feed these hungry pets. Then there is food and other survival supplies. Hence, for many people, the machete is a cheaper option, "the poor man's sword."[387]

Machetes have been proven to be effective killing blades, as shown by the 1994 genocide in Rwanda, where 500,000-800,000 Tutsi and Hutu opponents of President Habyarimana's regime were slaughtered by the Hutu, usually with machetes. The killing was known as the "interahamwe" ("those who stand together"). Here machetes were used to hack to death largely defenseless and helpless victims, rather than equal warriors. Most rural households had machetes, often crude choppers made out of car springs, but highly effective. However, machetes had also been imported from Belgium, and these were also readily available.[388] Machetes have been the weapons of the poorest people of the world, used in peasant uprisings and conflict in South America, Africa, and South East Asia because these weapons were available as agricultural tools. There

---

(Skyhorse Publishing, New York, 2010), p. 148.

[387] Martina Sprague, *Machetes, Kris, and Throwing Iron: Edged Weapons of Latin America, Indonesia, and Africa*, (Kindle, 2013).

[388] Philip Verwimp, "Machetes and Firearms: The Organization of Massacres in Rwanda," *Journal of Peace Research*, vol. 47, 2006, pp. 5-22.

are many news reports of people across the world being beheaded by crazies going berserk with machetes; usually the head is hacked off rather than lopped off as in one clean sweep associated with the iconic katana. Either way, you are just as dead.

In the Solomon Islands, PNG, and much of the South Pacific, machetes tend to be crude bits of spring steel, often with a handle made out of rubber wrapped around it, but the machetes have heft. In the Solomon Islands, there was a report in 2003 of an Australian missionary beheaded by a machete. Criminal gangs in the Solomon Islands use machetes as their weapon of choice, but not wimpy, whippy ones, rather, badass smashers.

Machetes may have a blade thickness of as little as 1 mm, making them light, and "whippy," and these types may stick or bend in combat since they are designed mainly to cut light grass. Thus, where there is thicker woody vegetation, as in South East Asia, the *parang* and *golok* are used, having shorter but much thicker blades. The ultra-slim machetes, if kept sharp, no doubt, will destroy flesh, but today there are cheap and effective alternatives. Cold Steel, for example, makes an array of cheap machetes in classic styles such as kukri, bolo, Latin, Thai, panga and katana etc. with a blade thickness of around 2.8 mm, made of 1055 steel. There are cheap machete versions of weapons, such as the gladius machete and the Bowie machete. I own most of these types and have used some in scrub clearing for many years; I have a Cold Steel Latin machete that has been sharpened so much from years of work that the blade looks like a large knife. For tough scrub, one needs a heavier blade and I have banged up some machete-swords 6 mm thick that can smash though small trees. However, as weapons, I think that Cold Steel's videos showing what their machetes can do to meat clearly shows the merits of the heavier machete as a weapon. It seems to me that if machetes were slightly thicker than the 2.8 mm (maybe even by 1-2 mms), without a radical increase in price, such "meta-machetes" would be a challenge to some of the sword markets at the utility/function end rather than the cultural/historical end. One could spend perhaps $500-1,000 US upwards on a Viking sword or a katana or buy 10-20 "meta-machetes," stocking oneself out for the apocalypse. Kershaw Knives' 1074 X Camp 18 (with its superb grip) and MTech's Tactical Combat Machete are both excellent, cost efficient choices here.

All this, though, is not an advertisement for Cold Steel, excellent as their products are, as there are many other brands of machetes which can be considered, such as Ontario Cutlery, Ka-Bar, CRKT, Kershaw, SOG, Bark River, Gerber, United Cutlery, MTech Machetes, Bellotto (Brazil), Bidor Tools (Malaysia), Imacasa Machetes (El Salvador), Hansa Machetes (Ecuador) and Condor Machetes. Condor Machetes, for example, has an 18-inch-long blade Thai Enep machete, which has a blade thickness of 1/8 inch, weight 1.3 lbs, made of 1075 high carbon steel with a black powder epoxy finish; tasty. Condor also has a 23-inch-long blade Bush Cutlass, with a D-guard, 1/8-inch-thick, weighing in at 2 lbs, made of 1075 high carbon steel. Then there are the superb workhorse machetes of Brazil's Tramontina, with a Latin bush machete with a 26-inch blade, being a five-star performer, and Imacasa (El Salvador) has a 28-inch blade Pata de Cuche machete with a crossguard for the bigger is better school.[389]

Axes and Hammers

In a jurisdiction where bladed weapons are heavily controlled, weapons such as axes and hammers are live alternatives.

The hammer was the weapon of Thor, the Norse god of thunder; hail Thor! *Mjölner*, Thor's hammer, was forged by the dwarfs Sindri and Brokkr and is a weapon of destruction, the "destroyer," "that which smashes," or "the pulverizer." Mjölner had the power to level mountains, and could be thrown, would never miss its target and return to Thor's hand. Mjölner has the mystical ability to send forth lightning bolts. This weapon, although having destructive powers, can also be used to heal people and animals. It appears to be the only weapon to survive the destruction of the universe at Ragnarök.

---

[389] See: https://www.machetespecialists.com/filter/brand/tramontina/.

We, alas, do not have Mjölner, but we do have a variety of hammers available as weapons. There are two basic categories: war hammers and hardware hammers, weaponized. The war hammer is a late medieval weapon designed to deal with plate armor which had become as hard as the edge of swords. Swords could not smash through this armor but glanced off. The war hammer, typically consisting of a hammerhead and a spike on the other end, could cause concussion through the armor, or smash the armor inward. The spike was capable of penetrating the armor, but the hammer spike could get caught in the hole that it had created in the armor, and as the knight dropped to the ground, the hammer would go down with the corpse. As well, knights could wear suits of chain mail under the plate armor to further minimize spike wounds. Thus, the important part of the hammer was the heavy head. The head of war hammers was originally flat, but later claw-like indentations were added to prevent glancing blows off the armor. The hammers came in various lengths, with short ones being about two feet and long ones about six feet, used to smash knights on horseback or even to break a horse's legs. It does so with with ease – I have seen an accident where a man was hit in the arm with a light sledgehammer (a bit heavier than a war hammer) and the bone at the impact point was smashed to pieces.

Amazon.com has many brands of war hammers available – from Cold Steel, General Edge, United Cutlery, to name a few. Generally, one can get a war hammer for around $50 US – very little for a weapon that could dispatch knights.

There is also another route and that is to use hardware hammers. A 14 lb sledge hammer is a fully committed weapon, but a lighter 2 kg hammer is an option. I have bought small hammers with a wedge splitter on one end for as little as the price of a burger. The short synthetic handle can be removed (usually by cutting it off and drilling out) and a hardwood handle added to increase length. Framing hammers, as used by Tyreese in AMC's *The Walking Dead*, have the advantage of usually having heavier heads than the standard claw hammer and straight claws, making them improvised mini war hammers. Many brands have drop forged steel shafts, and

Estwing makes the iconic classics such as the E3-28SM, 16 inches long, weight 2.3 pounds, and this looks like the beauty used in *The Walking Dead*. As a hammer facing tough work, Estwing is represented to give decades of faithful service (I have used other claw hammers where the drop forged handle gets bent slightly, but Estwings have strong shafts). They are magnificent and reasonably priced: buy some regardless of weapons issues. A hammer is a tool almost as useful as a knife.

One can obtain cheaper framing hammers with hickory handles, cut off the handle or bang/drill it out, and add a longer handle to make a poor man's war hammer. One could, in a pinch, lengthen an Estwing, not by cutting this beautiful tool, but by duct-taping the hammer handle to a longer piece of hard wood. The aim is not to break bricks and rocks all day, but self-defense at a pinch. At worst, a normal claw hammer could be used in this improvised duct tape fashion with the advantage of low maintenance as a "don't care" weapon. I have seen hammers in bargain bins for as low a price as a few dollars. In short, with the hammer, it is possible to have a highly effective melee weapon which is less expensive that even a standard machete. The hammer is the ultimate low maintenance weapon.

Barbarians who love hammers usually get excited contemplating axes. Here is a quintessential Viking weapon[390] as badass and proletariat as the hammer. The felling axe (usually with a two kg head) is something that every survivalist should have and there are many iconic axes, the Gránsfor American felling axe being one.[391] But, such axes, although delivering powerful blows—and many people have been killed or have had body parts chopped off by axes—are relatively slow compared to say a sword or machete. It has been suggested that one could remove steel from the axe head (stock removal) with an angle grinder (taking care to use the appropriately rated dust mask for lung protection, and keeping the axe head cool to avoid changing the tempering), but there are better ways to axe heaven, to be detailed shortly.

---

[390] See R. E. Wheeler, *London and the Vikings*, (London Museum, Catalogues, no. 1, 1927).

[391] Dudley Cook, *The Ax Book: The Lore and Science of the Woodcutter*, (Alan C. Hood and Company, 2005).

Today, there are many excellent tactical tomahawks available most of which are of such high quality that they can easily pierce medieval armor, especially those with a pick-like spike on the opposite side to the axe. The Cold Steel Trench Hawk has an overall length of nineteen inches, is made of 5150 drop forged carbon steel with a 3 ½ inch axe blade and a wedge-shaped spike. Cold Steel has many other "hawks," most with traditional old school American hickory handles, such as the 90 N Norse Hawk. Along traditional lines are the Cold Steel Trail Hawk, Frontier Hawk and Rifleman's Hawk, all very economically priced. Superb tactical tomahawks are produced by SOG (F01TN-CP, Tactical Tomahawk – an updated version of the Vietnam Tomahawk; F02T-N Battle Axe); United Cutlery (M48 Apocalypse Tactical Tomahawk Model: UC2946); CRKT (Choghan T-Hawk); MTech (Survival Hawk; Swift Hawk; Tactical Axe; Tactical Breaching Axe; Warfighter Tomahawk) as well as several tomahawks by the great Estwing (e.g., the EBTA tomahawk), being forged from one piece of steel. Tactical tomahawks have been used by American soldiers in every major conflict which America has been involved in and are thus tried and proven. These tools/weapons would be even more useful in the zombie apocalypse as close-range equalizers, perhaps delivering smashes more devastating than the iconic Bowies and kukris. Further, it is generally easier to master basic hawk fighting than many knife styles, making the hawk a must-have weapon.

Tactical hawks perhaps have one limit: they are small circle (close-range), compact weapons. At the other extreme is the majestic Dane axe; it has a blade thickness of 3 mm, a 9 5/8 hawk, handle length 48" and an overall length of 52." There are two "horns," the top one for stabbing and the shorter one for capturing shields and pulling them down. Tests posted on YouTube show that this weapon does indeed have "ferocious cutting power" and it could serve people where highly restrictive firearms and sword legislation is in place.

Most Viking axes were smaller than the mighty Dane axe so that they could be wielded with one hand, the other hand grasping a shield. Perhaps, the strongest of us could swing a Dane axe with a cut-down, reduced length handle, but it would not be a fast weapon.

Viking axes were light and fast; early era Viking axes had a cutting edge of 7-15 cms (3-6 inches) with hafts about 80 cms (32 in) long, but the length probably varied to suit the fighter.[392] The advantage of the axe over the sword is its concentration of force on a small cutting edge relative to the sword, with weight behind the edge, on a rigid body often as long as a sword, thus generating more angular momentum and pressure of the strike.

Thus, axes can smash through armor and unreinforced wooden shields, as well as depicted in the Viking sagas, splitting heads down to the shoulders. Unlike the sword (an exception being the "ears" of the Wing Chun Kung Fu butterfly knives and a few others), axes can be used to hook shields, weapons and limbs, as well as thrust using the horns of the blade. Some can be thrown in a last-ditch measure if one has two axes or another weapon (so as not to be, obviously enough, defenseless). The Viking sagas describe axes getting stuck after a blow (*Vatnsdaela Saga*), axe heads shattering and heads flying off the haft or the haft being broken from an opponent's blows (the opening scene of episode 1, season 1 of the History Channel's *Vikings* (2013)), has Ragnar Lothbrok's axe head get chopped off).[393] While this is always possible, the risk of a broken wooden haft could be minimized by adding protective langets, as with war hammers. Alternatively, and non-traditionally, the axe head could be welded onto a metal rod (correctly, so that cracking does not occur). Or carry a spare axe.

Cheap modern Viking axes could be made from hatchets and small axes with suitable relatively light but wide blades. Simply shape an approximately long piece of hard wood (e.g., American hickory, I use seasoned olive, which is inferior to American hickory, but good enough), pound on the axe head and add a strong glue that binds metal and wood. A fighting weapon can be made for less than US $10.

---

[392]   "Viking Axe," at http://www.hurstwic.org/history/articles/manufacturing/text/viking_ axe.htm.

[393]   Richard Underwood, *Anglo-Saxon Weapons and Warfare*, (Tempus, Gloucestershire, 1999), p. 73.

A fighting axe is of great merit and should be considered as a zombie apocalypse melee weapon, being relatively cheap, compared to swords. Paddy Griffith in *The Viking Art of War* said that in *The Olaf Sagas,* "it seems to have been proved that axes could beat swords in a stand-up fight."[394] Such was the high regard that the Vikings had for their axes. However, swords and especially good swords such as the *Ulfberht* were expensive and scarce, so the Viking had to adapt and use what weapons were available, just like us.

Swords

Swords are iconic, poetic weapons – and that includes *all* swords. Anyone doubting the sheer beauty that can be embodied in a sword should consult Steve Shackleford's *Spirit of the Sword: A Celebration of Artistry and Craftsmanship.*[395] Yes, even better than *Playboy,* in my opinion, now that the nudes have gone.

Swords have represented honor, and usually unlike weapons such as clubs and battle axes, often are personified with names: Arthur's *Excalibur,* Lancelot's *Arondight,* Siegfried's *Nothung,* Beowulf's *Hrunting* and *Naegling,* Roland's *Durendal* and Bilbo's *Sting,* to mention but a few. As the Estonian epic *Kalevipoeg* put it: "Who can separate a man and his sword? One is worth nothing without the other." Thus, "the history of the sword is the history of the Y chromosome."[396]

As Mike Loades has said: "From the great deeds of mythical heroes to the gentlemanly art of duelling and the swash and swagger of the silver screen, the sword remains at the heart of our romantic imagination. It is the weapon that gives the hope that skill can triumph over brute force. It is an enchanted weapon, the one with which the hero wins out over impossible odds."[397]

---

[394]   Paddy Griffith, *The Viking Art of War,* (Greenhill Books, London, 1995), p. 176.

[395]   Steve Shackleford, *Spirit of the Sword: A Celebration of Artistry and Craftsmanship,* (Krause Publications, Jola, 2010).

[396]   J. Christoph Amberger, *The Secret History of the Sword: Adventures in Ancient Martial Arts,* (Multi-Media Books, Burbank, 1999), p. 2.

[397]   Mike Loades, *Swords and Swordsmen,* (Pen and Sword Military, South Yorkshire,

Apart from the historical material, one can find a still relevant directory of US custom sword makers and companies making swords. Custom swords may cost from $2,500 up to $20,000 US and if jewels are embedded in the sword, the sky is the limit, with $ 250,000 US being but one figure. Even to buy a new good quality battle ready katanas and Viking swords from commercial sellers, in jurisdictions outside of the United States such as Australia, one may pay almost the price of a new rifle, or at least the price of a good second-hand firearm although, as with any rule, there are exceptions.

One can go down market, of course, and internet shopping now opens up a vast array of relatively cheap Chinese swords, especially katanas, for purchase, some claiming to be forged using traditional Japanese methods, with distinct hamons. For interest, I recently purchased two of these cheaper swords and put them to a torture test cutting masses of dry reeds. The blade of one so-called battle-ready sword bent. The other sword said to be full tanged, cut relatively well, but after a half a day's cutting the handle broke: it was only half tang. So, in the "spirit of the sword," I duct taped up the handle and use it now as a "machete," as Japan's persecuted minority Ainu people appear to do. It functions surprisingly well.

John Clements has concisely summarized the martial merits of medieval and most Renaissance swords (and the same point or with qualification arguably applies to the Japanese katana and Chinese dadao or war sword): "As chronicles and accounts document, the points of swords could often puncture through assorted armors and helms or pierce clean through a body. Edges of most blades were keen enough to shear through flesh and bone, sever limbs and heads with single swipes, cleave deep into torsos and even hit with enough force to pulverize flesh underneath the armour. The edge of a blade did not have to actually cut in order to deliver tremendous force onto a small spot of its target. It goes without saying that the human body does not respond well to forceful impacts of sharpened steel."[398]

2010), p. xiii.

[398] John Clements, "Echo of Steel," in Shackleford, as above, pp. 32-51, at p. 37.

In capable hands, swords have proved to be devastating weapons in melee combat. For example, the "Virginian giant," "the Giant of the Revolution," Peter Francisco (1760-1831), was a distinguished soldier in the American Revolutionary War. He was said to be strong enough to carry a 1,100 lb cannon to prevent it from falling into enemy hands, an effort recognized by the US Postal Service, who in 1975-1976, issued a commemorative stamp depicting this event. Francisco used a six-foot broadsword with a five-foot blade; at the Battle of Guilford House, March 15, 1781, Francisco killed 11 men in succession with this sword, another one whilst wounded and then another two.

On the medieval battlefield, though, axes, spears and pole arms were more commonly used than swords in both Europe, Japan and China.[399] With some notable exceptions, such as the larger *zweihänder* allegedly used to smash polearms, especially chopping the heads off pikes (difficult but not impossible to do), or at least disrupting pike formations, swords were largely for close-range personal defense. Further, sword fighting took longer to teach than axe/shield/armor or spear/polearm fighting, so that blade fodder could be got out to die and rot on the battlefield sooner. However, even with the katana, it is a gross exaggeration to suppose that swordsmanship skills with the katana take decades to acquire and only a few people on the planet can effectively use a katana in battle. To use a sword effectively, and with safety to oneself and others, will require intense training, perhaps for some years, but not decades. Nevertheless, if you want to put a lifetime of effort into it, one can get interesting results. I first used a katana at about age six and fifty plus years later have developed by own version of Miyamoto Musashi's *nitōken* method of fighting with two swords; Musashi used a katana and probably a wakizashi, but I prefer two katanas, used non-classically.[400]

---

[399] John Clements, *Medieval Swordsmanship: Illustrated Methods and Techniques*, (Paladin Press, Boulder, Colorado, 1988), p. 29.

[400] Fumon Tanaka, *Samurai Fighting Arts: The Spirit and the Practice*, (Kodansha International, Tokyo, 2003), p. 62 says that two sworded fighting in Japan replaced sword and shield fighting, so it was once well known.

Today, there is no shortage of information in book form and on-line on sword fighting, with virtually all swords known to man.[401] Many lifetimes could be spent absorbing all of this information, let alone engaging in practical training. I, myself after fifty plus years of dedicated martial arts training, am competent with the katana, Wing Chun butterfly knives, and some European swords such as the Viking sword and Two-Handed Great Sword.

I have done enough training with the rapier to see its merits as a contemporary melee weapon, where armor and shields are not involved. Yes, the rapier (be it the Spanish Bilbo, the Pilsen, Florentine, Italian, Deschaux rapiers, or European dueling sword),[402] with its relatively thin, light and the fast thrusting blade was "ineffective as a weapon of war..."[403] Yes, the rapier debates did reflect the conflict between the English and Italians, but none of these discounts the rapier as a personal melee weapon today, especially if one is trained in fencing. Good rapiers, although relatively poor at cutting compared to katanas and Viking swords, are not the weak and whippy slithers of metal of sports fencing, but are longer and stronger and have the capacity to deliver fast, penetrating stabs, far beyond that of any knife.[404] Cold Steel's videos of the Ribbed Shell Swept Hilt Rapier being put through its paces, well demonstrates the self-defense virtues of this fine type of weapon. On the negative side, the relatively poor cutting ability (compared to the larger blades), would make the rapier a less favored choice as a doomsday weapon, depending upon what other melee weapons are carried by friends and foes. Finally, it is well recognized that if there were *The Walking Dead* style zombies, capable of being readily dispatched only by brain destruction, the rapier would not be the weapon of choice for skull penetration and it is clumsy at close ranges. Every weapon has its merits and limitations.

---

[401] See http://www.thearma.org/manuals.htm.

[402] See http://www.swordworld.com.au/l2/period-swords/

[403] Terry Brown, *English Martial Arts*, (Anglo-Saxon Books, Frithgarth, Norfolk, 1997), p. 57.

[404] John Clements, *Renaissance Swordsmanship: The Illustrated Use of Rapiers and Cut-and-Thrust Swords*, (Paladin Press, Boulder, Colorado, 1997).

The European Long sword, two-handed sword, and Great Sword have been portrayed in the cinema, and by some Asian critics, as a club with an edge, a heavy, unsophisticated weapon.[405] As a matter of fact, the two-handed European swords, not used for ceremonial purposes, weighted from 1,500 g (3 lbs 3 oz.) to around 2,600 g (5 lbs 8 oz.). Historical weapons were not unwieldy or unpractically heavy.[406] The principles of fighting with the long sword were applied to other weapons such as the poleaxe and halberd.[407]

Even more myths and magic are associated with the Japanese katana, a good example of what swords scholar John Clements has called "candy coated mysticism and metaphysics."[408] This is unfortunate, even tragicomic, because the katana, used for its designed purpose, is a superb weapon, but treating it as a universal "light saber" á la *Star Wars*, a task which it cannot and should not achieve, degrades the weapon. It pisses off the spirits of the samurai, grasshopper, so be warned!

Katanas first gained Western interest after the opening up of Japan by Commodore Perry in 1853. As part of the joy of diversity and global cultural exchange, some Westerners were killed by Japanese wielding katanas, being split apart or decapitated. However, it is often not mentioned, as Lynn Thompson from Cold Steel puts it, that "when the Portuguese showed up in Japan there were a number of duals where Portuguese swordsmen equalled or bested Japanese swordsmen."[409] The katana, itself, hadn't made them invincible. How could it?

[405] T. Dawson, "A Club with an Edge," *Journal of Western Martial Art*, February, 2005, at http://jwma.ejmas.com/articles/2005/jwmaart_dawson_0205.htm.

[406] J. Clements, "The Weighty Issue of Two-Handed Greatswords," at http://www.thearma.org/essays/2HGS.html.

[407] John Clements, "The Centrality of the Longsword in the Study of Renaissance Martial Arts," at http://www.thearma.org/essays/Longsword_Centrality_in_RMA.htm.

[408] John Clements, "Fighting Skeptic – Of Martial Arts and Magic Arts," at http://www.thearma.org/essays/martial-arts-skepticism.html.

[409] Robert W. Young, "Tactical Folder Fighting: Cold Steel Founder Lynn Thompson Unveils the Truth Behind Knife Self-Defense!" In R. Horwitz (ed.), *The Ultimate Guide to Knife Combat*, (Black Belt Books/Ohara Publications, Valencia, 2007), pp. 267-272, cited p. 272.

In the civil war in Japan, between 1863 and 1868, European swords, including British-made swords such as the M1833 cavalry saber, were used, with the katana being relegated to a dress sword. The katana was only re-established as a sword of combat later.

In Feudal Japan, the katana, despite its mystique, was used as a backup weapon. The samurai in battle used a bow and arrows, yari (spear) and naginata (polearm), keeping the katana for personal defense and not as a principal battle weapon. The katana is designed for two-handed draw cutting/slicing, where the blade is pushed into a target and pulled through in a shearing and slicing action. Less effectively, it still can be used in a conventional European-style chopping motion, because sharpened steel is sharpened steel. Against flesh unprotected by armor, the katana is devastating. But, as the late sword master Hank Reinhardt (1934-2007) noted, the katana's wedge-shaped blade does not cut armor (including wood armor) well compared to the heavier but relatively thinner European blades, as the geometry of the wedge-shape means that even if the katana is used in a shearing action, it still has to move more armor-matter (metal, wood and/or leather) than the flatter European blade.[410] The katana did not cut Chinese armor effectively and its blade was found to chip when used against Mongol armor during the Mongol invasion of Japan in the 13th century.[411]

The point of the katana is not (steel plate) armor piercing; demonstrations of katanas going through car doors can be easily replicated with European swords. Indeed, car door material is relatively thin low carbon steel (or plastic/fiberglass, carbon fiber, and aluminum), and a good screwdriver or chisel can also penetrate.

Can katanas cut gun barrels? Clements has pointed out that most accounts of this are undocumented and unreliable.[412] Again, a wedge-shaped blade does not have the optimal geometry for

---

[410]   Hank Reinhardt, "Hype... As Ancient an Art as Sword Making," at http://www.thearma.org/essays/hype.htm.

[411]   J. Murdoch, *A History of Japan During the Century of Early Foreign Intercourse 1542-1651*, (Chronicle, Kobe, 1903), p. 343.

[412]   John Clements, "The Medieval European Knight vs. the Feudal Japanese Samurai?" At http://www.thearma.org/essays/knightvs.htm#.VZxm8i6qqko.

such a cut. Further, the harder the steel, the greater the likelihood of breakage and nicking, even when hitting softer metal. I have observed this first hand in my torture-test of a Chinese-made katana that I used for cutting reeds (my version of *tameshigiri*). I stuck a hidden stub of a rusty star dropper; the star dropper received a small cut in its fin, but the blade was chipped. Thus, I suspect that a very good katana could cut a relatively *thin* rifle (or shotgun) barrel of poor steel, but not without substantial damage. Birmingham sword maker Thomas Gill in 1786 tested his European blades for the East India Company by a public examination which in one test involved cutting a gun barrel. The sword did this, but the blade was essentially wrecked. All this though is not a point against the katana; who in their right mind would use a sword in combat to cut a rifle barrel, rather than using the side of the blade to parry the rifle (presumably used with a bayonet attached, rather than fired), and then use the sword to cut the rifleman down?

The katana is not a mystical, unique creation. As J. Kim Siddorn rightly observes: "the methods of pattern welding that the Japanese used were in place in Japan some 700 years after they had been superseded in the West."[413] The 700 year figure appears to be wrong; other authorities say that the Japanese used folding in blade making 200 years after the Vikings.[414] The Viking method involved taking strips of steel of various grades and twisting them together, then forging the weapon to produce lightweight and flexible blades. Hence, the katana does not have a unique, let alone magical method of forging. However, traditional Japanese sword forging became more complex than the Viking method, which is only to be expected, given its greater historical duration. There are now five traditional styles (*Go Kaden*), including the Soshu School-Style and Bizen-style, which produce different shaped katanas and hamons (the wavy differential hardening line).

---

[413] J. Kim Siddorn, *Viking Weapons and Warfare*, (Tempus Publishing, Gloucestershire, 2003), p. 83.

[414] Anthony Shore, "The Two-Handed Great Sword – Making Lite of the Issue of Weight," *Journal of Western Martial Art*, October 2004, at http://www.ejmas.com/jwma/articles/2004/jwmaart_shore_1004.htm.

Although the katana, used for its designed purpose, is a superb weapon,[415] it is not an "invincible weapon" as some untrained internet folk, from the safety of their parents' basements, seem to think. In the 1930s during the Second Sino-Japanese war, Chinese soldiers low on ammo used the *dadao*, the Chinese war sword against the katana-armed Japanese. The *dadao* has a blade 2-3 feet long and a handle long enough for two-handed use. The blade is thick and deeply curved with a point on the edge of the blade that is not efficient for thrusting – but one wouldn't want a jab in the eye with it. Hence, it was, and is still, a chopping weapon and a good one. At the battle of the Great Wall, the Chinese used the *dadao* against the katana-wielding Japanese to behead them.

During World War II, US service members sometimes battled Japanese soldiers in hand-to-hand combat. At the Battle of Iwo Jima, a US serviceman faced a Japanese soldier who had a katana held above his head ready for the classic samurai king chop (an unnecessarily open move). The American charged him and killed him with his Ka-Bar, receiving only a shallow cut to his back.[416] Another US marine grabbed the blade of the katana of a Japanese soldier, pulling it out of his hands. His hands were badly cut, but he survived – an incident illustrating the poor quality of swordsmanship of the Japanese soldiers compared to past noble traditions, as well as the extremely poor quality of the mass-produced *gunto showato* swords of the military period. Japanese purists are I think, correct in regarding these swords, often banged up by amateurs without *tamahagane* steel, as not genuine katanas, but pieces of shit.

There have been many attempts to compare the katana to other blades, such as the European long sword and Viking sword with respect to factors such as cutting ability, thrusting ability,

---

[415] "Man Uses Katana to Stop Home Invasion: This is the Gory Aftermath," April 11, 2015, at http://knowledgeglue.com/man-uses-katana-stop-home-invasion-gory-aftermath-nsfw/. This weapon was a mere decorative wall-hanger, not a battle ready blade, but it still did damage.

[416] Fred Hutchinson, *The Modern Swordsman: Realistic Training for Serious Self-Defense*, (Paladin Press, Boulder, Colorado 1998), p. 60.

guarding ability, speed, technical versatility, and durability.[417] There is a methodological problem in all such attempts as there is no standard of what is "typical," with no "generic" longsword or katana, even though each has a quantifiable characteristic. Even given this qualification, if one took representative samples of the "best" of each type of sword, there would still be no clear decision for any characteristic except, perhaps, handle durability. Here katanas are generally held together by a bamboo peg that could break but usually tends to last the distance. The traditional *tsuka* is made of wood and the *samegawa* wrapping is ray skin (cheaper swords often use plastic). All of this in principle, could start to deteriorate in a humid environment.

The same sort of indeterminacy arises when other sword characteristics are considered. For example, the katana may be thought to be superior at cutting because of its iconic sharpness and because, in principle, at least, a curved blade is arguably mechanically superior at cutting to a straight blade, all other things being equal, but they seldom are. Yet sharp straight-edged blades are more than adequate for all reasonable combat purposes and can easily destroy unarmored and often armored people. The longsword has, usually, a large cross bar for guarding, not only for the prevention of the hand sliding onto the blade but for hand guarding from blade and stick slide (a common Wing Chun 6 ½ pole tactic). But, the guard is only in one plane and a weapon with some flex can snap around it. Hand protection in a sword fight though is best obtained by skill and maneuverability, by not having one's hand in a vulnerable position in the first place.

As for blade speed, this is more a quality of the person when the blades are of roughly equal weight and size; specialized lighter rapiers are going to be faster in equally trained hands, all other things being equal.

The longsword has been regarded as technically more versatile because it can be used in "half-swording," grasping the presumably less sharp part of the blade closest to the hilt so that the sword can

---

[417]   John Clements, "Longsword and Katana Considered," at http://www.thearma.org/essays/longsword-and-katana.html#.VZxoBy6qqko.

be used as a short-range spear. Historically, this was done to dig at the gaps in plate armor, and the European masters documented this technique in their fight books/combat manuals (*Fechbücher*). So, of course, this can be done, but usually, there is an alternative (use of footwork) or use of a more practical weapon (e.g., war hammer against plate armour). The masters also recommended use of the *mordhau*, gripping the blade with both hands and striking with the pommel or cross guard, as depicted in the *Codex Wallerstein* (*Vonn Baumann's Fechtbüch* (Oettingen-Wallerstein Cod. I. 6. 4°. 2) and the Hans Talhoffer Fechtbuch, to name but two. This assumes that one has hand protection or that one's blade is ineffectively blunt unless serious injury was accepted. Surely, such a situation screams out for use of a more appropriate weapon, such as a war hammer, battle axe, club or even thick gauge steel water pipes or steel bar. Why use a cutting/stabbing weapon for less-than-effective bashing?

The blade of good katanas needs TLC with "sharpening" with "water stones" of various grit sizes, and the usual sharpening methods tend to wreck edges; diamond sharpeners will wear out blades, and non-traditional sharpening methods fail to get blades to the required level of sharpness. Actually, the katana is not "sharpened" as such, but is "polished" by hand using water stones, these being of increasingly fine grit. This taxing task can usually only be done a few times before the softer steel core begins to show through, leaving an aged blade. A blunt katana is not a good katana so that if one was in a *Mad Max/Road Warrior* situation with constant battles, as I envisage happening in the collapse, blade care for the katana could be an issue. Perhaps European blades would be easier to maintain in apocalyptic situations where traditional water stones are in short supply.

I do not agree with criticisms of the katana that because they are blade-heavy that they are "clumsy." There are no clumsy swords (within reasonable limits), only "clumsy" users. After fifty years of use I find the katana as feeling good and familiar to my hand, as one would expect with the long-term use of any such weapon. Traditionally, the sword was used two-handed because of the traditional method of draw-cutting, so that a shield could not simultaneously be used. Nevertheless, the katana can be used one-handed, as stated earlier, with some modification of the traditional draw-slices, and masters such as Miyamoto Musashi (1584-1645) in his *niten'ichi* ("two heavens in one") fought with a katana and a wakizashi. One can go further and fight with two katanas, or a katana and some other one-handed weapons, as mentioned previously.

Spears and Polearms

Long weapons such as spears, polearms, and the quarterstaff may not be of practical relevance in congested urban areas, but these melee weapons can still be relevant in rural areas, even up against guns (close range), if that is all one has. Further, the length of polearms, their principal virtue, is due to the length of the shaft; if necessary a polearm could have its shaft length reduced by cutting down the shaft so that the weapon instead of being over 6 feet, reduced to the length of a longsword, even a short sword. This could be done to make the polearm easier to use in urban settings. As well, many polearms are sold by the business end head only, the shaft to be supplied by the purchaser. Thus, a reasonably good French partisan head (defined below) can be had for under $100 US, and one would not get much of a sword for that.

A weighty book could be filled with describing European and Asian (East Asian as well as South East Asian) polearms. Here only a mention can only be made of each:

> *The Bill*: an English, Italian, and European weapon used around the mid-1500s consisting of a curved axe head, a fluke or spur for deflecting attacks and bringing down and/or hamstringing horses, openings to trap enemy weapons and a long spear point. The bill could hack off the heads of pikes and cut down cavalry. Its effectiveness was shown at the Battle of Flodden/Flodden Field (September 9, 1513), fought at Northumberland between the English under the Earl of Surrey and the Scots under King James IV. James himself was killed by a bill after being wounded by an arrow. The Scots favored the pike while the English used the bill and the hilly, slippery ground did not make the pike the superior weapon on the day.

Halberd: used around the 14th century this was a combination of staff, axe blade, and spear point, with a spike on the other side of the axe blade for parrying and using as a hook against cavalry. There are Swiss/German, Italian and English versions.

Poleaxe: a 14th century weapon used to attack plate armor, consisting of an axe, hammer and a long spike for spearing. The hammer sometimes had a spike on the otherwise flat hammer head surface for puncturing armor.

Bardiches: a popular Eastern European and Russian medieval weapon comprising an axe-like blade with a thrusting long spike.

Becs de corbin: a hammer with a long spike/ pick-like prong with a straight spike in the front of the weapon for thrusting.

Guisarmes: these had a spear with a needle-like point rather than a blade, and a parrying hook(s) for dismounting horsemen/hamstringing horses.

Glaive: a single-edged blade like the Japanese naginata, often with hooks on the blade to deal with cavalry. A polearm of the later Middle Ages.

Partisan: a spear or pike having a long tapering double-edged blade, usually with two curved blades/wings at the bottom of the blade used to hook, trap or strike.

Pikes: metal spearheads on a long pole, 3-4 meters or longer in length. The shaft of the pike came to be reinforced with metal strips near the head to try to prevent great swordsmen and halberd men smashing the heads of the pike. Pikes were used to great effect by commoners in battles such as the Battle of the Golden Spurs between France and the County of Flanders on July 11, 1302, where Flemish pikeman skewed the French cavalry.

Lance: generally, a smaller spear than the pike, typically without wings, used by mounted warriors for thrusting charges or throwing. Used throughout history, the weapon declined in use with the rise of medieval plate armor but then come back into vogue in the 18th and 19th century with the decline in the use of body armor.

Spontoon: similar to the pike (also called a "half pike"), but sometimes having crossbars for parrying. The length was about 6-7 feet. Some had a central blade with smaller curved blades on either side, giving the appearance of a trident/war fork.

Morning Star: a spiked club weapon, like a mace, only having long metal spikes. The Morning Star has a wooden handle up to six feet in length, and thus is longer than a mace, making such weapons genuine polearms.

Sword staff: a Scandinavian polearm used during the medieval period consisting of a blade at the end of a staff. It was used at the Battle of Effsborg (1502).

War scythe: made from a standard medieval scythe, this polearm consisted of a scythe blade on a pole. Sometimes the blade may have had a curved hook on it for dealing with cavalry. Such a weapon has been used in peasant revolts from ancient to modern times.

Guan dao: from China, the "reclining moon blade," a heavy curved single-edged chopping blade with a spike at the back of the blade for trapping of other weapons or to deal with horsemen and a pointed metal counterweight at the other end of the weapon. Although there is no objective historical evidence to support this, legend has it that General Guan Yu (died 219 AD) invented this weapon and as a hugely strong man wielded one between 18-48 kgs. Alternatively, the guan dao may have been an 11th century invention.

Naginata: a weapon used by early Japanese *sohei*, warrior-monks, against cavalry, and later as a self-defense weapon for Japanese women. It consisted of a curved blade on a pole, usually with a smallish round guard (tsuba), where the pole joined the blade to protect the hands in closer range fighting.

One of the most useful longer-range weapons was the spear, one of humanity's earliest weapons, probably being used after rocks and stone knives. Primitive spears have been made by chimpanzees and orangutans, using sticks from trees, sharpened with their teeth. Spears have been found at Schoningen, Germany, dated 400,000 BCE.[418] At Boxgrove, England, a rhinoceros scapula has been found with a circular hole in it that could have been made with a spear – dated 500,000 BCE.[419]

As a melee weapon for throwing, stabbing, or slashing, spears have been used in all human cultures and have been regarded as "the most effective hand-held bladed weapon humans ever devised."[420] The spear has reach, lethality and simplicity and is the only melee weapon originally devised to allow humans to hunt/fight non-

---

[418] H. Thíeme, "Lower Palaeolithic Hunting Spears from Germany," *Nature*, vol. 385, 1997, pp. 807-810.

[419] R. Dennell, "The World's Oldest Spears," *Nature*, vol. 385, 1997, pp. 767-766, cited p. 767.

[420] Robert E. Dohrenwend, "The Spear: An Effective Weapon Since Antiquity," *Journal of Asian Martial Arts*, vol. 16, no.1, Spring, 2007.

human animals. The ancient Greeks hunted lions in Macedonia and the Romans, leopards. Even in modern times, Len McDougall observes, "the power of the long spear is still demonstrated in the way African lions will actually withdraw at the approach of Masai tribesmen carrying their traditional long spears and shield."[421]

The spear, not the sword, was the principal weapon of pre-modern warfare across the Earth,[422] used by Europeans (especially the Vikings[423]), Mongols, American Indians (e.g., the Comanche), Chinese, Japanese, Australian Aborigines and used to great effect by the Zulus. For example, the Zulu iklwa proved to be a most impressive weapon. It was invented by King Shaka (died 1828), specially to defeat the style of fighting among Africans which was standard at the time. This involved carrying the shield in the left hand, long spear in the right, then raising the right arm, exposing the right side. As everybody fought like this, the weakness was not exploited. Shaka used a shorter spear to stab into the opening, with "iklwa" being, allegedly the sound of penetration/removal. This change in fighting methodology made the Zulus the pre-dominant tribe in Africa at the time.[424]

In the Battle of Isandlwana, January 22, 1879, the first major battle in the Anglo-Zulu war, 20,000 Zulu warriors fought 1,800 British, colonial and native troops and about 400 civilian fighters. The British had Martini-Henry breech-loading rifles, two "seven pounds" artillery pieces, and a rocket battery. The Zulus had some muskets and other rifles but were not trained in their use and, in any case, regarded firearms as a coward's weapon, killing at a distance, and I think there is something in that. They used their spears (assegai and iklwa), cow-hide shields, throwing spears and clubs.

[421] Len McDougall, *The Self-Reliance Manifesto: How to Survive Anything Anywhere*, (Skyhorse Publishing, New York, 2010), p. 145.

[422] A. Ferrill, *The Origins of War: From the Stone Age to Alexander the Great*, (Thames and Hudson, New York, 1985).

[423] See "Viking Spear," at http://www.hurstwic.org/history/articles/manufacturing/text/viking_spear.htm.

[424] Mervyn Mitton, "Iklwa – Early Zulu Fighting Spear," at http://gmic.co.uk/index.php/topic/38843-iklaw-early-zula-fighting-spear/.

Despite having guns, the Zulus defeated the British, killing more than 1,300 troops. About 1,000 Zulus died. The British loss was due to poor field tactics and a lack of ammo; the British fought, when their ammo was eventually expended, with fixed bayonets, but was no match for the spears and shields of the Zulus.

Nevertheless, the British got better at this quickly. At the Battle of Rorkes Drift (January 22, 1879-January 23, 1879), 150 British and colonial troops faced an attack of 3,000-4,000 Zulus, with the same assortment of weapons as used at the Battle of Isandlwana. There was also some hand-to-hand combat. The British fired about 19,100 rounds, killing, according to various estimates, 351 to 875 Zulus, with 17 British dead.

In modern times the fixed bayonet on a rifle has served as a spear when the ammo has run out. A British Army bayonet charge occurred in 2004 in Iraq at the Battle of Danny Boy, where the Argyll and Sutherland Highlanders bayonet charged a mortar position which nested over 100 Mahdi Army fighters. The British killed 40 with their blades. Successful British bayonet charges also occurred in Afghanistan in 2009 and September 2012.

Lt. Col. Dave Grossman in *On Killing*[425] has observed that it is generally easier for warriors to slash, chop or hack with bladed weapons, rather than to stab or skewer an adversary. This aversion to bodily penetration has been present throughout history. Thus, the Romans had the problem of soldiers not wanting to stab, but to cut. There are relatively less stab/penetration wounds compared to cuts/slashes at many historical battles such as Agincourt (1415) and Waterloo (1815). In modern times soldiers fighting at bayonet range have tended to use the butts of their rifles to smash rather than to skewer; soldiers may flee, and bayonet combat is rare. Grossman says: "To reach out and penetrate the enemy's flesh and thrust a portion of ourselves into his vitals is deeply akin to the sexual act, yet deadly, and is therefore strongly repulsive to us."[426]

---

[425] Dave Grossman, *On Killing: The Psychological Cost of Learning to Kill in War and Society*, (Little Brown and Company, Boston, 1996).

[426] As above, p. 121.

There is also a spear-variant, the goedendag, or a similar weapon, the *plançon à picot*. The goedendag was a weapon used by militias of Medieval Flanders in the 14th century, where it was called a spiked staff (*gepinde staf*). It consisted of a club of about 5 feet (150 cms) in length, with a diameter of four inches (10 cms) at the striking end, tapering down to a graspable handle. To this thickest end was attached a metal covering which had a sharp metal spike attached. The method of use was suggested by the nature of the weapon: used to spear knights or club them off their horses and then to spear them and/or club them to death. Flanders' guildsmen used this weapon to destroy French knights at the Battle of Courtrai/Golden Spurs near Kortrijk, Flanders, July 11, 1302. The weapon was capable of smashing the legs of horses, and the spike was strong enough to piece the armor of knights. The Flemish militia, along with the goedendags, were armed with maces and geldons (long spears). Their army was primarily infantry. The French army was largely cavalry, with a mix of aristocratic knights, squires, spearmen, and crossbowmen. The French were soundly defeated, I think in part because of the effective use made of the goedendags which neutralized any advantages armor had. The battle was named after golden spurs as the golden spurs of the French knights were collected and hung in the Church of our Lady in Kortrijk.[427]

Bludgeons: Fighting Sticks

Bludgeons are non-bladed rigid body impact weapons. Excluded by this definition are weapons such as whips and chains. Arguably, weapons such as the three-section staff and nunchakus fall into the bludgeon or bludgeon/flexible weapon hybrid camp. However, if one has not specialized in training with these, it is best to use more conventional bludgeons, for among other things, these sorts of traditional kung fu weapons are now highly regulated in many jurisdictions.

---

[427] J. F. Verbruggen, *The Battle of the Golden Spurs: Courtrai, 11 July 1302*, (Boydell Press, Woodbridge, 2002).

In China, where the baseball bat is one of the few weapons long-distance truckers can use (even the possession of kitchen knives is regulated in this communist paradise), some manufactures have produced steel-alloy baseball bat/clubs, which can smash red bricks to pieces without damaging the bat.[428]

Cricket bats are slightly heavier than baseball bats but are generally made from willow, a soft wood, and suffer the same fate of baseball bats in the longer run.

Let us not forget about walking sticks. Most of these are designed for urban environments as an "under the radar" weapon. The Irish shillelagh, though could be used as both a walking stick and a fighting stick. In the 18th century, England banned Irishmen owning weapons, so weapons had to be disguised as everyday objects such as walking sticks. The village of Shillelagh in the Wicklow Mountains, at the time, produced quantities of blackthorn which is a good timber for an impact weapon. Short sticks of around two feet were produced, but so were quarterstaffs of 6-9 feet in length. The martial art of Shillelagh bata developed around this fine weapon, but sadly today there are few practitioners.[429] While a blackthorn stick may not sound particularly deadly, "loaded sticks" can be made by adding molten lead to the end, which, when cooled, locks to the stick making a weapon capable of smashing out brains. No wonder Bing Crosby was so cheery singing: "With my shillelagh under my arm/and a twinkle in my eye/I'll be off to Tipperary in the morning."

"There's nothing like a good piece of hickory," the Clint Eastwood character ("Preacher") says in the movie *Pale Rider* (1985). The wood for impact weapons needs to be a hardwood, crush resistant, with the flexibility to a degree necessary to absorb shocks. Some woods with a high Janka scale hardness are not suitable for impact weapons as they may shatter with strong hits e.g. many tropical hardwoods,

[428] "Baseball Bat is a Hit as Defensive Weapon in China," November 1, 2011, at https://www.latimes.com/business/la-xpm-2011-nov-01-la-fi-china-baseball-bats-20111102-story.html.

[429] Maxime Chouinard, "The Stick is King: The Shillelagh Bata or the Rediscovery of a Living Irish Martial Tradition," at http://cimande.com/blackthorn/pdf/stick_edited.pdf.

Lignum Vitae, African Ebony.[430] The Japanese use evergreen white oak (*shiro kashi*) for training weapons, and the Chinese, white wax wood (*Ligustrum lucidum*). Some other choices are white ash, birch and (impact grade) hickory, as the *Pale Rider* character recognized.[431] Apparently, olive was used in Sicilian staff fighting, *paranza lunga*. The staff was called the *ulivastro* and was quite resilient, and was able to be bashed against metal or concrete without breaking. The *paranza* was devised by shepherds around AD 1200 as a defense against bandits, wolves and wild dogs.[432]

Swordmaster Miyamoto Musashi (1584-1645), on two recorded occasions, used a wooden sword, a bokken, to defeat an adversary using a katana. In his battle against swordmaster Sasaki Kojiro, renowned for using an extra-long katana which he called the "clothes-drying-pole," Musashi used a bokken fashioned from a boat oar that was even longer than Kojiro's sword. He smashed his skull with one blow.

The melee combat merits of the club were recognized by the Japanese in the mythical weapon of the *oni* (Japanese demons), the *kanabō*. The kanabō was a spiked or knobbed club made of hardwood or steel, a mace on steroids, and growth hormone. It ranged in length from two feet to the height of a man. Its shape could be straight from the handle to end or shaped like a huge baseball bat. Its purpose was to smash enemy armor and the legs of horses, and it could break or bend katanas or knock them out of an opponent's hands. Although the kanabō may have been mythical, there are similar medieval Japanese weapons such as the nyoibo, konsaibo, tetsubō, ararebo and kanemuchi.[433]

Club weapons have been used by all indigenous peoples, including the Australian Aborigines (with their war clubs and throwing clubs/sticks) and Native Americans. The gun stock

[430] "Woods for Weaponry," at http://todahabukoryu.org/wp/?page_id=33.

[431] James Goedkoop, "Woods for Training Weapons," at http://www.aikiweb.com/weapons/goedkoop1.html.

[432] "Paranza," at http://stephiblog.wordpress.com/tag/staff-fighting/.

[433] "Kanabō," at http://en.wikipedia.org/wiki/Kanabo.

club was primarily a weapon of the Eastern Woodlands Native Americans. It was based on the stock of a rifle, often having blades inserted on the side opposite the forward curve. A modern version is made by Cold Steel, as is the Indian war club.

The cudgel/club/staff was the most commonly used Shaolin weapon, and the Shaolin monastery was famous for staff techniques. The staff may have been first used in the late Sui Dynasty when the Shaolin monastery was targeted for attack by peasant rebel armies such as the Red Turbans.[434] Shaolin scholar Cheng Zongyou in 1610 completed a manual on staff fighting *Shaolin gunfa chan zong* (*Exposition of the Original Shaolin Staff Method*). Although he wrote treaties on archery, the spear, broadsword and crossbow (combined into one manual in 1621, *Geng yu sheng ji* (*Techniques for After-Farming Pastime*)), the staff was his favored weapon, having spent over ten years at the Shaolin monastery. Cheng Zongyou's staff manual was well received by Chinese martial artists at the time and Mao Yuanji (1549 c -1641) said: "All fighting techniques derive from staff methods, and all staff methods derive from Shaolin. As for the Shaolin method, no description of it is as detailed as … Cheng Zongyou's…" Mao Yuanyi incorporated this staff manual into his own treatise *Wubei Zhi* (*Treatise of Military Preparations*). For Cheng Zongyou, the staff was to be made of either hardwood or iron: wood, 8.2 to 8.7 feet length in weight and 3.2-3.9 lbs; iron, 7.7 feet in length, weight 19.5 to 20.8 pounds. References to Shaolin staff fighting techniques appeared in Late-Ming era military treatises such as Tang Shunzhi, *Wubian* (*Treatise on Military Affairs*) (c. 1540); General Qi Jiguang, *Jixiao xinshu* (*New Treatise on Military Efficiency* (1562)) and He Liangchen, *Zhenji* (*Records of Military Tactics* (1565)).

The club has the advantage as an of being cheap, readily available, and easy to improvise. Many forms of clubs also give one a fighting chance against an opponent with even a large fighting knife or a sword. The club requires much less training than a sword, and club training is itself a form of weight training: Indian clubs are sold today primarily as shoulder and arm training tools.

---

[434]   Meir Shahar, "Ming-Period Evidence of Shaolin Martial Practice," *Harvard Journal of Asiatic Studies*, vol.61, 2001, pp. 359-413.

For outdoor use, some versions of the staff or "long club" can be used. My training was initially with the Wing Chun six and a half pole (*luk dim boon gwun*). This pole is about 7 feet 2 inches long and was introduced into the system by the monk Shin Chi, who taught the techniques to Leung Yee Tai, according to one story. The pole used was known as the "rat's tail stick" and was quick and whippy, with perhaps a blade on the end of the pole. The idea was to have "six and a half" techniques so that the fighting system could be quickly passed on. Although the form incorporated a big horse stance (which doesn't occur in the rest of the Wing Chun system), this can be abandoned in practical fighting (see the 6 ½ pole fight scene in the movie, *Ip Man: The Final Fight* (2013) for example).

The "½ movement" is a concluding pushing movement in the form, but the six main movements are (1) a spear-like thrust (*biu gwun*); (2) pushing out (*tan gwun*); (3) & (4), thrust in the left and right (*chir gwun*); (5) snap of pole up (*til gwun*) and (6) snap of pole down (*jut gwun*). This is the half-staff grip of the European staff used in sporting applications: "half the staff's length is held between the hands, and the hands themselves are positioned equidistant from each end of the staff." [435] However, in the combat use of the European staff, about a quarter of the length of the staff is held between the hands, with the rear hand near the tip of the staff. This hand position was also advocated by English masters of arms such as Joseph Swetman, *The Schoole of the Noble and Worthy Science of Defence* (London, 1617).[436] The European and Asian methods are in full agreement, and I believe that a complete system can be constructed.

Many complicate this in the name of traditional purity, but it is unnecessary, or in the alternative, let them have the name and we keep the techniques. The pole is grasped at one end with standard dead lift grips, with the backhand palm-down, forward hand palm-up. As this weapon is primarily for longer range fighting, the pole is not grasped in the center as in close range European quarterstaff

---

[435]   Terry Brown, *English Martial Arts*, (Anglo-Saxon Books, Frithgarth, Norfolk, 1997), p. 65.

[436]   See: http://www.thearma.org/Manuals/Swetnam.htm.

fighting, but there is no reason why a fighter couldn't make such a transition if the need arose, moving from the Chinese system to the European: let a thousand flowers of violence bloom. The Wing Chun 6 and ½ pole technique incorporates both offence and defense, simultaneous attack and defense, especially through the "sticking pole" (*chi gwun*) techniques. The idea is to cling to an opponent's weapon, stick to it, feel the force, then redirect and drive through to destroy them. There is an emphasis on "inch force," explosive close range "snap." This is not unique to Wing Chun kung fu even though some of the clan like to think so. The Niulang staff, which combines techniques of the staff, spear and sword, is also used to detect, direct or deflect attacks and makes use of explosive power (*fajin*). Explosive power is, of course, well known in the use of the bō, the weapon of Okinawa and feudal Japan, as practiced in bō jutsu.

The staff was regarded as a superior personal self-defense melee weapon by a number of English masters of arms. George Silver in *Paradoxes of Defence* (1599)[437] praised the quarterstaff of "perfect length" of about 8-9 feet, determined by standing upright with the staff in one hand, close to the body, reaching up with the other hand fully extended, add to that length a distance sufficient to wield the weapon. [438] Silver saw "weapons of weight" such as polearms, battle axes, and halberds as superior to the sword alone or with buckler or dagger and arms of "perfect length" as superior to all melee weapons as well as to attacks by two men with swords and daggers. But, the quarterstaff, used in unarmored combat, was able to defeat "weapons of weight" (which defeat swords) because of "nimbleness and length," the weapon being faster than polearms. Silver, however, qualified his ranking of the quarterstaff, putting it below the Welch hook or forest bill. But, that ranking was only in one-on-one combat. In warfare with a multitude of men and weapons, the sword, battle axe and halberd were thought to be better weapons than the staff, being able to deal with armor, which explains why the staff did not

---

[437]   George Silver, *Paradoxes of Defence*, (London, 1599), at http://www.pbm.com/~lindahl/paradoxes.html.

[438]   Sydney Anglo, *The Martial Arts of Renaissance Europe*, (Yale University Press, New Haven and London, 2000), p. 166.

appear on the battlefield as such, even with an added spike and/or metal ferrule, although the club did in Nordic/Germanic fighting.

English master of arms Joseph Swetnam in *The Schoole of the Noble and Worthy Science of Defence* (1617),[439] said of someone who had mastered the rapier and dagger and the "staffe": "for those which have the skills of these two weapons may safely encounter against any men having any other weapon whatsoever." And: "I do affirme of a staffe against all long weapons." He differed from Silver in seeing the staff, in non-armored personal combat, as superior to all polearm weapons, including Silver's beloved Welch hook or forest bill. Polearms were, compared to staffs (even when the staff was steel capped) too top heavy, resulting in over commitment and a slower recovery time against a faster weapon.

Zach Wylde, the author of *English Master of Defence or The Gentleman's Al-a-mode Accomplish* (1711),[440] said of the staff that "a Man that rightly understands it may bid defiance, and laugh at any other Weapon." And: "No Weapon is learnt or understood so soon as this, because there is so little variety in it, and the Method so easy and plain." The German masters also agreed. Even Emperor Maximilian I was skilled in the use of the quarterstaff.

Many English martial arts books and articles mention with pride, and rightly so, the staff skills of Richard Peeke of Travistock, who fought simultaneously three Spanish rapier-and-dagger men in the presence of the Duke of Medina-Sidonia and other Spanish dignitaries at Xeres and defeated them all, using a quarterstaff. Richard Peeke recorded the battle in a pamphlet *Three to One: Being, an English-Spanish Combat, Performed by a Western Gentleman, of Tavistock* (1626).[441]

On October 22, 1625, Richard Peeke of Tavistock, Devon, was serving in an English naval squadron in the English-Spanish war. He

[439] Joseph Swetnam, *The Schoole of Noble and Worthy Science of Defence*, (London, 1617), (http://www.thearma.org/Manuals/swetnam.htm).

[440] Zach Wylde, *English Master of Defence or, The Gentleman's Al-a-mode Accomplish* (1711) at http://www.the-exiles.org/Manual%20Zach%20Wylde.htm.

[441] Richard Peeke, *Three to One* (1626) at http://martialhistory.com/reprints/peeke-three-to-one-1626/8/.

was with a group of English sailors who were sent ashore on October 24, 1625, to search for food, apparently oranges and lemons. Peeke searched on his own and was confronted by Spanish musketeers. After an intense fight, in which he was wounded, he was captured, and slung into chains and taken first to Cadiz then Xeres. Peeke was put on trial before four dukes, four marquesses and four earls. In the course of questioning Peeke was asked if he thought that the Spanish soldiers when they landed in England, would prove the English to be *gallinas* (chickens). Peeke replied that on the contrary, the Spanish "would prove to be pullets or chickens."

Duke Medyna then challenged Peeke to fight with one of these "Spanish pullets," which Peeke willingly agreed to. Peeke's chains were removed, and he was to fight with rapier and poniard a Spanish champion called Tiago. The battle ended by Peeke using the guard of the rapier to trap Tiago's rapier and using a leg sweep to put the Spaniard on his butt. Peeke then put his rapier to Tiago's throat and he surrendered.

The Spanish then asked Peeke is he would fight another man, and he said that he would if he could fight using a quarterstaff. This was given to him. Two swordsmen then confronted him. Peeke sarcastically asked for more opponents.

Duke Medyna asked how many, Peeke said any number under six. A third man then joined. Peeke killed one swordsman with one blow. Further blows injured the other two and disarmed them. Peeke was released by the Spanish.

This is a great quarterstaff story, but it could be false; one suggestion is that it was a piece of anti-Spanish propaganda or that the story was a product of literary forger, William Henry Ireland. On the other hand, a play *Dick of Devonshire* was produced in 1626, and Ireland did live in the late 18th century. There appears to be authentic reproductions of the cover of *Three to One* on-line,[442] so the story has some plausibility. There are certainly many documented cases in England of the quarterstaff being used to efficiently kill people.

---

[442]   Frank Docherty, "A Brief History of the Quarterstaff," *Journal of Western Martial Art*, May 2001, at http://ejmas.com/jwma/articles/2001/jwmaart_docherty_0501.htm.

The limit of the staff, like any melee weapon requiring two hands, is that it leaves one open and near-defenseless to projectile weapon attack by thrown objects such as axes, knives, throwing clubs and sticks and even rocks.[443] For such protection, one needs a shield that could perhaps be carried along with the quarterstaff, to safely drop away from an opponent if not used. Alternatively, a shorter one-handed weapon could be used, such as the *goedendag*.

Conclusion: Neo-Vikingism

In the artwork known as Trajan's Column, the largest artwork of ancient Rome, there is a portrayal of the Dacian wars (101-102 AD, and 105-106 AD). Pictured are Germanic warriors recruited into Roman forces. Some are bare-chested, some wearing bear-pelts (berserkers), others wolf-pelts, but many have clubs as a primary weapon.[444] The Germanic club-wielder fought in the front line of shield walls and used clubs, often with iron-studded knots, against armored horsemen. As Speidel puts it, "neither horsemen nor the tightly crammed foot soldiers of more advanced societies can easily dodge the crushing blows of clubs." In AD 312, the Battle at Torino was won for Emperor Constantine, primarily by club-wielders. Mention has already been made of the goedendags used by the Flemish to beat the French knights at Courtrai in 1302.

The mythology of the Vikings fits well with what I think is needed in a melee weapons philosophy. Vikings carried weapons even while doing ordinary everyday tasks and so will post collapse survivors. Further, as Martina Sprague has observed, the Vikings "excelled militarily because they ignored traditional western fighting methods"[445] This too, as I have argued in this book, will need to be done. The Vikings, as Sprague also said: "refused to be dominated

---

[443] "Other Viking Weapons," at http://www.hurstwic.org/history/articles/manufacturing/text/viking_misc_weapons.htm.

[444] Michael P. Speidel, *Ancient Germanic Warriors: Warrior Styles from Trajan's Column to the Icelandic Sagas*, (Routledge and Kegan Paul, London and New York, 2004), pp. 7-8.

[445] Martina Sprague, *Norse Warfare: The Unconventional Battle Strategies of the Ancient Vikings*, (Hippocrene Books, New York, 2007), p. 1.

or bound by the precepts of others and took the fight to their opponents." As the Hurstwic site says on Viking fighting in the sagas:

> They are direct, aggressive, efficient, and clever. They seize the initiative to take control of the fight. They do what is necessary to get the job done, when it is necessary to do it, using whatever tools are available. And so, they use clever and improvisational moves. They draw upon hidden weapons or reserve weapons as needed. They improvise weapons out of countless everyday objects that are at hand, using them in preference to conventional weapons at times when the improvised weapon has an advantage.[446]

Those who improvise, survive.

---

[446] "The Shape of Viking Combat," at http://www.hurstwic.org/history/articles/manufacturing/text/the_shape_of_viking_combat.htm; Hurstwic, *Viking Combat Training: Viking Fighting Moves from the Sagas*, (Hurstwic, DVD, 2013); Todd Palmer, "Viking Fighting Notes from 23 Sagas," at http://www.thearma.org/essays/vikingfight.htm#.Xg2tnUczaUk.

5.

Happiness is a Hot Gun:
Survival Guns and the Survival of Guns

> From inside fortifications, the gun has no equal among weapons. It is the supreme weapon on the field before the ranks clash, but once swords are crossed the gun becomes useless. -*Miyamoto Musashi*[447]

> There is something about a gun that captures the attention in a way no other weapon can. - *F. Kim O'Neill*[448]

Survivalist literature, being written by American authors, is heavily gun-oriented. The United States is one of the few jurisdictions in the Western world that still has a relatively libertarian attitude towards guns, permitting its citizens various gun rights under the Second Amendment to the United States Constitution. While gun-banners once claimed that this right to bear arms applied only to a "well-regulated Militia," the US Supreme Court has ruled that the right to bear arms is also an individual right.[449] However, that right has been held to be consistent with a range of prohibitory regulations, such as a prohibition of "assault weapons" and large capacity magazines.[450]

---

[447]   Miyamoto Musashi, *A Book of Five Rings,* (Axiom, 2006), p. 15.

[448]   F. Kim O'Neill, *The Ultimate Guide to Surviving a Zombie Apocalypse,* (Paladin Press, Boulder, Colorado, 2010), p. 28.

[449]   *District of Columbia v. Heller,* 554 U.S. 570 (2008); *McDonald v. Chicago,* 561 U.S. 3025 (2010).

[450]   *Dick Anthony Heller et al. v. District of Columbia et al., United States District Court,*

In the light of this case law, it is possible that either through mass US government ammo buy ups of billions of rounds or through the taxing of ammo, a *de facto gun* ban could occur in America, land of the once-free. Then, the apocalypse occurs …

In the context of the coming collapse of civilization the main physical threat to the survival of guns as personal weapons is not the maintenance of the physical hardware (most gun parts can be manufactured by hand by skilled gunsmiths as has been done by gunsmiths in Afghanistan), but the long-term viability of smokeless powder in cartridges. Some say that factory ammunition will last from 20-30 years if stored in a cool, dry place, other internet blogs state "indefinitely," but offer no supporting evidence. Even transporting powders constantly causes the grains to impact against each other, grinding into dust fragments, which are inclined to explode rather than "burn."

One could perhaps improvise black powder from sulphur, charcoal, and potassium nitrate (saltpetre) in a collapse survival situation (*disclaimer*: don't do this at home). However, making viable smokeless powder is entirely another matter. Smokeless powder is chemically more complex and dangerous to manufacture in sub-optimal conditions. The basic charge is nitrocellulose with nitroglycerine, nitroguanidine and a multitude of other chemicals, stabilizers, plasticizers, flash suppressants, deterrents, decoppering additives, opacifers and dyes, among other things.[451] Yet, without smokeless powder, weapons such as semi-auto rifles, shotguns and pistols relentless foul up and ultimately malfunction. Without constant cleaning, the reduced energy output may or may not generate cycling problems. But diligent cleaning of firearms will be the least of one's problems.

District of Columbia, March 26, 2010.

[451] Tenney L. Davis, *The Chemistry of Powder and Explosives,* (John Wiley and Sons, New York, 1992).

Survival Guns

Much has been written about guns for survival situations, but less for long-term, multi-generational breakdowns, and only one book, as far as I am aware, on survival guns for the collapse of civilization situations. In general, the recommendations at a minimum are that for self-protection each person should have at *least* one pistol, one shotgun and one semi-automatic rifle, and one long-range scoped bolt action rifle for precision shooting/sniping, although for hunting and protection against large dangerous animals (depending upon where one is in the world e.g. Africa), other specialized weapons would be needed.[452] The main areas of controversy in this field is: (1) How many guns are needed per person, all up? (2) What is the optimal or a satisfactory handgun for self-defense? (3) What is the optimal or a satisfactory factory semi-automatic rifle for self-defense? (4) What role is there for calibers such as the .22 LR?

On the question of how many guns should one need for a survival situation, most American survivalist's writers are heavily influenced by the much-loved book *Survival Guns* by Mel Tappan. Tappan was university educated (Stanford University) and had considerable technical and literacy skills. Tappan in this book and *Tappan on Survival*[453] considered survival situations where the survivalists would be on their own, facing bands of looters, well-armed and probably highly determined to take their stuff and probably their lives. Prolonged sieges could occur, making the issue of survival guns more than just a matter of home defense in civilized times. Against an attacker, in normal times, even a double-barrelled shotgun in 12 gauge and/or a .44 special double action revolver would do. In a collapse situation weapons require "the capacity of accurate, rapid and sustained fire at close, moderate and long range, utter reliability under heavy use, instant availability and one-shot stopping power."

---

[452] Duncan Long, *The Survival Armoury*, (Desert Publications, El Dorado, 1994); Max Velocity, *Contact: Tactical Manual for Post Collapse Survival*, 2nd edition, (Kindle, 2012); Stefan H. Verstappen, *The Art of Urban Survival*, (Kindle, 2010); W. S. Lind and G. A. Thiele, *4th Generation Warfare Handbook*, (Castalia House, Kouvola, 2015).

[453] Mel Tappan, *Tappan on Survival*, (Janus Press, Rogue River, 1981), *Survival Guns*, (Janus Press, Rogue River, 1977).

Defensive guns must be rugged and reliable with minimum maintenance, capable of rapid fire and with reasonable accuracy, capable of hitting a human torso; a pistol up to 75 meters, shotgun (shot) up to 50 meters; shotgun (slugs) 80 meters, and rifle up to 500 meters. The weapon should be heavy enough so that recoil from sustained fire does not affect accuracy. Tappan distinguished between working guns for hunting, pest control, and protection from dangerous animals and defensive weapons. The working gun requires greater precision than a defensive gun, firing bullets either with greater penetration to kill animals larger and tougher that humans, or with less penetration (e.g., 22.LR, .22 short) to kill small pests. Rapid fire is not generally necessary, but in some situations, rapid fire would be important.

The distinction between working guns and defensive guns led to Tappan and others recommending, for those contemplating collapse situations, virtually an entire gun shop of guns with massive quantities of ammunition, spare parts, gunsmithing tools, and reloading equipment. But, there is an opportunity cost of this "more is better" philosophy. On the limited budgets which most of us face, buying say a .22 LR pistol (useful for inexpensive target practice and killing small pests) would need to be traded (opportunity costed) against spending the cost of the pistol on either defensive ammunition or other supplies. The individual will need to decide how much and what can be got on a limited budget. In general, the gun survivalist literature, largely the product of good folk who have adequate supplies of money, do not consider the issues of cost constraints that sit over most of us.

Tappan's distinction between working guns and defensive guns is today only appropriately true. A pump, semi-automatic, or even lever action shotgun (in jurisdictions where the other types of repeating shotguns are banned) in 12 gauge could be loaded with birdshot shells to kill rattlesnakes up relatively close or to bag a duck for dinner.

In this context of "saving money," in an absolute financial pinch, it may be necessary to not have any working guns at all (except if one is in grizzly bear country). Outside of the United States, most people will not have any (legal) pistols, semi-automatic rifles and semi-automatic and pump action shot guns. In Australia in 2020, for example, long after the John Howard gun ban of 1996, even semi auto .22 LR rifles are banned (under a standard license). The only type of repeating weapons available are bolt, slide, lever action and more recently revolving action carbines. And, much of Europe is even more restrictive than Australia.

In summary, for most of us with limited resources, opportunity cost considerations and trade-offs will be central concerns in our choice of defensive firearms.

The Semi-Automatic Rifle

Survivalists generally support having a semi-automatic rifle, if one can legally possess it. The main debates are about the brands and which caliber: .223 or .308. I am not going to discuss the issue of brands here because there are few "lemons" that survive in the highly competitive gun market, especially here in the United States. I have owned a Colt AR in (.223), a number of Mini 14s (.223), an SKS, Maegan/AK 47 (7.62 x 39 mm calibre), HK 91 (.308/ 7.62 x 51 mm) and a number of sporting semi autos in .308 and a range of other calibres.

On the caliber issue, one can find in the literature considerable skepticism about the .223 as a fighting round for civilians in a collapse situation. Before discussing that issue, a matter of clarification. The .223/5.56 x 45 mm NATO and .308/7.62 x 51 mm NATO distinction should be noted. Commercial .308 ammunition may exceed the maximum pressure of the 7.62 x 51 mm round, so there could be problem using .308 ammo in military surplus rifles designed for a lower pressure. The .223 and 5.56 x 45 mm rounds have many of same external characteristics, but the leade or throat of the 5.56 round may be greater than that of the .223 round, so in some rifles chambering the 5.56 round there may be prior contact with the rifling before detonation, creating potentially dangerous pressures.

Thus, a 5.56 round in a .223 could be dangerous, but in general, a .223 round in a 5.56 gun may not be. Therefore, if one is intending to use any cheap surplus ammo or interchange rounds like this, check the matter out first with a qualified gunsmith.

Tappan saw the .223 round as "flat shooting and very accurate to about 300 yards, it has negligible recoil and offers reasonable stopping power at reasonable ranges." Although the .223/5.56 x 45 mm was seen by Tappan as a reasonable round in its range, he was critical of the AR15's of his time for jamming after a bit of firing, and thus he did not recommend its inclusion in a battery of survival guns. He said the .308 Winchester/ 7.62 x 51 mm NATO round, "[f] or defensive use … is the best rifle cartridge yet developed anywhere in the world," being powerful enough for most tactical uses and controllable in rapid fire. If he could have had only one fighting rifle, it would be a battle rifle in .308/7.62 x 51 mm. The military moved to the 5.56 x 45 mm round for logistic reasons (primarily to increase enemy wound rates and tie up resources; lightness in the field etc.), but those factors are not relevant for civilian survivalists. On the jamming of the AR 15, that seems to have been a problem of the past; and while most AR 15s are not as robust as the iconic AK 47, they are generally regarded as good enough for most survival situations, with a modest bit of cleaning. What, then, about the caliber issue?

In another iconic book, *Boston's Gun Bible* by Boston T. Party,[454] it is stated that in a survival situation the .308 is preferred to the .223 due to (1) its greater penetration of cover and vests; (2) long range accuracy and lethality (.223's lethality over 300 meters is "marginal at best"); (3) the .308 has greater "stopping power"; (4) although the .308 round is 1.5 times bigger than the .223, it may require more rounds to stop an enemy. He concluded that in *Mad Max/ Road Warrior* "end-of-the-world" scenarios, a battle rifle in .308 is needed, and he favored the HK 91 in a collapse situation. Updated to 2020, following US import bans of many weapons, the Heckler and Koch, SR9 (SR9 (T) Target) could be a choice. More powerful still is the HK SLB 2000, a semi auto sporting rifle firing the iconic .30-06 round, in up to a 10-round magazine. The M1A, the civilian version

---

[454] Boston T. Party, *Boston's Gun Bible*, (Javelin Press, Ignacio, 2002).

of the M14, produced for example by Springfield Armory, is another .308 alternative to those who do not like the growing AR family of weapons in .308.

Colonel Jeff Cooper was a strong critic of the "assault rifle," seeing it as a "poodle shooter, a small, clumsy, fully automatic, sub-caliber piece with a high rate of fire, but inferior in range, power, and practical accuracy."[455] Cooper's skepticism applied to civilian versions of these weapons as well.[456] In more recent times, the late Chris Kyle (*American Sniper* (2014)), a man who had over 150 kills confirmed by the Pentagon, said of the 5.56 x 45 mm round: "the 5.56 is not a preferred bullet to shoot someone with. It can take a few shots to put someone down, especially the drugged-up crazies".[457]

Far be it for me to argue with such authorities about the combat satisfactoriness of the .223/5.56. Fine – go with the .308 in a battle rifle. However, I think today AR-style rifles are coming to dominate the US defensive rifle market, so perhaps a .308 from one of the numerous AR manufacturers is an option.

Those in jurisdictions which have banned all semi auto rifles will have to make do with bolt action, lever action, pump action, and revolving carbine rifles. There will be no tendency for a mass fire "spray 'n' pray," and marksmanship will once again be of key importance in the art of the rifle. Jeff Cooper said in 1983: "...the farmers who fought the Boer War shot weapons that were vastly superior to those which are issued to American or Russian soldiers today..." And: "... the notion that quality and rapidity of fire can make up for marksmanship is nonsense. Fifty misses do not constitute firepower. One hit does." He also said: "Good shooting can make up for poor equipment, but equipment cannot make up for poor shooting."[458] The need to recover the art of rifle marksmanship is one of Cooper's themes in his now classic *The Art of the Rifle*,[459]

[455] Jeff Cooper, "The Fighting Rifle: Forgotten but Not Gone," *Special Weapons*, vol. 2 no. 1, 1983, pp.18-23, at p. 18.

[456] See Jeff Cooper, "Cooper's Corner," *Guns & Ammo*, July, 1994, pp. 105-106.

[457] Chris Kyle (with Scott McEwen and Jim DeFelice), *American Sniper: The Autobiography of the Most Lethal Sniper in U.S. Military History*, (William Morrow, New York, 2012), p. 100.

[458] Jeff Cooper *Guns & Ammo*, May, 2006, p. 10.

[459] Jeff Cooper, *The Art of the Rifle*, (Paladin Press, Boulder, Colorado, 1997).

which survivalists should study, along with combat strategies and tactics.

In a jurisdiction such as Australia, which for the time does permit bolt, slide/pump, lever action, and revolving carbine rifles, one could perhaps secure weapons including the World War II era bolt action battle rifles, such as a Lee Enfield in .303 British. Enfield MK 2 in .308 are sold in Australia from time to time. A locally modern made version in .308/ 7.62 x 51 mm was made by Australian International Arms, the AIA No 4 Mk IV, which uses modified ten shot M14 magazines and may still be available. Other guns such as the Tula TOZ-122, a Russian bolt action, also in .308, are options.

Better though would be Ruger's Gunsite Scout, a .308 bolt action featuring a 10 round detachable magazine and forward mounted Picatinny rail enabling an intermediate eye relief scope for quick target acquisition. The Scout rifle was one of Jeff Cooper's great ideas, a general-purpose rifle, especially for a lone military scout (or survivalist) in enemy territory. In 1998, Steyr Austria produced its version of the Scout, now called the "Jeff Cooper Commemorative Scout," but the gun came at a premium price. Ruger has given a less costly alternative. The Scout rifle should be a repeater "capable of taking game both large and small; able to dispatch varmints and garden raiders with extreme prejudice; a useful tool for recreational shooting and marksmanship training; and capable of defending family and property from two-and four-legged miscreants."[460] The rifle should be capable of killing "any living target of reasonable size," up to an arbitrary mass figure of about 400 kg. At the upper levels, the .308 will be inadequate, so Cooper was probably asking too much. The Scout's principal aim was to be a general-purpose weapon for use against two-legged predators.

In this context, lever action rifles in 30-30, .44 Magnum, and .45-70, produced by many firms including Marlin and Henry, could serve as lever action "assault rifles." Kevin Steele described in a 1995 article how one US gunsmith was customizing the Marlin M1895 (.45-70), Marlin M336 (.30-30), and Marlin M1894 (.44 Magnum), to produce

---

[460] David M. Fortier, "Scout's Honour," *Rifle Shooter*, May/June, 2011, pp. 22-28, cited p. 22.

general purpose rifles along the Scout line, with the intermediate eye relief scope and other features.[461] Jeff Cooper himself praised the .30-30 lever action carbine and considered that it was a superior weapon to the standard "assault rifle."[462]

James Ballou, in his excellent book, *Arming for the Apocalypse*,[463] would seem to support this conclusion. Commonly held guns, such as for in Australia the bolt action Lee Enfield, or lever action Marlin, are likely to be frequently used by shooters throughout their lives so that they will be highly familiar with the gun. ("Fear the one-gun man.") Post-Apocalyptic guns do not need to be "pretty," they need to be able to effectively work for the individual. Thus, many of us may already be adequately armed for the apocalypse. There is just the need to secure an adequate supply of ammo and reloading gear.

Before turning to the vexed handgun question, I will make some brief comments about the shotgun. T. F. Swearengen summed up the merits of the fighting shotgun in these words:

> Throughout its active life, the fighting shotgun has exhibited an important characteristic that has made it a superior fighting weapon. This is the lethality of its multiple-projectile ammunition. The shotgun-ammunition combination has always been the most lethal short-range weapon in existence.[464]

In general, multiple shots are deadlier that single shots in proportion to the square of their number. The 12-gauge slug, as Mel Tappan put it: "delivers a blow like the hammer of Thor at short distances," and under 60 yards has killed grizzlies and even Cape buffalo, something one shouldn't try.

The shotgun has a relatively small spread pattern at close range, so accurate shot placement is needed, but not as exact as with a handgun. But, the firepower of a good combat shotgun will dwarf

[461]   K. E. Steele, "Lever-Rifle Revolution," *Guns & Ammo: Rifle and Shotgun Annual*, 1995, pp. 14-17; Rick Hacker, "Unlikely Home Defence Guns," *Guns & Ammo*, August, 2006, pp. 44-49.

[462]   See Jeff Cooper, "Practical Defensive Carbines," *Guns & Ammo*, Annual, 1993, p. 90.

[463]   James Ballou, *Arming for the Apocalypse*, (Paladin Press, Boulder, Colorado, 2012).

[464]   T. F. Swearengen, *The World's Fighting Shotguns*, (TBN Enterprises, Alexandria, 1978), p. 19.

most standard handguns. Thus, one should acquire a repeating autoloader, pump, or if these are illegal, a lever action shotgun. The single shot, double (and now triple) barrel (side-by-side or over-and-under) or less common bolt action (e.g. the Savage Model 210 FT), are limited compared to the repeaters, having only one, two, or three shots. As for the double/triple barreled shotguns—one can imagine getting into trouble in a SHTF situation with multiple attackers—thus, far better to use a carbine. A couple of decades ago survivalists usually recommended using a pump action shotgun such as the Remington 870 because of its reliability. The Mossberg 500 is excellent, but almost all existing brands of repeating shotguns will see you through if you can have one.

In the United States, a wide range of reliable non-magazine fed semi-auto shotguns are available, which with a tube extension, can hold up to twelve 12-gauge shells. There may be a higher chance of malfunctions during feeding and ejection of shells with some autoloaders than with pump actions. That slight risk needs to be balanced against the stunning firepower that a weapon such as a gun like the Saiga 12 shotgun has, which shreds opponents, as dramatically shown in *The Expendables* (2010). This gun, modelled on the AK 47, is a rotating bolt, gas-operated weapon fed from a box magazine. They are regarded as highly reliable.

Pistols

There is perhaps no area of intense controversy in the gun world as the choice of a pistol for self-protection against other humans (rather than say wild animals). Handguns are generally less powerful than rifles (ignoring exotic handguns firing rifle bullets, although these too will be less powerful than their rifle analogues). This underpowered weapon has the overwhelming merit of convenience, of being readily attached to the person, so that this gun goes with one: "have gun, will travel." In urban pre-collapse society, handguns are a first-line of protection for police and security personnel, enabling them to perform their duty with hands free until the weapon is drawn. For civilians, pistols enable concealed carry to occur, protection within polite society that would not be so polite if long arms were carried.

The revolver vs. semi-auto pistol debate has gone on as long as the semi-auto pistol has existed. Suffice to say that each has its advantages and disadvantages relative to purpose and function. Semi-auto pistols spit empty brass away from the shooter, an advantage in combat, but not for collecting the brass for reloading in a grid down situation. Revolvers can use a variety of loads sitting next to each other, from birdshot to more powerful loads to kill larger animals. Revolvers can generally fire more powerful rounds than auto pistols, which could be useful when faced by dangerous animals (see appendix). The revolver, both single and double action, can be carried for long periods fully loaded and combat ready without the potential problem of long-term spring fatigue in auto pistol magazines (solved by cycling the magazines). And, so it goes on. Overall, for combat, most authorities favor the auto pistol over the revolver, not only because revolvers are more complicated mechanisms, whose cylinders can be frozen by dirt and grime, but also because auto pistols can offer more rounds in their magazines. The Glock family of pistols, for example, are highly reliable and pistols such as the double-action Glock 17 in 9 mm Parabellum have a 17-shot detachable magazine with one round in the chamber. The Glock 21 in .45 ACP even has a 13-round magazine, which would be handy for the zombie apocalypse to say the least.

There have been perennial debates about the issue of handgun stopping power throughout the 20th and the 21st centuries. As has been said, the early concern came from the problem of the *Moro juramentado* in the Philippines who attacked American officers and administrators with the kris, kampilan, or barong, in suicide missions, as already mentioned, but it won't hurt to have a brief revision in this context. The US sidearm at the time, the Colt Model 1894 .38 revolver, did not reliably stop them, even if they ultimately died. The .45 (Long) Colt Single Action Army (Peacemaker) was brought back and legend has it that the Colt .45 ACP was invented to stop the Moros. But, this is mythology, as although the Colt .45

ACP 1911 was adopted as a side arm of the US forces in March 1911, it did not reach US army units in the Philippines until mid-1913 and at that time battles against the Moros had ended, primarily by use of the .45-70 Springfield Trapdoor Carbine and the Winchester 97 12-gauge pump action shotgun. As said earlier, even these guns sometimes failed.

Warriors in the Boxer Rebellion had been known to take rifle bullets and kill before dying. There are cases of people receiving multiple 7.65 x 21 mm bullets to the heart and not being immediately incapacitated. One goblin took a 12 gauge shotgun blast to the chest at 3-4 meters but was still able to run on 20 meters.[465] New York police officer Jim Cirillo has seen felons hit with oo and No. 4 shot, a 12 gauge slug, 200-and 230-grain .45 ACP hollow points and still keep coming.[466] He has personally seen a gunman cock his revolver after being hit by No. 4 12 gauge buckshot which severed the spine, pierced the heart and put five pellets in the lungs.

Nor is it universally true that a head shot will instantly incapacitate an attacker; there are cases of people attempting suicide by a shot to their heads surviving and some people have had their heads partly shot away and not been instantly incapacitated, although, obviously enough, blowing the entire head off is a winner

Attempts to formulate formulas to measure the effectiveness of cartridge stopping power typically link bullet diameter, kinetic energy, momentum, and some "efficiency" factor. This is not the place for any detailed critique of these formulas, but in general, although some capture our intuitions and experience about what is effective, the formulas are usually question-begging and constructed to get the results the creators wanted, often to make big diameter bullets, such as the .45 ACP, superior to most other pistol rounds.[467]

[465] B. Karger, "Penetrating Gunshots to the Head and Lack of Immediate Incapacitation. I. Wound Ballistics and Mechanisms of Incapacitation," *International Journal of Legal Medicine*, vol. 108, 1985, p.53-61.

[466] Jim Cirillo, *Guns, Bullets, and Gunfights: Lessons and Tales from a Modern-Day Gunfighter*, (Paladin Press, Boulder, Colorado, 1996), p. 57.

[467] "Measuring Effectiveness of Cartridges: Taylor KO Factor," December 19, 2012, at http://firearmshistory.blogspot.com.au/2012/12/measuring-effectiveness-of-cartridges_19.html.

Most of these formulas generate anomalies. Thus, the Taylor Knock Out Factor (TKO) for the 5.56 x 45 mm NATO round, bullet diameter 0.224 (in) traveling at 3,100 fps, has a TKO factor of a lowly 6.12 and the .223 Remington, mass 55 gr, bullet diameter also 0.224 in, traveling even faster at 3,300 fps has a TKO factor of only 5.78. But the 9 mm Parabellum, a pistol bullet, 115 gr mass, bullet diameter 0.355 in, velocity 1,250 fps has a TKO factor of 7.31.[468] Hydrostatic shock factors, energy transfers, bullet yaw and bullet construction and expansion, are not usually considered by these ballistic formulas, so counter-experiential results follow.

Tappan gave the following formulas for comparative stopping power (CSP):

CSP = (Bullet weight in grains) x (Muzzle velocity) x

(Sectional area of the bore in square inches) x

(Empirical efficiency evaluation of bullet shape).

The "efficiency factor" is an "arbitrary" factor based on experience. Tappan gave 0.9 for round nose bullets and 1.0 for blunt and slightly flat points.[469] He noted, rightly, that actual velocities used for pistol factory data is optimistic, usually determined using test barrels longer than actual guns. Using CSP, Tappan concluded that a minimum one-shot stopping power for a round was 22 and above. Thus: .38 special, 13.77; 9mm Parabellum, 13.37; .357 Magnum, 22.72; .44 Special, 27.11; .44 Magnum, 51.50; .45 ACP, 31.08; .45 Colt, 34.87. He thus agreed with other authorities (such as Hatcher's RSP) that the 9 mm Parabellum fails as a defensive round, being "completely inadequate" and "having less than half the stopping power of the .45 ACP," even though the 9 mm was, and is, widely used in the military and police, with both successes and failures. Tappan concluded: "the 9 mm is one of the most unsuitable selections you could make." Interestingly enough, Tappan also regarded the .357 Magnum as

---

468   "Measuring Effectiveness of Cartridges: Thorniley Stopping Power," December 22, 2012, at http://firearmshistory.blogspot.com.au/2012/12/measuring-effectiveness-of-cartridges_22.html.

469   Tappan, *Survival Guns*, p. 38

"marginal in power." On Tappan's CSP scale, the .357 magnum, a round which in quality long-barreled revolvers has destroyed wild animals larger than humans, or tougher, comes out on the CSP as inferior to the .44 Special. The .45 ACP is the only auto pistol with "decisive" stopping power, Tappan believed. Thus, continued the Church of the .45 ACP.

However, Evan Marshall and Edwin Sanow in *Handgun Stopping Power*[470] assembled a persuasive argument that: "[s]topping power is an illusion… There are no magic bullets. There are no manstopping calibers. There is no such thing as one-shot stopping power." Their methodology was to look at actual shootings to determine the efficiency of handgun ammunition. Without a direct and destructive hit to the brain stem, there is no reason why instant (i.e., 1-2 seconds) incapacitation should occur by conventional handgun bullets. It may take 30-90 seconds for a stop, with the goblin being hostile for 10-15 seconds.

Contrary to Julian Hatcher and Tappan, the .45 ACP 230-grain FMJ hardball from street gunfights was found to be "a marginal stopper at only 61- to 64 percent effective." Marshall and Sanow observed that .45 ACP supporters are "extremely smug about the fact that none of the horror stories told about stopping-power failures with other calibers exist about the .45 ACP." But the .45 ACP has failed, dramatically, just as the 9 mm has as well, and all standard handgun rounds. Marshall and Sanow cite the example of a scumbag taking seven rounds of .45 ball to the chest and surviving and another goblin soaking up four .45 ball to the chest and still walking four hours later.

The 9 mm round's most spectacular failure was the infamous April 11, 1986, Miami shootout between two felons armed with Ruger Mini-14s firing the 5.56 mm NATO round (although they probably had .223 ammo in it). One goblin was hit six times with 9 mm and .38 special rounds and the other, an amazing 12 times, with the same combination of ammo. Sadly, two FBI agents were killed and five others wounded. The FBI on September 15, 1987, had

---

470   Evan P. Marshall and Edwin J. Sanow, *Handgun Stopping Power: The Definitive Study*, (Paladin Press, Boulder, Colorado, 1992).

a wound ballistics workshop at the F.B.I. Academy in Quantico, Virginia. The experts concluded that apart from destructive hits to the central nervous system, standard handguns cannot deliver instant incapacitation, even from heart hits. Consequently, agents should keep shooting until the felon goes down and out. The experts were also critical of the performance of the 115-grain 9 mm Silvertip bullet, but Marshall and Sanow say in rejoinder that the bullet did perform as it was supposed to do, expanding in the soft tissue and that the .45 ACP would not have given a better result.

The Miami shootout led to law enforcement moving to the .40 caliber family of handguns, but recently the FBI has made a move back to the 9 mm with new projectile technology which enables, they believe, 9 mm projectiles to outperform .40 S&W and .45 ACP projectiles. Accuracy, the FBI sees, is an important issue, with agents missing 70-80 percent of shots fired in a firefight. Hence, having more shots is an advantage, especially given the low recoil of the 9 mm weapon. But, while that may be sound policy for a government agency, civilians prepared to devote considerable time to training may prefer still to remain with .45 ACP and .40 S&W if they do not have the FBI superior rounds.

In short, any pistol is backup, not a primary weapon. Outside of the United States, most people are not going to have them. For those lucky enough to have pistols as backup weapons, Boston T. Party, in my opinion, was right in concluding: "there's no longer time to endlessly debate 9 mm versus .45. Pick a quality, reliable gun you like in the most powerful cartridge you can handle, use reliable ammo, pay for the best training, dry fire daily, shoot weekly, and carry it every hour. If you do that, it won't really *matter* if it's a Glock or a Colt, a 9 mm or a .45. Carry a good gun with you daily, have the skill to use it instantly – and you're 98% there."[471]

---

[471] Boston T. Party, as above, p. 25/2.

What About a .22 LR rifle?

The .22 LR is probably the world's most shot round. Growing up, outside of martial arts training, I would take to the West Texas hills, and shoot either a Browning auto in .22 LR (SA-22) or an old single shot bolt action, brand I remember not. The Browning I could fire holding in one hand as my "pistol," and I got quite accurate with it, being able to shoot a leaf off of its sprig from about 15 feet, one hand. The Browning is now long gone, but I can still, over 70 years of age, split a playing card edge-on, holding the bolt action .22 out with one hand, at a distance of about 20 feet, as well as hitting a plastic bottle thrown into the air, with the rifle drawn from my side, firing with one hand. In the early 1990s, I had a superb Ruger 10/22 with a 4x scope; I could shoot the heads off of matches, from a rest, at standard pistol range distance. I once cut the plastic rim that goes around some plastic fruit juice/water containers, edge-on, firing from a tree stump rest, downhill, at a distance of about 75 meters. This is not stated to be impressive, as plenty of folk does far better than that. It does show what the humble .22 can do for an average shooter. For such shooters, the virtually no-recoil .22 LR enables one to train to reach a level of super-close-range accuracy.

One can, in a bug out situation, carry in a backpack, along with other gear, perhaps 1,000 rounds or more of .22 LR without too much trouble. The .22 LR can be lethal. Jeff Cooper has said that "The .22 long rifle is, for its size, the most lethal caliber in the world." Marshall and Sanow say: "Despite its diminutive ballistics, the .22 long rifle is responsible for sending as many people to the morgue as any other caliber of handgun, shotgun, or rifle." And they say that a ".22-caliber hole in the aorta will put down an assailant as fast as a .38 or .45 caliber hole." Fired from a rifle, a 40-grain lead bullet has a velocity of 1,150 fps and 117 foot-pounds of energy at the muzzle exit and a velocity of 976 fps and 85 foot-pounds of energy at 100 yards. Perhaps using multiple rounds, easy enough from large capacity magazines which one can obtain for guns such as the Ruger 10/22, one could have most of the benefits of a pistol with less of its disadvantages. The .22 LR can penetrate the human skull, especially form the side (sometimes with internal ricochet within the cranium.[472])

However, I do not believe that the .22 LR should be one's *first line* of defense as a survival gun, but only a supplementary weapon. There is no doubt that the .22 LR guns have merits as numerous assassinations demonstrate. Generally, .22 LR guns can be readily suppressed, especially if sub-sonic rounds are used, but before this book is published Rump may ban suppressors. Against human, rather than hypothetical enemies, the .22 LR round has great killing potential when no medical aid is available, and its wounding capacity may tie up attackers. The round thus has merit in the defense of a fixed position as it could supply suppressing fire at low cost, preserving centerfire ammo. But, if I had only one gun to take in bugging out, regardless of how much ammo one could lug, I would not take a .22 LR rifle because, in a life-or-death firefight, I would not trust my survival solely to the .22 LR. Others are free to differ, and will. Good for them.

The major problem with the .22 LR round is that this small, mass produced cartridge is more likely to fail than centerfire rounds, due to manufacturing defects such as breaks in the impact-sensitive explosive pasted inside the rim. The firing pin may strike such a break, and the gun not fire, just when your life depends upon it. Thus, a rimfire rifle should only be used in defensive situations if this is all one has, or in situations where a jam is not an immediate disaster, say in defense of a fixed position. Therefore, there is a place for the .22 LR in post-apocalyptic self-defense, but in a backup role, not as a primary defensive weapon. Earlier in this book, I was critical of the use of the .22 LR in hunting all but small game because of the general lack of stopping power of the round, if that concept still has any utility.

---

[472]   Malcom J. Dodd, *Terminal Ballistics: A Text and Atlas of Gunshot Wounds*, (CRC/ Taylor and Francis, Boca Raton, 2006), p. 41.

After the Gun

In Post Apocalyptica, in the United States, guns will be the most common doomsday weapon, but this will not be so in many other jurisdictions. In the early days in gun restricted areas, thugs and their gangs will be well armed with illegal guns and will prey upon the unarmed, pillaging, raping, torturing and murdering along the lines of the present-day farm killing sprees in South Africa, raised to the exponential power of many thousands. Perhaps some folk in desperation may acquire illegal guns at a premium price, but most people will not. It will be necessary then to have a sub-optimal means of self-protection, and as argued in the previous chapter, "go medieval." Having a ballistic shield that is maneuverable, but still capable of stopping rifle bullets, potentially gives one a chance of charging a lone gunman and taking him down at close range with a battle axe, war hammer or short sword. Not having such a ballistic shield, one could use an improvised shield of wood and steel and hope that the bullet doesn't penetrate, or is deflected. Once I charged two gunmen intent on a home invasion, armed with a homemade heavy shield of wood and steel and a Viking spear. Probably one will be wounded but you might last long enough to send your opponents to *Hel.*

Range weapons that could be used from a protected position include all sorts of throwing weapons, throwing spears and axes, and archery. Throwing weapons include knives, sharpened steel rods, sticks and rocks. Greek, Roman and Viking warriors, used slings to hurl rocks. Xenophon (431- ?355BC), a Greek general, said that sling users could shoot further than Persian archers.[473] Roman slingers could hit a man at over 200 meters with a rock and sometimes the Romans used cast-lead projectiles. The staff sling, *fustibalus,* was often used by Roman soldiers as a range weapon instead of bows and arrows, as it required less training. The weapon consisted of a 1-1.5-meter staff with a leather sling attached to one end of the staff.

---

[473]   J. Jim Siddorn, *Viking Weapons and Warfare,* (Tempus Publishing, Gloucestershire, 2003), p. 106.

Rocks, lead and "Greek fire" grenades could be hurled up to 150 meters.[174]

At closer ranges throwing knives, steel rods, throwing axes, and spears could be used. The range of the spear could be improved by using an atlatl, a spear-thrower. This is a 15-20-inch extension of the arm, with the focus of force concentrated at the end of the spear rather than in the middle, as in hand-throwing ones. Even relatively large game can be taken, and in self-defense, there does not appear to be any stopping power debate, for being impaled with a large spear in the chest is highly likely to stop a human, as the heart can be literally churned out.

Although all of the above weapons will prove useful in a Post Apocalyptical world without guns, the bow and arrow will once again be the principal range weapon. This is not the place for a detailed discussion of survival bowmanship, but some parting shots can be made.

Crossbows are the easiest for rifleman to use but are slow to reload. That could problematic if the crossbow was one's only weapon – which it should not be. All other bows—long bow, recurve bow and compound bow are faster—although some say that a compound bow is about the same speed as a crossbow.[475] For distance shots in a multi-generational collapse scenario, the crossbow is preferable to the compound bow. Crossbows are hard on strings due to the amount of friction, and wear out relatively fast, requiring string replacement in as few as 200 shots. However, strings can be stockpiled (or improvised), and if stored in a cool, dry place out of sun light, will last indefinitely. The compound bow, using a levering system of pulleys and cables is much more problematic to repair in a SHTF situation if a pulley is damaged. Even replacing the strings may require a bow press. And, compound bows and wood arrows don't mix because of the pressure on the arrow shaft: if cracked the

[474] Robert Dohrenwend, "The Sling – Forgotten Firepower of Antiquity," *Journal of Asian Martial Arts*, vol. 11, 2002, pp. 28-49.

[475] "10 Myths vs 10 Facts on Contemporary Crossbows," April 9, 2011, at https://beckettcrossbows.wordpress.com/2011/04/08/ten-myths-and-facts-on-contemporary-crossbows/.

shaft may break and enter the archer's forearm, which at worst could severe arteries in the forearm, leading to a bleed-out; next worse, put you out of the fight. As arrows will ultimately need to be constructed of wood, the compound bow will be limited in multi-generational use.

The compound bow will be slower than a recurve or longbow to fire because in a compound bow, there is reduced mechanical advantage at the beginning of the draw, but less force will be needed as the bow is pulled further back, "letting off" to a lower holding weight. This has advantages insofar as the bow can be held at full draw relatively easily compared to a recurve or longbow, allowing more careful target acquisition, but it will be slower to get shots off. That will probably not matter for longer-range shots.

However, as in the past, there will be a need for faster, closer-range shots that the recurve and long bow can deliver. The traditional long bow, constructed out of yew or ash, decided battles such as the battle of Agincourt (1415).[476] The bodkin point was quite capable of penetrating mail armor and can penetrate some bulletproof vests of today.

The Mongols, as another example, came close to ruling the world, and they did it, in part, with a preference for shooting their enemies rather than hand-to-hand combat. The Mongol bow was highly effective with a maximum range of 300 meters but was mainly used for getting off fast shots on horseback. A thumb ring was used to pull the bow string back enabling the use of a strong bow, but with less effort in the shots.[477]

Humanity after the age of gun has ended will return to traditional weaponry, so it would be good for our tribe to preserve such skills, and the weapons themselves, and pass on this knowledge for the sake of the survival of the tribe, for the relatively little time still remaining in the human tragicomedy.

---

[476]   E. G. Heath, *Archery: A Military History*, (Osprey, London, 1980).

[477]   Timothy May, *The Mongol Arts of War: Chinggis Khan and the Mongol Military Systems*, (Pen and Sword Military, Barnsley, 2007), p. 50.

APPENDIX

The Return of Nature, Red in Tooth & Claw: Fighting Wild Animals

You hear its deep, savage growls as it tastes your blood and ignores your seemingly futile resistance while it continues to tear at your left shoulder with determination, leaving your right arm free to fight back. At this point, you realize this bear intends to kill and eat you. It was not a defensive or reactionary attack, and the bear did not leave you alone after knocking you flat and delivering the first bite to your left arm as you tried to go into a submissive position. Fighting back is your only chance, but how are you going to defend yourself against several hundred pounds of muscle, tooth, and claw? - *Scott B. Williams*[478]

This chapter will consider whether or not wild animals will be a threat to the remnant who survive after the collapse of civilization. *An important disclaimer:* the author and publisher do not condone the killing of animals save in circumstances when it is a life or death emergency, and the animals pose a risk to human life. The point of this chapter here is to advise on how to deal with feral animal attacks in a post apocalyptic world where the present rule of law has collapsed and all firearms, weapons, wildlife, and game Acts and regulations no longer exist, and there are no emergency

---

[478]   Scott B. Williams, *Getting Out Alive: 13 Deadly Scenarios and How Others Survived,* (Ulysses Press, Berkeley, 2011), p. 223.

services that will protect an individual from animal attacks, that is, the time of the end of the rule of law. The chapter is provided for self-defense in hypothetical post-apocalyptic environment only. At present, some people have been prosecuted for illegally killing bears that have attacked them. Hence, *avoid* any situation, if at all possible, where one may need to defend oneself against any animal protected by legislation. But, our concerns are when that regime crumbles and reality drives out illusion. The considerations of this chapter are solely with the "End of the Rule of Law," and if you square off against wild animals now, expect to be either killed or arrested and then maybe killed in jail.

The phrase "red in tooth and claw" was in popular use in the 1800s and occurred in Canto 56 of Alfred Lord Tennyson's poem *In Memoriam A.H.H* (1850), expressing the sentiment of the cruelty, if not viciousness, of nature and the possibility of the human race itself, ultimately being "blown about the desert dust." While some environmentalists generally have a warm and fuzzy view of nature, the world outside the womb of modern liberal consumer society is grim and tough, as Kenneth M. Weiss describes: "Every creature dies and most of us will die in grim ways we would not choose. In the animal and plant world, it usually means being torn apart while still alive. Even those who escape big predators are often taken down by microbial ones who eat us alive from the inside out, needing neither teeth nor claws to do it. Nature is certainly as Tennyson described it."[479] Civilization has hidden, to some degree this "struggle for life" as Darwin described it in *Origin of Species*,[480] but it is set to return with a vengeance.

---

[479] Kenneth M. Weiss, "Nature, Red in Tooth and Claw," So What?" *Evolutionary Anthropology*, vol.19, 2010, pp.41-45, cited p. 43.

[480] Charles Darwin, *Origin of Species*, (John Murray, London, 1859), p. 425.

Fighting Real Wild Animals in the Collapse

Back to the "real" world. In countries such as Africa, wild animals are, and have always been, a threat, and the native people have learnt to live with them. Before they had firearms, people survived in this land with weapons such as clubs and spears and did fine, apart from those that got torn apart and eaten alive/dying. For many African tribes in the past, young men faced a test of warrior-hood by fighting and hopefully killing a lion with a spear; many no doubt got chomped, but some presumably succeeded, so killing a lion with a spear can be done.

However, as long as firearms are available and ammunition preserved and reloaded, dangerous African animals are likely to be dealt with rounds designed for dangerous game. Calibers for game such as elephants, rhino, and buffalo begin at .375 H&H Magnum and include the .404 Jeffery, .416 Rigby and the elephant calibers: .450 Nitro Express, .458 Winchester Magnum, .458 Lott, .460 Weatherby Magnum; .470 Nitro Express and .500, .700 and .800 Nitro Express.[481] In particular, the .505 Gibbs is said to be capable of stopping any land animal on Earth, including Cape buffalo; the round has a Taylor knock-out value of at least 80 (for what that is worth), with 6,000 foot-pounds of kinetic energy at the muzzle, and bullets ranging from 525 grain to 700 grain. All of these calibers can be used against lions and tigers, with over-kill, but other calibers which can be used include .338 Winchester Magnum; .340 Weatherby Magnum; .350 Remington Magnum and .358 Norma Magnum.

We move now from Africa to another "wild" country, Australia. In general, Australia does not have the same sorts of predatory animals that could become troublesome in post-apocalyptic times in Africa and, indeed, North America. Dingos may eat human babies (e.g., the Azaria Chamberlain case), but are generally timid around adults. The Northern Territory has crocodiles, but they seem to be only a problem for those who stray off the beaten track. Buffalo are tough and can get aggressive. The skin of the northern

---

[481] Chuck Hawks, "Rifles for Dangerous Game," at http://www.chuckhawks.com/rifles_dangerous_game.htm.

buffalo is about 20 mm thick and they do not bleed out readily. Such buffalo have been known to soak up slugs of lesser rounds and then take the shooter apart with horns and hooves.[482] Some hunters have seen buffalo hit by well-placed .375 H&H Magnum and .458 Winchester Magnum rounds, which have not finished the beast off, as the rounds were not loaded to the claimed ballistics.[483] American gun legend Elmer Keith[484] could have been thinking of Australia's buffalo when recommending that one should use "enough gun."[485] The big game round should have "enough" kinetic energy to pass through the animal creating great damage and blood loss. The bullet should have a large sectional density and hold together. If a modern controlled expansion bullet is used, which expands and stays in the animal, it needs to be able to penetrate deeply, punching through flesh and bone. Aussie hunter Barry Jones has said: "I would not feel safe, nor in a position to ensure the safety of my clients, with anything less than .400 caliber and close to 5,000 ft/lbs of energy, and then only if it was loaded with the strongest and heaviest soft nosed or solid bullets." There is no cartridge too big, or bullet too tough for such creatures.

These sorts of dangerous animals are not likely to be any more of a problem then they already are for people living in areas already shared with them. Nevertheless, dangerous animals, such as the big cats could confront people if they are let out or escape zoos.[486] Most major western cities have a zoo which has such dangerous animals, and some cities have on their outskirts, or within the distance of a tank of fuel, lion parks, and the like. If there is even a small, but not unreasonable risk of such dangerous animals ending up on the doorstep of your retreat, an appropriate rifle, as previously mentioned would be wise to have available.

---

[482] M. Graham, "Buffalo Kills Hunter," *Sporting Shooter*, August, 2005, p. 8.

[483] Barry Jones, "Cartridges for Dangerous Game," *Australian Shooter's Hunter 2000 Special*, pp.79-81, cited p. 81.

[484] Elmer Keith, *Big Games Rifles and Cartridges*, (Sportsman's Vintage Press, 2013).

[485] See also Robert Ruark, *Use Enough Gun: On Hunting Big Game*, (Safari Press, 1997).

[486] Piero San Giorgio, *Survive the Economic Collapse: A Practical Guide*, (Radix/Washington Summit Publishers, Whitefish, 2013), pp. 378-379.

Americans who are "jackasses," or unlucky, face a danger of alligator attacks in swampy regions such as Florida. In Florida from 1948 to March 2008, 21 people were killed by alligators, and there were 449 attacks, 150 attacks since the year 2000. Alligators can grow to over 14 feet and weigh over 1,000 pounds. Hence, exercise common sense and keep away from them. Unlike most animals, crocodiles and alligators are almost invulnerable to body shots. They are mini dinosaurs.

Mountain lions can be dangerous, and many reach a weight of 250 pounds. California has had 17 attacks on humans by mountain lions from 1890 to January 2008, with 13 attacks since 1992. There have probably been more attacks; for an attack to be official strict criteria must be met. Nevertheless, by these statistics mountain lions are not a serious threat to humans, until, of course, you meet one and it wants to eat you.

Coyotes have also killed humans. The smaller cats can be handled with the .223 fired from popular rifles in the AR series and other sporting semi-autos such as the Mini 14. Lever action and pump action rifles in Western action calibers such as .44 Magnum and .30-30 would do the job and offer fast follow-up shots. Revolvers in .44 Magnum and higher calibers (e.g., Smith & Wesson Model 460 XVR and Model 460V in .460 S&W Magnum) and the S&W Model 500 in .500 S&W Magnum, should teach these pussies who's boss. Then of course, there is always the 12 gauge.

Doggy-Style: Man's Best Friend?

Today, the dog is your friend, slobbering over your face, but in a Post Apocalyptica, once he/she becomes feral, the "call of the wild" will lead to packs of feral dogs roaming the land, preying on livestock and humans. In October 2004, there were media reports of the small northern Albanian town of Mamurras facing the onslaught of a snarling pack of 200 stray mountain dogs that attacked at least nine people in the middle of town. People were dragged to the ground suffering serious wounds.

189

Police and hunters killed 20 dogs, including the alpha male. In 2011, residents in the small US town of Deer Park, 40 miles north of Spokane, Washington, were on "high alert" after a pack of dogs killed, between late-March and mid-June, 100 animals, including a 350 lb llama. Various animals, including goats, were killed, but no people were attacked. These dogs were apparently abandoned pets left to fend for themselves and they did so by reverting to the pack animals of their racial memory in authentic multicultural style. Such feral dogs can carry rabies and are generally unafraid of humans, making them a potentially potent threat. The horror film *Cujo* (1983, Stephen King) is a dramatization of the dark side of the dog.

Dog attacks are a far more serious threat to Americans, both today and will be in Post Apocalyptica, than any other animal, because, of course, Americans have millions of dogs – the estimated dog population in 2013 being around 77.5 million.[487] Feral dog damage in the US is estimated to be greater than US $620 million annually, and in my home state of Texas alone, US $5 million, primarily from livestock destruction, with the annual damage projected to increase.[488] Each year 4.7 million Americans are bitten by dogs. The breeds that are primarily responsible for *adult* attacks are, predictably enough, large fierce dogs such as pit bulls, Rottweilers and wolf hybrids. Between 1979 and 1996, over 300 people died from dog attacks in the US, with one quarter of these attacks being from feral dogs. Feral dogs kill an average of 19 people per year in the US and transmit multiple diseases and parasites, including rabies and Rock Mountain Spotted Fever (RMSF).[489] In the US in 2013, 32 dog attacks resulted in death, with 18 child victims and 14 adult victims.

Feral dogs are becoming a threat to livestock and humans across the world. In Australia, feral dogs (note that the domestic dog itself is

---

[487]   D. Bergman (et al.), "Dogs Gone Wild: Feral Dog Damage in the United States," USDA National Wildlife Research Centre Staff Publications, Paper No 862, 2009, at http://digitalcommons.unl.edu/cgi/viewcontent.cgi?article=1866&context=icwdm_usdanwrc.

[488]   D. Pimental (et al.), "Update on the Environmental and Economic Costs Associated with Alien-Invasive Species in the United States," *Ecological Economics*, vol.52, 2005, pp. 273-288.

[489]   P. Daszak (et al), "Emerging Infectious Diseases of Wildlife – Threats to Biodiversity and Human Health," *Science*, vol. 21, 2000, pp. 443-449.

only 0.2 percent genetically different from the grey wolf), often are a mixture of dingo and escaped or abandoned pet dogs and weigh up to 40 kgs. These dogs have attacked sheep across Australia, killing up to 70-80 percent of lambs in paddocks. Some farmers have had up to 40 lambs and sheep attacked in one night. The Australian Bureau of Agricultural and Resource Economics and Sciences (ABARES) estimated that for 2009 sheep losses were AUS $50 million. But today the cost of feral dogs and dingoes, for both damage and control in the state of Queensland alone is AUS $67 million, and increasing rapidly, as wild dogs numbers are now regarded as "out of control" by a leading Queensland Agforce wild dog expert. Annual livestock losses are between AUS $48.3-48.7 million in northern Australia, and losses for the beef industry, AUS $23.4 million.

Farmers believe that feral dogs are "changing their behavior, getting smarter, learning, evolving and becoming more aggressive," and this has left farmers "fearing for their family's safety and that of their workers." Dogs have become bolder, now coming up to homesteads and even savaging to death cattle as part of a "thrill-seeking" mass attack by bigger packs, according to researchers from Australia's National Invasive Animals Co-operative Research Centre. It is estimated that there are now tens of thousands of wild dogs in the Australian outback and many have come to prey in peri-urban zones such as the Sunshine Coast and Gold Coast hinterland. Australia's Agricultural Minister (in 2012), John McVeigh, agreed at the time that "wild dogs are out of control right across the state of Queensland."

In Italy, in 2009, there were an estimated 500,000 stray dogs roaming the country, mainly in the south. A 2009 attack led to a boy being mauled to death and in Sicily, a German tourist was attacked by a pack of eight dogs on a beach. A woman, 24 years-of-age, had her face badly disfigured and ended up in a "desperate" condition in hospital. A witness to this said: "They (the dog pack) were tearing her apart and they would have killed her if people hadn't intervened."[490]

---

[490]   N. Squires, "Italy Targets Stray Dogs after Fatal Attacks," March 19, 2009, at http://www.telegraph.co.uk/news/worldnews/europe/italy/5013717/Italy-targets-stray-dogs-after-fatal-attack.html.

A pack of stray dogs killed a 10-year-old boy, pulling him from his bicycle.

In Bucharest, there are an estimated 65,000-100,000 stray dogs. During the first eight months of 2013, almost 10,000 people in Bucharest were treated for dog bites. There have been some deaths, such as a Japanese tourist in 2006, and on September 12, 2013, a four-year-old boy was mauled to death by a pack of stray dogs.

As noted, there is a feral dog epidemic in most US cities, with 100 million+ feral dogs and cats relearning how to hunt, kill, and eat prey.[491] In depopulated Rust Belt cities, feral dogs have become the new rulers. In Detroit, there are an estimated 20,000-50,000 stray dogs, usually roaming in packs. Detroit has been described as "almost post-apocalyptic, where there are no businesses, nothing except people in houses and dogs running around."[492] Detroit even has its own type of pit bull, known as the "Highland Park Red," which primarily protects the drug business. People, especially postal workers, arm themselves with pepper spray. The feral dog problem is occurring across the US, especially in Los Angeles, New Orleans, Cleveland, New York, Baltimore, Houston, Indianapolis, Santa Fe and Pittsburgh. Strays are aggressive enough to kill humans.

The stray dog problem will get worse because, unlike wolves, which have only one breeding cycle per year, domestic dogs have 2-3, and one domestic female dog and offspring can produce hundreds of pups over a six year + period.

There are some excellent books written by experts in dog handling dealing with the subject of self-defense against dog attacks, primarily in "normal," not collapse situations.[493] Articles often advise that one does not run (and hence become prey), keep calm, show confidence/dominance, make oneself appear bigger (e.g., holding

---

[491]   Will Doig, "The Secret Lives of Feral Dogs," January 15, 2012, at http://www.salon.com/2012/01/14/the-secret-lives-of-feral-dogs/.

[492]   C. Christoff, "Abandoned Dogs Roam Detroit in Packs as Humans Dwindle," August 21, 2013, at http://www.bloomberg.com/news/articles/2013-08-21/abandoned-dogs-roam-detroit-in-packs-as-humans-dwindle.

[493]   Loren W. Christensen, *Self-Defence Against a Dog Attack*, (Turtle Press, Amazon Digital Services, Kindle edition, 2012).

and waving hands), yell and not play dead. Common sense measures include not leaving food scraps around the exterior of one's house and for rural properties, having secure fencing.

In jurisdictions where people have been completely disarmed, it is best not to attempt to fight savage dogs, but to leave poison bates for them – in times of collapse, of course. There is no shortage of information on the internet. Commercial poisons such as strychnine may be available at present in various jurisdictions for farmers. Check local laws.

Without a firearm, how would one fight a savage dog? Dog repellent spray, and certainly bear spray, are good options if the wind is not blowing towards you.

Wolf Age

Outdoorsman Len McDougall, in *The Self-Reliance Manifesto*, states that he has had considerable experience with wolves and has spent nights alone in the woods in their habitat without any trouble from them.[494] Wolves are, he believes, not a problem, if non-rabid. Undoubtedly, there is a type of "wolf hysteria" linked to a deep human racial memory. In modern times, the US livestock industry is particularly concerned about stock losses from wolves, although most of these losses are less than one percent of total losses, and feral dogs are a much greater threat.

Wolf attacks on humans are uncommon, but the frequency has varied throughout history and geography. Historically, wolves in Europe have been more aggressive then wolves in North America, perhaps due to human culling: North Americans have had freer access to firearms, and the more aggressive wolves have been shot.

Wolves in Western Europe, and sometimes today in remote parts of Russia, have been a problem. In France between the years 1580-

---

[494]   Len McDougall, *The Self-Reliance Manifesto: How to Survive Anything Anywhere*, (Skyhouse Publishing, New York, 2010).

1830, 3,069 people were killed by wolves, and 1,857 were killed by non-rabid ones. In British India in 1878, 624 people were killed by wolves. In the 1980s there were over 100 deaths from wolves in one year alone in India. Deaths from wolf attacks continue to the present day in Iran and rural China. T. R. Mader observes that: "The areas of Asia where [there are] wolf attacks on humans are the same areas where people have no firearms or other effective means of predator control."[495]

In North America from the years 1950-2000, there were 13 confirmed cases of non-fatal wolf attacks on humans, but no documented cases of people in North America being killed by wolves in the 20th and 21st centuries.[496] The situation was different in previous centuries in North America. Packs of non-rabid wolves (generally wolves with rabies are lone wolves) have been reported to have attacked and killed adults in the 1800s. T. R. Mader says that American naturalists such as John James Audubon (of whom the Audubon Society is named), documented wolf attacks on humans.

In one such attack, occurring in about 1830, two men were traveling in Kentucky near the Ohio border in winter, with wood-chopping axes for self-defense. They were attacked in a heavily wooded area by a pack of wolves; fighting back with their axes, they were knocked to the ground and severely wounded. The wolves killed one man and the other dropped his axe and fled up a tree, spending the night there. By morning, the wolves had left. He climbed down the tree to find his companion's bones in the snow and three dead wolves. This was a pretty good effort for the last stand and could have been better if more combat-orientated weapons were carried. The wood chopping axe can deliver a powerful first strike but its weight, usually of about 2 kgs, makes it cumbersome, so that quick follow-up strikes are difficult. Lighter axes of the type used by the Vikings would have been better, as discussed in chapter 3. But, the power of

---

[495]   T. R. Mader, "Wolf Attacks on Humans," at http://www.aws.vcn.com/wolf_attacks_on_humans.html.

[496]   J. D. C. Linnell (et al.), *The Fear of Wolves: A Review of Wolf Attacks on Humans*, (NINA/LCIE, Trondheim, 2002), at http://www.wwf.de/fileadmin/fm-wwf/Publikationen-PDF/2002.Review.wolf.attacks.pdf.

a wolf should not be underestimated. Wolves have been kicked by half-ton moose, only to shake-off the pain and continuing attacking the animals. In Bondurant, southeast of Jackson, Wyoming, in March 2016, a wolf pack killed 19 elk in one night.

Another report in 1888 from New Rockford, Dakota, was of a father and son who were clearing a path around a haystack when they were attacked by a wolf pack and eaten. The mother, who had a baby, saw the attack from the house. The wolf pack then attacked the house but did not get inside. They then left to return to the hills.

In 1942 Michael Dusiak, a section foreman for the Canadian Pacific Railway, was attacked by a wolf. He had been patrolling the track on a speeder, a small open railway car. He fought the wolf with two axes and hit it a number of times. Fortunately for him, a train came by and stopped and three men got off armed with picks and other tools and killed the wolf. The wolf was inspected by a conservation officer and found to be without rabies and healthy.[497]

Mader mentions a number of wolf attacks. In one, in 1980, a forester in British Columbia was attacked by three wolves and fled up a tree. The alpha wolf was later shot by conservation officers with the Ministry of Environment and found to be non-rabid and healthy, as was the wolf who in August 1987 bit a 16-year-old-girl in Algonquin Provincial Park in Ontario. In the same park in August 1996, an 11-year-old child was bitten on the face by a wolf and dragged from a sleeping bag. The child's face was ripped open requiring 80 stitches. In the year 2000, a healthy wolf at Ice Bay, Alaska, attacked a six-year-old boy, without provocation. On Vargas Island, British Columbia, a 23-year-old male, was bitten on the hand and head, the head wounds alone requiring 50 stitches. Teachers out jogging also seem to attract the attention of wolf packs, as a number of Googleable articles indicates.

For wolf attacks to be "documented," Mader notes, there are some unreasonable criteria that need to be met, which make it difficult to document wolf attacks in the first place. For a start, the person must

---

[497]   R. Peterson, "A Record of Timber Wolf Attacking a Man," *Journal of Mammology*, vol. 28, no. 3, August, 1947, pp. 294-295.

die from the attack – bites are not classified as attacks! There need to be independent eye witnesses and it must be proven that the wolf has never been kept in captivity.

Wolves may attack humans because of: (1) extreme hunger; (2) rabies infection and other diseases; (3) familiarity – losing the fear of humans and (4) threat to young or perceived threats to prey that have been killed. Mader says that there are many well-documented cases of wolf attacks on humans, such as when wolves have been kept in zoos. Typically, kiddies climb into the enclosure to pat the nice "doggy," who turns out to be rather unfriendly and shreds them. Sometimes, adult humans have been killed by wolves in zoos.

McNay states that in a study of 80 wolf-human encounters in Alaska and Canada, 39 cases had elements of aggression among healthy wolves; 12 cases were suspected of rabies, and there were 29 cases of fearless behavior among non-aggressive wolves (in six cases people had dogs).[498] Aggressive, non-rabid wolves bit people in 16 cases, with six bites being severe, but none life threatening. Dog-wolf hybrids can also be a problem.

A "super pack" of about 400 wolves killed 30 horses in four days in Verkhoyansk, Russia, in 2011. Teams of hunters firing from helicopters dispatched them. The "super pack" was made up of hundreds of packs who came together because of the harsh cold killing off prey: temperatures plummeted to -49 C.

Professor Emeritus Valerius Geist, in his paper "When Do Wolves Become Dangerous to Humans,"[499] noted that well-fed wolves with abundant prey, with little contact with humans, or where they are hunted, are not dangerous to humans. He concluded:

> Therefore, to minimize danger to humans there needs to be (1) a low ratio of wolves to prey, and (2) an occasional, rare visit by humans or (3) a self-confident, fearless, even arrogant demeanor of persons traveling in areas with wolves. Such a confident, fearless way of walking and acting is associated with

---

[498]   Mark E. McNay, *A Case History of Wolf-Human Encounters in Alaska and Canada*, (Alaska Department of Fish and Game Wildlife Technical Bulletin no. 13, 2002).

[499]   Valerius Geist, "When Do Wolves Become Dangerous to Humans?" At http://wolfeducationinternational.com/wp-content/uploads/2014/04/Carnegie-No.1-edited.pdf.

carrying arms. When we are armed we are sending a message of confidence and courage with our very movement. And this is intimidating to all large mammals I have worked with in my field studies as an ethologist. It is not the act of hunting or shooting that makes wolves and other predators weary, but the confident, self-assured manners of armed persons. Healthy wilderness wolves under these conditions are so shy and weary that they are not vulnerable to regular hunting methods, especially to stalking. It may be counterintuitive, but inefficient hunting is an excellent protector of large carnivores.

Signs of weakness, running, stumbling, even screaming, done in the typical Hollywood movie fashion, would be good ways of bringing on wolf attacks. Potential prey acting bold and fearless disrupts the "hard cage of interlocking instincts and imprint-like learning" and attacking new, potentially dangerous prey "requires the dismantling of what they learned and a slow process of re-learning, guided by observational learning about the new prey and a very cautious approach to attacking." Nevertheless, as wolves come in contact with humans, they gradually lose their natural caution, first moving into human territory in an incremental fashion, then observing humans, making exploratory bites before attacking people.

Wolves in a pack are formidable fighters and seemingly have a "group mind," which is greater than the sum of the parts. Geist says that "wolves as pack hunters are so capable of predation, they may take down black bears, even grizzly bears." Wolf scat examined by Canadian researchers was found to contain the fur and claws of both black bears, even grizzly bears.

In Post Apocalyptica, the threat of wolf attacks could either decrease or increase depending upon the nature of the apocalyptic threat that took us down and other environmental conditions. If the numbers of wolves decreased as well as the numbers of humans, the relative proportion of wolf attacks could decrease. If human numbers crashed (due say to a human-specific pandemic) but wolf numbers remained constant, the proportion of attacks could decrease because of more available non-human prey and much less human-wolf interaction. But, if wolf numbers remain high, but available non-human prey decreases, humans could be back on the menu. Therefore, it is prudent to prepare wolf defenses if one is in regions where wolves are.

The movie *The Grey* (2011), starring Liam Neeson as John Ralph Ottway, gives a worst-case scenario of wolf attacks. To spoil the movie, if you haven't seen it, Ottway is the last of a group of Alaskan plane crash survivors, the others being killed either by a pack of super-huge (CGI generated) wolves, or their own stupidity and he probably dies in a final battle (which we do not see) with the largest male gray alpha. His weapons are broken bottles taped to his hands. This portrayal of wolves is essentially mythical; the claim made in the movie that the gray wolf is the only animal other than man that seeks revenge, is anthropomorphic nonsense. It is possible though that *The Grey*, based on Ian MacKenzie Jeffers' novella *Ghost Walker*, is actually a psychological drama, where the gray wolves are not real, but symbols of his inner demons. Who knows; literary film interpretation, like the law, is "some tricky shit."

Attacks by packs of wolves are not unheard of, we have seen, but unlikely. What should one do to survive? Oliver Starr who had his forearm crushed by the incredible jaw strength of a wolf (bite strength of a wolf 406 pounds, Rottweiler, 328 pounds makes these sensible recommendations: don't run, you will become prey; don't stare or turn your back; make your appearance large; grab a few stones to throw; back slowly away. For more than one wolf, he recommends curling up into a tight ball, protecting your head, neck, face, and sides. But, if the wolves are serious, "this strategy would only be effective for a very short time." It sounds like a good way of making oneself into a meatball and ultimately wolf crap.

Warriors following the barbarian way are more in tune with the advice given by Professor Emeritus Valerius Geist of projecting strength. Firearms are obviously the weapons of choice, and firepower and accuracy is needed. Opening up on the pack with a semi-auto shotgun or rifle should solve the problem – after the end of the rule of law, of course. I personally would not want to kill creatures that are truly magnificent unless it was them or me, but then they are no longer "magnificent," and sentimentality goes with rapid trigger pulls.

The interesting question is, in Post Apocalyptica, after the ammo (including reloading) runs out, then what? The last section of this chapter will discuss in detail melee weapon defense against wolves and bears. For the moment, let us note that there are some rare cases cited of humans defeating wolves and leopards unarmed. (I personally doubt such reports). Nevertheless, with weapons, as we have seen, humans have prevailed against wolves. In 2013 a 56-year-old Russian grandmother in rural Dagestan killed a wolf with a wood chopping axe, smashing it on the head, and a shepherd in Bosnia killed a brown bear with an axe, almost decapitating it.

Bear Attacks

The average adult male black bear is about 300 pounds but can reach up to 800 pounds after having laid on pre-winter fat, although it is rare for males (who are 33-50 percent larger than females) to reach more than 600 pounds.[500] The grizzly bear is genetically the same as the Alaskan brown bear or Kodiak bear. Adult grizzlies can reach 700 pounds or more. The adult male bears of Kodiak Island can reach 1,500 pounds, being five feet tall at the shoulder when on all fours and 10 feet tall when standing on hind legs. Polar bears are even more formidable, with adult males reaching up to 1,700 pounds, being five feet or more on all fours, and 11 feet or more standing on their hind legs. The front claws of a grizzly can be up to six inches long. Bears can generally run at up to 40 mph (humans top speed about 27 mph) over short distances. Hence, the often-told story: two men face a bear attack. One man quickly puts on running shoes. The other informs him that he can't outrun a bear. He says, running off, that he only has to outrun him. What are friends for? But consider: perhaps the bear quickly kills the slower mate, then catches up to running man, and shreds him?

---

[500] Army Rost (compiler), *Survival Wisdom and Know-How: Everything You Need to Know to Subsist in the Wilderness*, (Black Dog and Leventhal Publishers, New York, 2007), p. 34.

Bears are extremely agile for their size; agile enough to catch ground squirrels. Their strength is astonishing; grizzlies have been known to snap in half a piece of six-inch diameter pine with one bite. They can tear apart rotten stumps and logs to search for insects and are strong enough to kill most prey with a single swipe. Hell, they even tear (parked) planes apart![501] Layers of fat and very thick fur acts like a type of natural armor.

Bears have been known to have been cleanly shot in the heart by an arrow fired from a compound bow, and while dying, hang on long enough to tear the archer apart. However, well-placed .44 Magnum slugs, fired from a single action revolver from a distance of about 10 feet, put down a large grizzly.[502] Talk about a lucky ducky.

Although polar bears, when hungry, will readily prey on humans, bears do not generally hunt humans, unless under special circumstances. There is a low frequency of bear attacks on humans in North America compared to dog attacks. In the 1990s, bears killed 29 people in the US and Canada; grizzlies 18, black bears 11, and there were 162 bear-inflicted injury cases in Canadian and US national parks between 1900 and 1985.[503] The number of fatal bear attacks in North America has increased in recent times; between 1900 and 1990, 40 fatal bear attacks were recorded; between 1990 and the summer of 2010, 54 fatal attacks (brown and grizzly bears, 27 attacks, black bears, 26, with one death from a polar bear), with other authorities stating that black bears alone killed 63 people from 1900-2009.[504] Predatory attacks by bears have often been on women, children and the elderly[505] – it is sometimes said that bears

---

[501]   "Grizzly Bear Attacks Plane," at http://www.blackbearheaven.com/bear-rips-plane-appart.htm.

[502]   "The Longest Minute - Terrifying Bear Attack," *The Great White Hunter*, at http://thegreatwhitehunter.wordpress.com/the-longest-minute-terrifying-bear-attack/.

[503]   T. Y. Cardall (et al.), "Grizzly Bear Attacks," *Journal of Emergency Medicine*, vol. 24, no. 3, 2003, pp. 331-333.

[504]   S. Herrero, "Fatal Attacks by American Black Bear on People: 1900-2009," *Journal of Wildlife Management*, vol. 75, 2011, pp. 596-603.

[505]   S. C. Whitlock, "The Black Bear as a Predator of Man," *Journal of Mammology*, vol. 31, no. 2, 1950, pp. 135-138.

are choosing easy targets, but all humans compared to bears are easy targets. It is more likely that such people have relatively less physical prowess in escaping bear attacks. Furthermore, wilderness attacks usually occur when there are only one or two people, and bears seldom attack groups of (robust) humans greater than six persons, but if they did it would be effortlessly easy for them to defeat even six unarmed humans.[506]

The standard recommendation for avoiding bear attacks is to avoid bears, not to be in their territory. If it is unavoidable to be in their territory, common sense precautions include storing and cooking food away from camp, keeping rubbish away from camp, and avoiding areas where bears are likely to be, such as thickets and streams. If confronted by a bear the general advice is to: (1) avoid direct eye contact with the bear and aggressive behavior, backing away slowly, talking in a monotone voice; (2) bears often make bluff charges so one should stand one's ground and never run away (indicating that one is prey); (3) if the bear makes contact, one is supposed to roll up in a ball, play dead and hope that the bear will lose interest and depart. With black bears and polar bears, this advice gets qualified because if there is no reaction from you, a predatory bear may start eating you. Grizzlies may stop attacking if they think that you are dead if the attack is non-predatory. If predatory and you are in your ball, you may become a meat snack. Even a non-predatory grizzly may get curious with the ball of meat it has just found and toss you around: recall that these incredible hulks kill stronger animals with just one swipe of their great paws![507] The received strategy hence doesn't make much sense to me, because I haven't found in the literature any certain way of pre-emptively distinguishing predatory from non-predatory attacks. It seems to be based too much on how men are presently supposed to behave in this society – i.e., roll up into insignificant balls of meat and fat and hope that the social predators, the Social Justice Warriors, don't "kill" them too quickly.

---

[506] S. Herrero, "Human Injury Inflicted by Grizzly Bears," *Science,* vol. 170, 1970, pp. 593-598.

[507] L. Mueller and M. Reiss, *Bear Attacks of the Century,* (Globe Pequot, Guilford, 2005).

If it is correct that there is no certain method of determining *before* the actual attack whether a bear is acting defensively or as a predator and an attack is possible from any charge, being rolled up in a ball is hardly a good position to begin a life-or-death fight against a bear, even if one has bear spray.

Thus, in Stephen Herrero's now classic book, *Bear Attacks*,[508] one man began to fight back against the bear that was eating his thigh by hitting the bear – the bear then rips three ribs loose from the man's spine and opens up his chest cavity. This man was only saved by his partner showing up. In another example, an unarmed female geologist was attacked by a black bear. She played dead, and the bear began to gnaw her arms. Although she escaped with her life, she needed artificial arms.

Herrero says that "[t]rying to fight an attacking grizzly during a sudden encounter can't be ruled out as a strategy based on the data."[509] He cites a number of cases where bears have been killed by melee weapons. In May 1983, for example, in central Saskatchewan, a black bear stalked three men, killing one and attacking the other two. One man fought it with a mere filleting knife and killed it. Herrero said that he knew of three incidents of predatory black bear attacks where the bear was killed by people who did not have a firearm. In two cases, the bear was knifed to death, and in the third, the bear's skull was crushed by a small boulder.[510] These are all inferior melee weapons compared to what one could have.

Authorities recommend using capsicum spray against attacking bears over firearms, probably from a combination of legal/politically correct conservation reasons, and from the difficulty of shooting an attacking bear under stress. Tests done by Herrero found capsicum spray 100 percent effective with aggressive black bears (but there was a limited sample of four bears) and 94 percent effective against

[508] Stephen Herrero, *Bear Attacks: Their Cause and Avoidance*, (Revised edition), (The Lyons Press, Guilford, Connecticut, 2002).

[509] As above, p. 18, Table 2.

[510] "Fraser Graham Kills Grizzly Bear with Knife while Hunting in Chain Lake Areas of Alberta," November 1, 2013, at www.huffingtonpost.ca/2013/11/01/fraser-graham-kills-grizzly-bear-knife_n_4194910.html.

grizzly bears.[511] Since these tests, bear sprays have been widely used and have been found to be highly effective on American and Canadian bears.[512] Evidence of effectiveness on polar bears is more limited. Bear spray prevents injury in most, but not all cases. Under ideal conditions, the optimal range is 20-25 feet, but this range is affected by environmental factors such as strong wind (blowing in your direction), rain, cold temperatures and dense vegetation. Some bears are not deterred by substantial doses of spray and others need to be sprayed multiple times.[513] Mechanical problems can in principle, develop with spray canisters, but there does not appear to be any cases of this happening in the field in a bear attack. Mechanical failures, of course, can happen with any mechanical device, including firearms, and the human body, which is also a weak meat machine.

Fighting Bears in the Collapse

Bears are protected under US *Endangered Species Act,* and use of firearms and other weapons used against them is justified only on self-defense grounds. Further, firearms are generally banned from US national parks, so bear spray (and to be argued, after The Collapse, melee weapons) and common sense are campers' main forms of protection. In a collapse situation, after the present rule of law has ended, if in journeys bears are likely to be encountered, those bugging out need to carry bear spray, firearms and melee weapons. In fact, even if one is bugging out in regions where bears are not generally found, bear spray is an excellent weapon as well against two-legged predators. That is, for as long as it lasts, unless more can be brewed.

---

[511] S. Herrero and A. Higgins, "Field Use of Capsicum Spray as a Bear Deterrent," *Ursus,* vol. 10, 1998, pp. 533- 357.

[512] "Top 5 Questions about Grizzly Bear Attacks," at http://www.glacier-national-park-travel-guide.com/grizzly-bear-attacks.html.

[513] L. L. Rogers, "Reactions of Free-Ranging Black Bears to Capsaicin Spray Repellent," *Wildlife Society Bulletin,* vol. 12, no. 1, 1984, pp. 59-61.

Bears are well-known to have taken fire from serious rifles and to have still kept coming and have taken the rifleman apart. Bullet placement is crucial in bear defense. The bear may ultimately die from a less-than-optimal shot, but it will not be stopped soon enough, but you might be. Head and neck shots at a charging bear are extremely difficult as the bear may be moving at a speed of up to 44 feet per second, and you will be under stress, also affecting shot accuracy. Typically, it is necessary to put the first shot through the shoulder into the body to cripple the bear and a fast second shot in a vital zone in the front of the bear under the head.[514] A bear gun needs to be highly reliable, accurate to at least 50 yards, capable of a fast second shot (usually there is only time for two shots). Generally, a high-powered repeating rifle is regarded as the most effective bear-killing firearm. The round must have high knockout power and not breakup on impact, penetrating deeply to maximize destructive impact, with controlled expansion. The round should have a high sectional density.[515] (The sectional density (SD) is the ratio of the bullet's weight in fractions of a pound, to the square of the diameter in inches.)

As with all dangerous game, the maxim "use enough gun" rings true. Black bears have been killed at close range using 12-gauge shotguns with slugs.[516] But, bear expert Herrero regards the shotgun with slugs as a "[w]eapon of last resort to be used at close range only." The shotgun is just as heavy as a rifle, less accurate, and shotguns slugs lack sectional density. Hence, there is less penetration from such a short, thick projectile.

The US Forest Service researchers in Alaska recommend these four cartridge-bullet combinations for bear defence: .458 Winchester Magnum with 520-grain soft-point bullets if the recoil can be

<hr>

[514] As above.

[515] W. R. Meehan and J. F. Thilenius, *Safety in Bear Country: Protective Measures and Bullet Performance at Short Range*, (General Technical Report PNW-152, US Department of Agriculture, Forest Service, Pacific Northwest Forest and Range Experiment Station, Portland, 1983).

[516] L. Kaniut, *Alaska Bear Tales*, (Alaska Northwest Publishing Company, Anchorage, 1983).

tolerated; (2) .375 H&H Magnum with 300-grain-soft-point bullets; (3) .338 Winchester Magnum with 300-grain bullets and (4) .30-06 with 220-grain bullets. These rounds are usually delivered by bolt action rifles, but an option is the Browning BLR, a long action .30-06 lever action, a superb and reliable gun and fast on follow-up shots. The CZ 550 Safari Magnum comes in .375 H&H, .458 Winchester Magnum, .416 Rigby, and is an excellent, reasonably priced rifle.

A number of authorities favor using lever action rifles in calibers such as .45-70, .450 Marlin, and .454 Casull. Gun shops in remote regions of North America may not stock exotic dangerous game calibers; hence bring plenty of ammo if you have such a gun. The advantage of the use of those lever action guns is that they can double-up as more politically correct (or less politically incorrect) self-defense guns. Wild West Guns makes two suitable bear defense guns based on a modified Marlin 1895 lever action. The .457 Wild West Magnum delivers an extra thick-jacketed bonded core bullet, delivering 3,760-foot pounds of energy. The even more impressive .50 Alaskan fires a 450-grain bullet traveling at 2,250 fps, yielding 4,200-foot ponds of energy. As far as semi-autos go, Alexander Arms produces an AR-style rifle in .50 Beowulf which can be used on all North American game. Eskimos have killed bear using .308 semi autos, presumably with multiple shots.

Robert F. Petersen killed a polar bear measured standing upright at 12 foot 8 inches and weighing 1,500 pounds on February 26, 1965, in the village of Kotzebue, Alaska. He used a .44 Magnum revolver with 240 grain Norma bullets, shot within 25 yards, and blasted it with five shots. Thus, in a pinch, and with a bit of luck, even a heavy-caliber handgun could save one's bacon. But, in general, though, it won't.

Bare Against the Bear

What does one do in a Post Apocalyptica when the ammo runs out, but bear numbers are high? The internet presents many opinions, mostly crazy, typed by armchair warriors in their parents' basements, about how to fight a bear without a gun. Fire is a favourite, particularly hosed from a flamethrower to burn the bear's fur and then cook the bear. Perhaps in a pinch, a quarterstaff, the end wrapped in cloth and soaked in a flammable chemical (petroleum jelly) could act as a deterrent if environmental conditions such as wind and rain were favorable. In movie fashion, incendiaries, improvised napalm, and explosives have been suggested, along with various forms of traps which seemed to work fine for Arnie against the alien in *Predator* (1987). Just. Don't. Do. It.

One person, Jim West, was attacked by a black bear on October 7, 2008, in British Columbia and killed the bear in a life-or-death battle with an improvised club, smashing its skull.[517] Professor Dohrenwend says in his paper "Dangerous Animals and Asian Martial Arts,"[518] that there are records of men killing large animals such as bears with knives, apparently, thrusting a padded forearm into the animal's mouth and then stabbing it. In my opinion, these reports are probably bullshit, as the bear's jaw strength surpasses even the wolves. Bears have been known to bite and bend (obviously not bite through) two-inch (hollow) steel fencing posts to get food. Thus, the padded arm would be crushed, and a steel armored arm would be used to get a secure bite to toss the knife attacker like a rag doll, ripping the arm away from the body. Cases from North America where a knife has been used in defense against a bear attack usually involve serious injuries to the knife man.[519] Where a bear has

---

[517] Frank Minister, *The Ultimate Man's Survival Guide; Recovering the Lost Art of Manhood*, (Regnery Publishing, Washington DC, 2009); "B. C. Man comes Out Swinging in Bear Attack," October 8, 2008, at https://www.cbc.ca/news/canada/british-columbia/b-c-man-comes-out-swinging-in-bear-attack-1.756707.

[518] Robert E. Dohrenwend, "Dangerous Animals and the Asian Martial Arts," *Journal of Asian Martial Arts*, vol.19, no.1, Spring, 2000, (9 pages).

[519] F. Manfred, *Lord Grizzly*, (University of Nebraska Press, Lincoln, 1983).

been only modestly aggressive, they have been driven off by attacks such as an arrow stabbed into the bear's throat.

As a last-ditch self-defense strategy, a large bladed stabbing-type of knife, such as a Bowie or tanto, with a blade of around 12 inches plus, should be your faithful companion in Post Apocalyptica. The blade needs to be long enough to reach vital organs through the bio-armour of fur, hide, and fat. Such armor renders slashing and chopping weapons (e.g., the kukri or katana used not to thrust, but to slice) ineffective against bears unless a lucky smash to the skull can be delivered. No doubt, a man equal to Frisian warrior Pier Gerlofs Donia (c.1480-1520) would have a better chance than most of us in smashing the bear's skull with a 7 ft (2.15 meters) in length and 14.6 lb (6.6 kilograms) "greatsword" (*zweihander*). "Grutte Pier" was a human "bear" and strong enough to bend coins using only his thumb, index and middle finger. He was said to be able to behead a number of people (seven in one story) with one swing of his sword and to split a man from head to groin, with one stroke. Even so, my money would be on the bear in a Grutte v Brute grudge match.

The spear, in various guises, has been used to kill all animals on Earth, and as a harpoon, to hunt whales. A throwing spear launched from a "spear chucker" was used by Gene Morris to kill a lion, Cape Buffalo, a wolf, two bears, 283 alligators and in total 592 animals.[520] Brazilian hunter Sasha Siemel (1890-1970), killed over 300 jaguars single-handed with a spear. He, in neo-Viking style, favored a spear, with a shield, over a gun, to be "perfectly equipped." The Brazilian jaguar weights up to 300 pounds.[521]

The spontoon or half-pike was about 6-7 feet long and had a central blade with smaller curved blades either side, giving it the appearance of a trident. Around the mid-17th century until modern times, it was carried as protection against bears.

Bear hunting was popular in Russia in the 1800s. The Russian nobility and aristocrats enjoyed watching the hunts by skilled hunters

---

[520] "Hunting with Spears," at http://www.huntingwithspears.com/photogallary/tabid/219/galleryType/SlideSHow/ItemID/32/Default.aspx; D. Morris, *The Washing of the Spears*, (Simon and Schuster, New York, 1965).

[521] Sasha Siemel, *Tigrero!* (Prentice Hall, New York, 1953).

(*rogatchik*). The hunters used large bear spears (*rogatina*) containing a large bay leaf-shaped blade with a cross section piece to stop over-penetration.[522] One such Russian hero was Mihail Andrievskiy, huntsman of great duke Nikoday Romanov. He published an article in 1894 in the magazine *Nature and Hunting* about bear hunting with a spear.[523] In recent times, men have killed black bears with spears.[524]

The Alutiiqs (Kodiak natives) hunted Kodiak grizzlies for food, making clothes and tools. They used bows and arrows and spears. Across Alaska, native people in the past killed grizzlies using bows and arrows and the predominant hand weapon of the spear.[525] The strategy has been the one used for as long as the human species has wielded weapons: to hunt in a group and work together to overcome the bear's obvious physical advantages.[526] In the coming apocalypse, the wolf age of the collapse of civilization, human safety will once again depend upon prowess with weapons and belonging to a tribe of similarly endowed fighters.[527]

Conclusion

This chapter has examined the question of animal threats to survivors after the collapse of civilization. In the West, dangerous animals such as wolves and bears could become isolated threats under special circumstances, primarily when survivors need to journey through their territory, but this is no more a problem than already exists. Bear spray, rifles, and even melee weapons such as special spears can be used to battle wolves and bears, if necessary. Generally, these animals are "timid" and avoid human contact. With

---

[522] "Bear Hunting by Spear," at http://www.besteuropeanhunts.eu/bear-spear-hunting/.

[523] http://www.eaglehunter.co.uk/Vadim_Gorbatov_Portfolio/VGAP010_Bear_Hunt.html.

[524] https://www.mirror.co.uk/news/world-news/hunter-who-used-7ft-spear-8636150.

[525] Sidney Huntington, *Shadows on the Koyukuk: An Alaskan Native's Life Along the River*, (Alaskan Northwest Books, 1993).

[526] Gaston Phoebus, *The Hunting Book*, (Regent Books/ Hightext, London, 1984).

[527] R. Poortvleit, *Journey to the Ice Age*, (Harry N. Abrams, New York, 1994).

a die off of the human population, it is possible that there will be less contact between these animals and human survivors in the future. Scenarios depicted in *The Grey* (2011) and *The Edge* (1997) (stalking of two men who survive a plane crash by a Kodiak bear), is possible, but not highly probable.

www.ingramcontent.com/pod-product-compliance
Lightning Source LLC
Chambersburg PA
CBHW031253090426
42742CB00007B/438